P.118

P.206

P.212

P.210

P.120

P.200

P.206

P.210

P.210

D0945189

P.234

P.216

P.218

P.232

P.236

P.230

P.220

P.238

P.246

P.236

P.236

P.244

P.254

P.252

P.268

P.270

P.260

P.264

P.266

P.266

P.268

P.268

P.298

P.266

P.294

P.284

P.194

P.294

P.300

P.298

P.298

P.300

A Field Guide to the Birds of Japan

Text by   Wild Bird Society of Japan
Joseph A. Massey
Shogo Matsui
Tsutomu Suzuki
Elizabeth P. Swift
Akira Hibi
Noritaka Ichida
Yozo Tsukamoto
Koichiro Sonobe

Illustrations by   Shinji Takano

Distribution maps by Nobuyuki Monna

Editor in Chief   Koichiro Sonobe
Editor   Jane Washburn Robinson

Wild Bird Society of Japan

KODANSHA INTERNATIONAL LTD.
TOKYO, NEW YORK & SAN FRANCISCO

DEDICATION
This book is dedicated to the wild birds of Japan
and to those individuals and organizations whose
objectives and activities contribute to the
protection of those birds and to the conservation
of their natural habitat.

Publication of this book was assisted by a grant from the
Commemorative Association for the Japan World
Exposition.

Distributed in the United States by Kodansha
International/USA Ltd., through Harper & Row Publishers,
Inc., 10 East 53rd Street, New York, N.Y. 10022; in the
United Kingdom by Harper & Row Ltd., Publishers, 28
Tavistock Street, London WC2E 7PN; in Australia by
Harper & Row (Australasia) Pty., Ltd., Corner Frederick
Street & Reserve Road (P. O. Box 226), Artarmon NSW
2064.

Published by the Wild Bird Society of Japan, Aoyama
Flower Bldg., 1-1-4 Shibuya, Shibuya-ku, Tokyo 150, Japan,
in cooperation with Kodansha International Ltd., 12-21,
Otowa 2-chome, Bunkyo-ku, Tokyo 112, Japan, and
Kodansha International/USA Ltd., with offices at 10 East
53rd Street, New York, N.Y. 10022 and The Hearst Building,
5 Third Street, Suite No. 430, San Francisco, California,
94103.

First edition, 1982
Fifth printing, 1988

Library of Congress Cataloging in Publication Data
Main entry under title:

A Field guide to the birds of Japan.

  Bibliography: P.
  Includes indexes.
    1. Birds—Japan—Identification. I. Massey, Joseph A.
II. Takano, Shinji, 1926– . III. Sonobe, Koichiro.
IV. Robinson, Jane Washburn. V. Nihon Yachō no Kai.
QL691. J3F54 1985   598.2952   82-80650
ISBN 0-87011-746-7
ISBN 4-7700-1246-2 (in Japan; Kodansha International Ltd.)
ISBN 4-931150-04-7 (in Japan; Wild Bird Society of Japan)

Contents

FOREWORD by Sir Peter Scott

The publication of a new field guide is a very important event for everyone concerned with birds and their conservation, and the appearance of such a book for Japan is most welcome.

The Japanese Archipelago, fringing the eastern edge of Asia, has a rich avifauna, including what is probably the rarest bird in the world —the Toki or Japanese Crested Ibis, and one of the most recently discovered birds —the Okinawa Rail (both of which, of course, figure in this book).

The Wild Bird Society of Japan — one of the country's most active and effective nature conservation organisations — is to be applauded for presenting so attractively 537 species in colour, with distribution maps for 497 of them. I am particularly pleased to learn that they will be sending 500 copies of the book to various appropriate organisations throughout Asia.

The Field Guide principle was invented by the distinguished American bird painter Roger Tory Peterson, whose 'Field Guide to the Birds' appeared in 1934. It covered only the birds of eastern North America. But the principle has been extended to cover birds, and many other groups of animals and plants, in many other parts of the world. It was a brilliant invention which revolutionised the study of nature, and it had deep philosophical implications, because it provided a whole new set of out-door objectives. People who used the books in the field became interested in what they identified and were content to list the species they saw, regarding this as an end in itself, instead of always wanting to kill, 'collect', or otherwise molest them. Whilst making their lists, they spent more time watching and so developed an interest in the lives of the animals and plants they saw, and this led them to care for nature and its conservation. For this reason the value of field guides in public awareness and education can scarcely be exaggerated.

This new Japanese Field Guide fully maintains the high standards set by those published for other areas, and I should like, in conclusion, to congratulate its 8 authors, for the knowledge they have brought together and crystallised so comprehensively. I must also congratulate Mr. Takano for his beautiful and highly authentic illustrations, and finally I wish to thank them all and the Wild Bird Society of Japan for allowing me to become associated, through this foreword, with so excellent and useful a book.

Peter Scott.

Slimbridge
April 1982

Introduction

This is the first English language field guide to the birds of Japan to cover in text and illustrations all of the bird species known to occur in Japan. In recent years more interest has been shown in Japanese birds by both foreign visitors and Japanese residents. There has been an increase in bird observation and study not only by professional ornithologists but by a regularly expanding corps of experienced amateur birders led by the Wild Bird Society of Japan (WBSJ). The WBSJ, through the efforts of its network of members, has made national censuses of the breeding bird population, studied the migratory habits and routes of Japanese raptors, and has done semi-annual censuses of waders and annual censuses of waterfowl. Japanese bird experts have monitored threatened species like the Japanese Crested Ibis and the Short-tailed Albatross. As a result of these activities much has been learned about the breeding places, behavioral characteristics, and seasonal ranges of Japanese birds. Numerous new species have been added to the list of Japanese birds including a species new to science, the Okinawa Rail (*Rallus okinawae*), discovered on that island in 1981.

This book brings together the new information on Japanese birds that until now has been available only in Japanese and makes it accessible to birders around the world. It is a guide to the field identification of every bird species that has been recorded in Japan up to March 1982. There are color illustrations and descriptions of the 524 species known to have occurred in the wild and the 13 species introduced by man.

Range and Maps

The area covered in this book is shown on the map on the inside back cover. The maps which accompany the species descriptions show the breeding range in red and the wintering range in yellow green. The area where the bird may be found in either season is indicated in brown. The maps have been researched and prepared by the Wild Bird Society of Japan.

Geography, Climate, and Habitat

The Japanese islands covered in this guide extend from Hokkaido in the north to the southern Ryukyu Islands in the southwest and the Ogasawara and Iwo Islands in the southeast. The main archipelago forms an arc 3,000 kilometers long, located 200 to 700 kilometers off the eastern coast of the Asian mainland. The four major islands are Hokkaido, Honshu, Shikoku, and Kyushu. They lie at about the same latitude as the eastern United States from Maine to Georgia and have a similar, but somewhat wetter, temperate climate. About 66% of their surface is mountainous and heavily wooded, with steep slopes and narrow ravines the norm. Peaks in the Northern and Southern Alps range to over 3,000 meters. Mt. Fuji, 100 kilometers southwest of Tokyo, at 3,776 meters is Japan's highest mountain. There are, however, several large plains on Honshu. Tokyo is located on the Kanto Plain of eastern Honshu, while Osaka lies on the Osaka Plain of western Honshu. In contrast to the mountains, which are relatively sparsely inhabited and heavily forested in second growth, the plains are densely populated and intensively cultivated, with wet rice agriculture predominant. Northern Japan, especially Hokkaido, has somewhat more rolling, less steep terrain with some areas of the plains having undergone less intensive cultivation. The Sarobetsu Plain in northern Hokkaido is an unusual and noteworthy example of a relatively undisturbed wet grassland habitat in Japan.

Hokkaido and the Japan Sea side of Honshu northward from the Northern and Southern Alps receive substantial snow, with some areas recording the deepest snowfall at that latitude anywhere in the world. In contrast, Japan extends to the south into the subtropics, both in the southern Ryukyu Islands and in the outlying Ogasawara Islands and Iwo Islands. The habitat of these islands differs in important respects from that which prevails on the mainland. The southern Ryukyu Islands, in particular, have extensive mangrove forests which harbor birds and animals closely related to those of the southern Asian jungle.

Besides the birds that are year-round residents and those that breed in Japan, there are many breeding birds from southeast Asia and many wintering birds from Siberia, the Aleutians, and other northern parts of the Eurasian continent. Still others pass through each fall and spring in the course of their migration between wintering areas in southeast Asia and breeding areas in Siberia. And an impressively large number of seabird and shorebird species roam the Japanese seas and the shoreline. The foreign birder in Japan may see uniquely Japanese species such as the Okinawa Rail, Pryer's Woodpecker, and Bonin Islands Honeyeater. And, with luck and perseverance, he can find rare species.

Order of Presentation

This guide is intended to assist birders in identifying birds under field conditions that are often adverse. To make it easier in those circumstances, we have departed from the standard taxonomic order in which the families of birds are usually presented. The order we use here groups families of birds together according to their shared visual and behavioral characteristics. We have followed the order and terminology used in Roger Tory Peterson, *A Field Guide to the Birds, East of the Rockies* (Boston, Houghton Mifflin, fourth edition 1980) modified to suit the Japanese birds, as follows:

i)   Swimmers — Ducks and duck-like birds
ii) Aerialists — Gulls and gull-like birds
iii) Large waders — Cranes, storks, herons, bustards, and other large long-legged birds
iv) Small waders — Plovers, sandpipers, etc.
v)   Birds of prey — Hawks, eagles, and owls
vi) Fowl-like birds — Pheasants, quails, etc.
vii) Nonpasserine land birds — Kingfishers, woodpeckers, swifts, etc.
viii) Passerine (perching) birds — Swallows, thrushes, finches, etc.

Identification

A. Species' Names Names are given for each species in English, Latin (the scientific name), and Japanese. Where North American and European English names differ, both versions are given. Generally the European name is in brackets. With minor modifications (e.g. Storm Petrels instead of Fork-tailed Petrels) the names used are based on those adopted by the Ornithological Society of Japan, *Check-list of Japanese Birds 1974,* as updated in 1975 and 1978.

B. Measurements The length of each species given in the identification is as measured from the tip of the tail to the tip of the bill with the bird outstretched. Birds in the field will look shorter. Wingspans are given for appropriate large species. They are measured at the point of greatest distance across both wings when spread out flat.

C. Similar Species A separate heading is given in the identification for similar species where necessary and appropriate. In many cases, birds in a particular family are so alike that the central description is the appropriate place for discussing the key differences.

D. Voice Wherever the voice is a distinctive aid in field identification and adequate information about it exists, a description has been given. These are based for the most part on those given in two works by Shinji Takano: *Yacho Shikibetsu Handbook* (Tokyo: WBSJ, 1980) and *Nihon-san Chorui Zukan* (Tokyo: Tokai Daigaku Shuppankai, 1981). In addition, reference has been made to Ben F. King and Edward C. Dickinson, *A Field Guide to the Birds of South-East Asia* (London: William Collins Sons & Co., Ltd., 1975), and to Roger Tory Peterson, Guy Mountfort, and P.A.D. Hollom, *A Field Guide to the Birds of Britain and Europe,* third edition (London: William Collins Sons & Co., Ltd., 1974).

E. Status Under this heading information is given about the relative abundance of the species, the season in which it is found in Japan, its preferred habitat, and its known breeding areas. Statements of relative abundance pertain to the main portion of the range and habitat. We have followed the criteria used by Chandler S. Robbins et al., *Birds of North America: A Guide to Field Identification* (New York: Golden Press, 1966). An *abundant* bird may ordinarily be seen in large numbers every time one visits the proper habitat during the proper season. A *common* bird will probably be found most of the time in the right habitat and season, but perhaps in smaller numbers. An *uncommon* bird will likely be found only in small numbers, although it may occur regularly. A *rare* bird is, by definition, hard to find. It may occur only in a highly specific or limited habitat. *Accidentals* or *stragglers* are the rarest birds since they do not normally occur at all in a given region but are found there as a consequence of some unusual circumstance. Such rarities are excluded from most field guides. We have included them here because some of those birds may prove to be rare but regular visitors.

TOPOGRAPHY

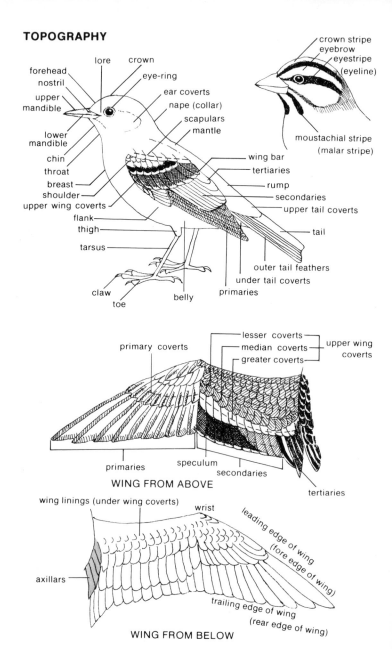

crown stripe
eyebrow
eyestripe (eyeline)
moustachial stripe (malar stripe)

lore
crown
forehead
nostril
eye-ring
upper mandible
ear coverts
nape (collar)
scapulars
mantle
lower mandible
chin
throat
breast
shoulder
upper wing coverts
flank
thigh
tarsus
claw
toe
belly
primaries
under tail coverts
outer tail feathers
tail
upper tail coverts
secondaries
rump
tertiaries
wing bar

primary coverts
lesser coverts
median coverts
greater coverts
upper wing coverts
primaries
speculum
secondaries
tertiaries

WING FROM ABOVE

wing linings (under wing coverts)
wrist
leading edge of wing (fore edge of wing)
axillars
trailing edge of wing (rear edge of wing)

WING FROM BELOW

Terms and Abbreviations Used in this Book

♂: male
♀: female
Adult: a bird which has attained its definitive plumage.
Subadult: a bird about to acquire its adult plumage. The term is generally used for birds which take more than a year to acquire definitive plumage.
Immature (imm.): a bird in a plumage in between juvenile and adult.
Juvenile (juv.): a bird in its first plumage.
Chick: a newly hatched bird unable to fly.
Summer or breeding plumage: a different plumage acquired by many species during the breeding season.
Winter or non-breeding plumage: the plumage worn by birds when they are not breeding; refers to those species which have different plumage in breeding season.
Eclipse plumage: a dull-colored plumage stage of short duration which occurs in some species, most notably male ducks, between the breeding plumage and the winter plumage. Ducks in eclipse can be seen in Japan from late August through November.
Molt: the process of shedding feathers and replacing them with new ones. All birds molt at least once a year.
Resident: a bird which lives in the same location all year.
Transient or passage migrant: a bird which regularly passes through an area on its migration without remaining there for either the summer or the winter.
Summer visitor: a bird which comes to an area for breeding.
Winter visitor: a bird which comes to an area to spend the winter.
Endemic: used to describe a species which is restricted to a certain area.

Acknowledgements

The Wild Bird Society of Japan has published this field guide in the hope that it will promote international cooperation for the protection of birds, especially in Asia and the Pacific. More than most books, field guides are works of collective effort and enthusiasm. This one was made possible by the cooperation and contributions of many people from Japan, the United States, and Great Britain, many of whom generously volunteered their time and expertise.

First we want to express our deep appreciation to Sir Peter Scott for writing the foreword for this book and for his encouragement to our society, and to the Commemorative Association for the Japan World Exposition for providing the funds which enabled us to publish this guide. We are most grateful to Shinji Takano for his illustrations and advice and to Jane Washburn Robinson for editing the text.

This field guide was written by the people listed below: Text: Dr. Joseph A. Massey (Gaviiformes through Pelecaniformes, Anseriformes, Charadriiformes in part — Families Stercorariidae through Alcidae, and the Introduction), Koichiro Sonobe (Ciconiiformes, Identifying Birds with this Book, and Birdwatching Guide for Japan), Shogo Matsui (Falconiformes through Gruiformes), Tsutomu Suzuki (Charadriiformes in part — Families Jacanidae through Glareolidae, Passeriformes in part —Family Motacilidae), Elizabeth P. Swift (Columbiformes through Piciformes and Passeriformes in part — Family Pittidae), Yozo Tsukamoto (Passeriformes in part — Families Alaudidae, Hirundinidae, and Campephagidae through Prunellidae), Akira Hibi (Passeriformes in part —Families Muscicapidae through Emberizidae), and Noritaka Ichida (Passeriformes in part — Families Fringillidae through Corvidae and Birdwatching Guide for Japan). All manuscripts were reviewed and amended by Koichiro Sonobe and Jane Washburn Robinson. Illustrations: Shinji Takano.

Editor in Chief: Koichiro Sonobe. Editor: Jane Washburn Robinson. Editorial assistants: Katsuaki Shibahara, Mitsuo Ishiai, Toyoko Ichida, and Masaomi Yamamoto. Distribution maps: Nobuyuki Monna. Book design: Minoru Imai. Advisory group (approved the species to be included in this book and reviewed the plates and the distribution maps): Teruaki Morioka, Takuya Kanouchi, and Masumi Shimura. Assisted with the preparation of manuscripts: Samuel C. Morse, Anne N. Morse, Nobuko Sasaki, Tsutomu Suzuki, and Noritaka Ichida. Dr. Massey's manuscript was written with the cooperation of Kimiko Nakashima. Typing: Noriko Niijima, Emiko Kume, and Liz Walkington. Proofreading: Hideyo Morita and Dr. Lowell Adams. The research of copyright on layout: Tetsuo Shimizu, Marks & Clerk (London), and Gee & Co. (London).

We are grateful to Roger Tory Peterson and Houghton Mifflin Company (Boston) for permitting the use of the Peterson system of indicating field marks with arrows on the plates. We want to thank Dr. Robin J. Robinson and Esso Production Japan for contributing the services of a secretary and the use of a word processor, and especially Michiko Mori who typed the entire text, including numerous editorial changes, on the word processor.

Seiichi Yamashita
President
Wild Bird Society of Japan

Checklist of Japanese Birds

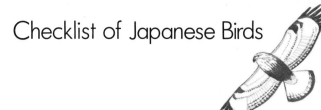

●ORDER GAVIIFORMES
Family Gaviidae
___ Red-throated Loon
___ Arctic Loon
___ Pacific Loon
___ Yellow-billed Loon

●ORDER PODICIPEDIFORMES
Family Podicipedidae
___ Little Grebe
___ Eared Grebe
___ Horned Grebe
___ Red-necked Grebe
___ Great Crested Grebe

●ORDER PROCELLARIIFORMES
Family Diomedeidae
___ Wandering Albatross
___ Short-tailed Albatross
___ Laysan Albatross
___ Black-footed Albatross
Family Procellariidae
___ (Northern) Fulmar
___ Kermadec Petrel
___ White-necked Petrel
___ Hawaiian Petrel
___ Bonin Petrel
___ Black-winged Petrel
___ Stejneger's Petrel
___ Bulwer's Petrel
___ Streaked Shearwater
___ Wedge-tailed Shearwater
___ New Zealand Shearwater
___ Flesh-footed Shearwater
___ Sooty Shearwater
___ Short-tailed Shearwater
___ Christmas Shearwater
___ Audubon's Shearwater
Family Hydrobatidae
___ Wilson's Storm Petrel
___ Fork-tailed Storm Petrel
___ Leach's Storm Petrel
___ Swinhoe's Storm Petrel
___ Band-rumped Storm Petrel
___ Sooty Storm Petrel
___ Matsudaira's Storm Petrel

●ORDER PELECANIFORMES
Family Phaethontidae
___ Red-tailed Tropicbird
___ White-tailed Tropicbird
Family Pelecanidae
___ Spot-billed Pelican
Family Sulidae
___ Brown Booby
___ Masked Booby
___ Red-footed Booby
Family Phalacrocoracidae
___ Great Cormorant
___ Temminck's Cormorant
___ Pelagic Cormorant
___ Red-faced Cormorant
Family Fregatidae
___ Great Frigatebird
___ Lesser Frigatebird

●ORDER CICONIIFORMES
Family Ardeidae
___ (Eurasian) Bittern
___ Chinese Little Bittern
___ Schrenck's Little Bittern
___ Cinnamon Bittern
___ Black Bittern
___ Japanese Night Heron
___ Malay Night Heron
___ Black-crowned Night Heron
___ Rufous Night Heron
___ Green-backed Heron
___ Chinese Pond Heron
___ Cattle Egret
___ Great Egret
___ Intermediate Egret
___ Little Egret
___ Chinese Egret
___ Eastern Reef Heron
___ Gray Heron
___ Purple Heron
Family Ciconiidae
___ White Stork
___ Black Stork
Family Threskiornithidae
___ Spoonbill
___ Black-faced Spoonbill
___ Japanese Crested Ibis

___ Oriental Ibis

●ORDER ANSERIFORMES
Family Anatidae
___ Canada Goose
___ Brant
___ Graylag Goose
___ White-fronted Goose
___ Lesser White-fronted Goose
___ Bean Goose
___ Snow Goose
___ Emperor Goose
___ Swan Goose
___ Mute Swan
___ Whooper Swan
___ Whistling Swan
___ Indian Whistling Duck
___ Ruddy Shelduck
___ Common Shelduck
___ Crested Shelduck
___ Mandarin Duck
___ Mallard
___ Spot-billed Duck
___ Green-winged Teal
___ Baikal Teal
___ Falcated Teal
___ Gadwall
___ (Eurasian) Wigeon
___ American Wigeon
___ Pintail
___ Garganey
___ (Northern) Shoveler
___ Red-crested Pochard
___ Pochard
___ Canvasback
___ Ring-necked Duck
___ White-eyed Pochard
___ Baer's Pochard
___ Tufted Duck
___ Greater Scaup
___ Steller's Eider
___ King Eider
___ Black Scoter
___ White-winged Scoter
___ Surf Scoter
___ Harlequin Duck
___ Oldsquaw
___ Common Goldeneye
___ Bufflehead
___ Smew
___ Red-breasted Merganser
___ Common Merganser

●ORDER FALCONIFORMES
Family Accipitridae
___ Osprey
___ Honey Buzzard
___ Black Kite

___ White-tailed Eagle
___ Steller's Sea-Eagle
___ (Northern) Goshawk
___ Chinese Sparrow Hawk
___ Japanese Lesser Sparrow Hawk
___ (European) Sparrow Hawk
___ Rough-legged Buzzard
___ Upland Buzzard
___ Common Buzzard
___ Gray-faced Buzzard-Eagle
___ Hodgson's Hawk-Eagle
___ Spotted Eagle
___ Imperial Eagle
___ Golden Eagle
___ (European) Black Vulture
___ Crested Serpent-Eagle
___ Northern Harrier
___ Pied Harrier
___ Marsh Harrier
Family Falconidae
___ Gyrfalcon
___ Peregrine Falcon
___ Hobby
___ Merlin
___ Amur Red-footed Falcon
___ Lesser Kestrel
___ (Eurasian) Kestrel

●ORDER GALLIFORMES
Family Tetraonidae
___ Rock Ptarmigan
___ Hazel Grouse
Family Phasianidae
___ Common Quail
___ Bamboo Partridge
___ Copper Pheasant
___ Common Pheasant

●ORDER GRUIFORMES
Family Turnicidae
___ Barred Buttonquail
Family Gruidae
___ Common Crane
___ Japanese Crane
___ Hooded Crane
___ Sandhill Crane
___ White-naped Crane
___ Siberian White Crane
___ Demoiselle Crane
Family Rallidae
___ Water Rail
___ Okinawa Rail
___ Banded Crake
___ Baillon's Crake
___ Ruddy Crake
___ Swinhoe's Yellow Rail
___ Ashy Crake
___ White-breasted Waterhen

___ Common Gallinule
___ Watercock
___ (European) Coot
Family Otidae
___ Great Bustard
___ Little Bustard

●**ORDER CHARADRIIFORMES**
Family Jacanidae
___ Pheasant-tailed Jacana
Family Rostratulidae
___ Painted Snipe
Family Haematopodidae
___ Oystercatcher
Family Charadriidae
___ Ringed Plover
___ Little Ringed Plover
___ Long-billed Ringed Plover
___ Snowy Plover
___ Mongolian Plover
___ Greater Sand Plover
___ Caspian Plover
___ Dotterel
___ Lesser Golden Plover
___ Black-bellied Plover
___ Gray-headed Lapwing
___ (Northern) Lapwing
Family Scolopacidae
___ Ruddy Turnstone
___ Western Sandpiper
___ Little Stint
___ Rufous-necked Stint
___ Long-toed Stint
___ Least Sandpiper
___ Temminck's Stint
___ Baird's Sandpiper
___ Pectoral Sandpiper
___ Sharp-tailed Sandpiper
___ Rock Sandpiper
___ Dunlin
___ Curlew Sandpiper
___ Red Knot
___ Great Knot
___ Sanderling
___ Spoon-billed Sandpiper
___ Ruff
___ Buff-breasted Sandpiper
___ Stilt Sandpiper
___ Broad-billed Sandpiper
___ Long-billed Dowitcher
___ Asiatic Dowitcher
___ Spotted Redshank
___ Redshank
___ Lesser Yellowlegs
___ Marsh Sandpiper
___ Greenshank
___ Greater Yellowlegs
___ Spotted Greenshank

___ Green Sandpiper
___ Wood Sandpiper
___ (American) Wandering Tattler
___ Gray-tailed Tattler
___ Common Sandpiper
___ Terek Sandpiper
___ Black-tailed Godwit
___ Bar-tailed Godwit
___ (Eurasian) Curlew
___ Australian Curlew
___ Slender-billed Curlew
___ Whimbrel
___ Bristle-thighed Curlew
___ Little Whimbrel
___ (European) Woodcock
___ Amami Woodcock
___ Common Snipe
___ Pintail Snipe
___ Swinhoe's Snipe
___ Latham's Snipe
___ Solitary Snipe
___ Jack Snipe
Family Recurvirostridae
___ Black-winged Stilt
___ Avocet
Family Phalaropodidae
___ Red Phalarope
___ Northern Phalarope
Family Glareolidae
___ Indian Pratincole
Family Stercorariidae
___ Great Skua
___ Pomarine Jaeger
___ Parasitic Jaeger
___ Long-tailed Jaeger
Family Laridae
___ Great Black-headed Gull
___ Little Gull
___ Black-headed Gull
___ Herring Gull
___ Slaty-backed Gull
___ Glaucous-winged Gull
___ Glaucous Gull
___ Mew Gull
___ Black-tailed Gull
___ Saunders's Gull
___ Sabine's Gull
___ Black-legged Kittiwake
___ Red-legged Kittiwake
___ Ross's Gull
___ Ivory Gull
___ White-winged Black Tern
___ Whiskered Tern
___ Black Tern
___ Caspian Tern
___ Greater Crested Tern
___ Gull-billed Tern
___ Common Tern

___ Roseate Tern
___ Black-naped Tern
___ Aleutian Tern
___ Spectacled Tern
___ Bridled Tern
___ Sooty Tern
___ Little Tern
___ Blue Noddy
___ Brown Noddy
___ Black Noddy
___ White Noddy
Family Alcidae
___ Thin-billed Murre
___ Thick-billed Murre
___ Pigeon Guillemot
___ Spectacled Guillemot
___ Marbled Murrelet
___ Ancient Murrelet
___ Japanese Murrelet
___ Crested Auklet
___ Whiskered Auklet
___ Least Auklet
___ Parakeet Auklet
___ Rhinoceros Auklet
___ Horned Puffin
___ Tufted Puffin

●**ORDER COLUMBIFORMES**
Family Pteroclididae
___ Pallas's Sandgrouse
Family Columbidae
___ Japanese Wood Pigeon
___ Ryukyu Wood Pigeon
___ Bonin Wood Pigeon
___ Collared Turtle Dove
___ Red Turtle Dove
___ Rufous Turtle Dove
___ Emerald Dove
___ Japanese Green Pigeon
___ Red-capped Green Pigeon

●**ORDER CUCULIFORMES**
Family Cuculidae
___ Horsfield's Hawk-Cuckoo
___ Indian Cuckoo
___ Common Cuckoo
___ Oriental Cuckoo
___ Little Cuckoo
___ Red-winged Crested Cuckoo

●**ORDER STRIGIFORMES**
Family Strigidae
___ Snowy Owl
___ Eagle Owl
___ Blakiston's Fish-Owl
___ Long-eared Owl
___ Short-eared Owl
___ Scops Owl

___ Collared Scops Owl
___ Boreal Owl
___ Brown Hawk-Owl
___ Ural Owl
Family Tytonidae
___ Grass Owl

●**ORDER CAPRIMULGIFORMES**
Family Caprimulgidae
___ Jungle Nightjar

●**ORDER APODIFORMES**
Family Apodidae
___ White-throated Needle-tailed
  Swift
___ House Swift
___ White-rumped Swift

●**ORDER CORACIIFORMES**
Family Alcedinidae
___ Greater Pied Kingfisher
___ Black-capped Kingfisher
___ Ruddy Kingfisher
___ Collared Kingfisher
___ Miyako Kingfisher
___ Common Kingfisher
Family Meropidae
___ Australian Bee-eater
Family Coraciidae
___ Broad-billed Roller
Family Upupidae
___ Hoopoe

●**ORDER PICIFORMES**
Family Picidae
___ Wryneck
___ Japanese Green Woodpecker
___ Gray-headed Woodpecker
___ Pryer's Woodpecker
___ Black Woodpecker
___ White-bellied Black
  Woodpecker
___ Great Spotted Woodpecker
___ White-backed Woodpecker
___ Lesser Spotted Woodpecker
___ Japanese Pygmy Woodpecker
___ (Northern) Three-toed
  Woodpecker

●**ORDER PASSERIFORMES**
Family Pittidae
___ Fairy Pitta
Family Alaudidae
___ Bimaculated Lark
___ Short-toed Lark
___ Lesser Short-toed Lark
___ Skylark
___ Horned Lark

Family Hirundinidae
___ Bank Swallow
___ Barn Swallow
___ Pacific Swallow
___ Red-rumped Swallow
___ House Martin
Family Motacillidae
___ Forest Wagtail
___ Yellow Wagtail
___ Citrine Wagtail
___ Gray Wagtail
___ White Wagtail
___ Japanese Wagtail
___ Richard's Pipit
___ Godlewski's Pipit
___ Tree Pipit
___ Indian Tree Pipit
___ Pechora Pipit
___ Red-throated Pipit
___ Water Pipit
Family Campephagidae
___ Lesser Cuckoo-Shrike
___ Ashy Minivet
Family Pycnonotidae
___ Chinese Bulbul
___ Brown-eared Bulbul
Family Laniidae
___ Thick-billed Shrike
___ Bull-headed Shrike
___ Brown Shrike
___ Northern Shrike
___ Chinese Great Gray Shrike
Family Bombycillidae
___ Bohemian Waxwing
___ Japanese Waxwing
Family Cinclidae
___ Brown Dipper
Family Troglodytidae
___ Winter Wren
Family Prunellidae
___ Alpine Accentor
___ Siberian Accentor
___ Japanese Accentor
Family Muscicapidae
(Subfamily Turdinae)
___ Japanese Robin
___ Ryukyu Robin
___ Swinhoe's Red-tailed Robin
___ Siberian Rubythroat
___ Bluethroat
___ Siberian Blue Robin
___ Siberian Bluechat
___ Daurian Redstart
___ Stonechat
___ Gray Bushchat
___ Isabelline Wheatear
___ Wheatear
___ Desert Wheatear

___ Pied Wheatear
___ Blue Rockthrush
___ White-breasted Rockthrush
___ Siberian Thrush
___ White's Ground Thrush
___ Bonin Islands Thrush
___ Gray-backed Thrush
___ Gray Thrush
___ Blackbird
___ Brown Thrush
___ Izu Islands Thrush
___ Pale Thrush
___ Gray-headed Thrush
___ Black-throated Thrush
___ Dusky Thrush
___ Fieldfare
___ Redwing
(Subfamily) Paradoxornithinae
___ Bearded Tit
(Subfamily) Sylviinae
___ Short-tailed Bush Warbler
___ Bush Warbler
___ Japanese Marsh Warbler
___ Gray's Grasshopper Warbler
___ Middendorff's Grasshopper
Warbler
___ Lanceolated Grasshopper
Warbler
___ Black-browed Reed Warbler
___ Great Reed Warbler
___ Thick-billed Reed Warbler
___ Yellow-browed Warbler
___ Pallas's Willow Warbler
___ Arctic Warbler
___ Pale-legged Willow Warbler
___ Crowned Willow Warbler
___ Ijima's Willow Warbler
___ Goldcrest
___ Fan-tailed Warbler
(Subfamily) Muscicapinae
___ Tricolor Flycatcher
___ Narcissus Flycatcher
___ Mugimaki Flycatcher
___ Red-breasted Flycatcher
___ Blue-and-White Flycatcher
___ Sooty Flycatcher
___ Gray-spotted Flycatcher
___ Brown Flycatcher
___ Ferruginous Flycatcher
(Subfamily) Monarchinae
___ Black Paradise Flycatcher
Family Aegithalidae
___ Long-tailed Tit
Family Remizidae
___ Penduline Tit
Family Paridae
___ Marsh Tit
___ Willow Tit

___ Coal Tit
___ Varied Tit
___ Great Tit
Family Sittidae
___ Nuthatch
Family Certhiidae
___ Brown Creeper
Family Zosteropidae
___ Japanese White-eye
___ Chestnut-flanked White-eye
Family Meliphagidae
___ Bonin Islands Honeyeater
Family Emberizidae
___ Yellowhammer
___ Pine Bunting
___ Siberian Meadow Bunting
___ Japanese Reed Bunting
___ Tristram's Bunting
___ Gray-headed Bunting
___ Little Bunting
___ Yellow-browed Bunting
___ Rustic Bunting
___ Yellow-throated Bunting
___ Yellow-breasted Bunting
___ Chestnut Bunting
___ Black-headed Bunting
___ Japanese Yellow Bunting
___ Black-faced Bunting
___ Gray Bunting
___ Pallas's Reed Bunting
___ Reed Bunting
___ Lapland Longspur
___ Snow Bunting
___ Fox Sparrow
___ White-crowned Sparrow
___ Golden-crowned Sparrow
___ Savannah Sparrow
Family Fringillidae
___ Brambling
___ Oriental Greenfinch
___ Siskin
___ Common Redpoll

___ Hoary Redpoll
___ Rosy Finch
___ Scarlet Finch
___ Pallas's Rosy Finch
___ Pine Grosbeak
___ Red Crossbill
___ White-winged Crossbill
___ Long-tailed Rose Finch
___ Bonin Islands Grosbeak
___ Bullfinch
___ Chinese Grosbeak
___ Japanese Grosbeak
___ Hawfinch
Family Ploceidae
___ Russet Sparrow
___ (Eurasian) Tree Sparrow
Family Sturnidae
___ Daurian Myna
___ Silky Starling
___ Red-cheeked Myna
___ Gray-backed Myna
___ (European) Starling
___ Gray Starling
___ Crested Myna
Family Oriolidae
___ Black-naped Oriole
Family Dicruridae
___ Black Drongo
Family Artamidae
___ White-breasted Wood-Swallow
Family Corvidae
___ Jay
___ Lidth's Jay
___ Azure-winged Magpie
___ Black-billed Magpie
___ Nutcracker
___ Jackdaw
___ Rook
___ Carrion Crow
___ Jungle Crow
___ (Northern) Raven

Identifying Birds with this Book

Although 524 species of birds have been recorded in Japan so far, identifying a particular bird usually is not too difficult. As in developing any skill, however, a bit of pleasant effort is required. Ultimately, proficiency is achieved only through practice looking at birds in the field. But field observations must be supplemented with study of a field guide. Here are a few pointers to help the beginning birder learn to identify birds more quickly.

Determining the correct identity of a bird is essentially a process of elimination. First you must be able to recognize the family to which a bird belongs, for example if it is a seagull, a woodpecker, or a heron. To do this you must pay close attention to the size and shape of the bird and in many cases to its bill. Study the field guide, including the pictures on the inside front cover, to become familiar with the bird families which occur in Japan. Then look through the pictures to see the birds you might encounter in the field. Pay special attention to the arrows on the pictures which point to the field marks so you will learn the kinds of things to look for when you see a new bird. You will see that the yellow tip of the bill of the Spot-billed Duck, the blue back of the Common Kingfisher, and the crest of the Lapwing are field marks which will help you to identify these birds at a glance. Some will be more difficult because there are species which look almost alike, but the distinguishing characteristics can be learned with study and practice.

In the field train yourself to observe birds in flight, carefully looking for colors and patterns, silhouette, the way the wings are held, and the manner of flight. The behavior of a bird can also give important clues to its identity. Pay attention to such things as how it flies, how it swims, how it moves its tail, whether it walks or hops, and if it occurs in flocks. From the beginning take note of calls and songs. Most species have distinctive voices. Knowing them can be an invaluable aid in identification.

Additional factors which will be helpful in narrowing your options are season, habitat, and location. For example, the Common Cuckoo cannot be found in Japan during the winter, seagulls cannot be found in the mountains, and often similar species do not occur in the same parts of Japan. In most cases there is little likelihood of finding a bird in a habitat totally different from the kind it normally prefers. Of course it is exciting to find a bird where it doesn't belong or at a time of year when it does not normally occur in Japan, but until you have become more proficient it is best to assume you have selected the wrong species. For this information please refer to the status and the distribution map for each species.

Don't expect to be able to identify every bird you see. You should, however, soon learn to know within two or three possibilities what bird you have seen. There will always be birds on any day in the field which you will not see well enough to identify. Good birders recognize this and avoid guessing when they have not seen a bird well enough to make a positive identification.

For a start, note the following:

VISIBLE FIELD MARKS
I. Size and Shape
Compare the overall size of the bird to that of familiar species:

Body Shape: Is the bird plump like a Hawfinch or slender like a wagtail?

Bill Size and Shape: Is the bill short or long? Thick or thin? Straight or curved?

Tail Length and Shape: Is the tail long or short? Is it square, rounded, notched, forked, or wedge-shaped?

Wingspan and Shape: Are the wings long or short? Pointed or rounded?

II. Color and Patterning
Look for distinctive color combinations or patterning such as stripes or barring on:

Face and Head: Does it have a stripe through the eye or crown? A ring around the eye?

Underparts: Is its belly light or dark, barred, plain, or patterned?

Upper Surfaces of Wings and Body: Are there distinctive marks, spots, or stripes?

Rump and Tail: Is the rump light or dark? What about the tail? Does the tail have a dark or light band at the tip?

Wings: Are there prominent bars or stripes on the wings? Do the wings contrast with the back?

III. Behavior
Posture at Rest: How does the bird sit or perch?

Tail-wagging: Does it wag its tail? If so, is it up and down or in a circle?

Tree Climbing: Does it climb straight up like a woodpecker, in spirals like a creeper, or go down head first like a nuthatch?

Flying: A. Does the bird dip up and down in flight like a woodpecker or fly straight like a Gray Starling?

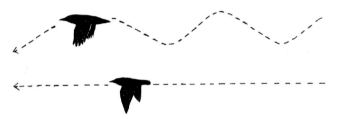

B. Does it soar?

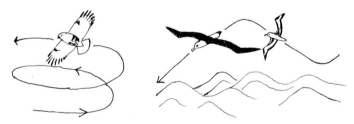

C. Does it hover?

Loons (Divers)

Family *Gaviidae* (World: 5 species; Japan: 4 species) Medium to large aquatic birds with thick necks and sharply pointed bills. Dive from surface with a forward plunge or submerge gradually and quietly. Take off from water with long running start. In flight appear hunchbacked with outstretched necks tilted slightly downward and feet extended beyond short tails. Usually silent in winter. Sexes alike.

RED-THROATED LOON [RED-THROATED DIVER] *Gavia stellata* <Abi> L 63cm. Slightly *upturned thin bill,* small slim head habitually tilted upward. **Summer:** *Reddish-brown. throat patch,* gray head, plain dark back. **Winter:** Extensive white area on face and neck. Paler, finely speckled gray back. **Similar species:** Arctic and Pacific Loons have *straight* bills and hold heads level. Yellow-billed Loon has large upturned yellowish bill. **Status:** Common winter visitor to coasts and bays throughout Japan.

PACIFIC LOON [PACIFIC DIVER] *Gavia pacifica* <Shiroeri-ōhamu> L 65cm. Slightly smaller than Arctic Loon from which it cannot be distinguished in winter (and with which it is grouped into a single species by some authorities). In summer Pacific has *paler crown and nape;* dark throat patch has *purple* (not green) *iridescence.* **Similar species:** See species listed under Arctic Loon. **Status:** Common winter visitor to coasts and bays, especially along the Pacific.

ARCTIC LOON [BLACK-THROATED DIVER] *Gavia arctica* <Ōhamu> L 72cm. *Slender, straight bill.* **Summer:** Pale gray crown and nape; four distinct checkered areas on dark gray back; dark throat patch has green iridescence. **Winter:** Black forehead, dark gray back, white on neck more sharply defined from black than in Red-throated. **Similar species:** See the Pacific Loon. Winter Red-throated is paler; bill is *upturned.* Yellow-billed is much larger with *upturned yellowish bill.* **Status:** Uncommon winter visitor; coasts and bays.

YELLOW-BILLED LOON [WHITE-BILLED DIVER] *Gavia adamsii* <Hashijiro-abi> L 89cm. Significantly larger than the other loons found in Japan, with larger head and fairly thick neck. The large *upturned yellowish bill* is straight on top, angled upward on the bottom. **Summer:** Glossy black head and neck with necklace and two striped half-collars; back checkered black and white. **Winter:** Dark gray-brown back; pale face and foreneck with whitish area around eye. **Similar species:** See other loons. **Status:** Uncommon winter visitor to northern Japan.

Loons

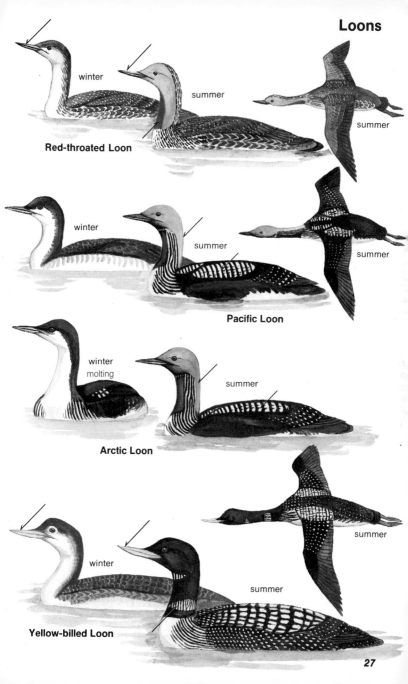

Red-throated Loon
winter
summer
summer

Pacific Loon
winter
summer
summer

Arctic Loon
winter
molting
summer

Yellow-billed Loon
winter
summer
summer

27

Grebes

Family *Podicipedidae* (World: 20 species; Japan: 5 species) Diving and swimming birds, smaller than loons, appear tailless. Often dive rather than fly to escape danger. Flight is weak, preceded by a running take-off. Small heads are held low in flight on extended thin necks. Sexes alike.

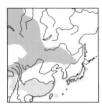

GREAT CRESTED GREBE *Podiceps cristatus* <Kanmuri-kaitsuburi> L 56cm. Largest grebe in Japan. **Summer:** Black crest and *black-tipped chestnut fringe* around white face; black bill. **Winter:** Blackish cap; gray-brown nape and back; *white neck, throat, and face; black lores;* pale bill. **Similar species:** Winter Red-necked Grebe has shorter gray neck; back of head more rounded. **Status:** Breeds locally in n. Honshu (Aomori Pref.). Uncommon winter visitor to coasts and some inland lakes.

RED-NECKED GREBE *Podiceps grisegena* <Akaeri-kaitsuburi> L 47cm. Larger; longer neck and bill than Eared and Horned Grebes. **Summer:** *Light cheek, rufous neck.* **Winter:** Grayish overall; *white crescent on cheek.* Yellow bill has black tip. **Similar species:** Winter Great Crested Grebe has white above eye; back of head more pointed. See description. **Status:** Breeds in lakes and marshes in Hokkaido. Common winter visitor; coasts and estuaries, Honshu southward.

HORNED GREBE [SLAVONIAN GREBE] *Podiceps auritus* <Mimi-kaitsuburi> L 33cm. Straight black bill with light tip. **Summer:** Black head with *golden ear tufts; chestnut neck.* **Winter:** *Black cap stops at eye line;* white cheek and *foreneck.* **Similar species:** Eared Grebe has higher forehead; see description. **Status:** Uncommon winter visitor; coasts.

EARED GREBE [BLACK-NECKED GREBE] *Podiceps nigricollis* <Hajiro-kaitsuburi> L 31cm. Bill slightly upturned. **Summer:** *Black neck* and head; golden ear tufts. **Winter:** *Gray neck;* ill-defined dark cap *extends below eye.* **Similar species:** Horned Grebe has flatter forehead; see description. **Status:** Common winter visitor to coasts, estuaries, ponds, and lakes throughout Japan.

LITTLE GREBE *Podiceps ruficollis* <Kaitsuburi> L 26cm. Smallest grebe in Japan. Blunt rounded body; short neck and bill. **Summer:** *Chestnut cheek* and neck; *light patch at base of bill.* **Immature:** Striped face and neck. **Winter:** Paler upperparts. **Similar species:** Other grebes have longer necks and bills. **Status:** Common resident; lakes, marshes, and rivers throughout Japan.

Grebes

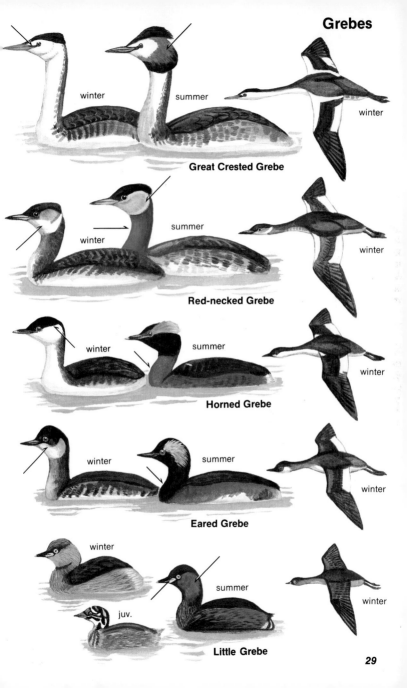

winter

summer

winter

Great Crested Grebe

winter

summer

winter

Red-necked Grebe

winter

summer

winter

Horned Grebe

winter

summer

winter

Eared Grebe

winter

summer

juv.

winter

Little Grebe

Cormorants

Family *Phalacrocoracidae* (World: 30 species; Japan: 4 species) Large, predominantly black, diving birds with webbed feet, long stiff tails, long necks, and slender bills hooked at the tip. With necks outstretched, usually fly low over water (higher over land) in long lines or wedges. Often perch with wings spread. Breed in colonies on cliffs or inland in trees. Sexes alike.

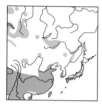

GREAT CORMORANT [CORMORANT] *Phalacrocorax carbo* <Kawa-u> L 82cm. W 135cm. Large, with glossy blue-black body and dull *bronze upper wing coverts.* Naked skin on face yellow; cheeks white. **Summer:** White plumes on head and neck, white patches on flanks; both absent in winter. **Immature:** Brown above, paler below. **Similar species:** See Temminck's Cormorant. **Status:** Locally common breeding resident in Aomori, Tokyo, Aichi, Shiga, and Oita Prefs. Breeds in tree colonies. Habitat includes shallow coastal waters, estuaries, and inland waters.

TEMMINCK'S CORMORANT [JAPANESE CORMORANT] *Phalacrocorax filamentosus* <Umi-u> L 84cm. W 137cm. Nearly identical to Great Cormorant. Adults distinguished by *greenish gloss on bronze upper wing coverts;* shorter tail; wings joined to rear half of body, center of body in Great. Without gloss, immature not easily distinguished. **Status:** Locally common breeding resident of rocky seacoast from Kyushu northward. Winters Honshu southward. Rarely found in inland waters.

RED-FACED CORMORANT *Phalacrocorax urile* <Chishima-ugarasu> L 76cm. Similar to the Pelagic Cormorant, but has *bluish-white bill, larger head,* slightly thicker neck, and *red forehead in summer.* **Status:** Breeds on cliffs and islands off the coast of the Nemuro Peninsula in e. Hokkaido; winter area uncertain.

PELAGIC CORMORANT *Phalacrocorax pelagicus* <Hime-u> L 73cm. W 98cm. Smaller than Great and Temminck's Cormorants. Entire plumage glossy greenish-black. Head small; neck long and *thin.* Naked skin on *face red,* but *forehead black, bill blackish brown and thin.* **Summer:** Black crests on crown and nape; white patch on each flank. **Winter:** Crests and flank patches absent; face skin covered. **Immature:** Brown overall. **Similar species:** See Red-faced Cormorant. **Status:** Locally common breeder on cliffs and rocks along coast of n. Japan; winters throughout Japan.

Cormorants

winter

Great Cormorant

imm.

summer

winter

winter

drying its wings

juv.

imm.

summer

Temminck's Cormorant

summer

summer

Red-faced Cormorant

imm.

summer

summer

winter

imm.

summer

Pelagic Cormorant

winter

Swans

Family *Anatidae* in part (World: 6 species; Japan: 3 species) Large swimming birds with long necks. Northern Hemisphere adults are all white, often stained orange on head; young birds gray brown. Distinguished in flight from other large white birds by all-white wings, long outstretched necks, and feet which do not project beyond tail. Feed mainly on aquatic plants and seeds by upending or by immersing head and neck. Migrate in lines or wedges, flying with slow, powerful wingbeats. Inhabit inland lakes, slow-running rivers, sheltered bays, and coastal waters. Sexes alike.

MUTE SWAN *Cygnus olor* <Kobu-hakuchō> L 152 cm. *Orange-red bill has a black knob* at the base. Swims with neck curved and wings sometimes arched upward. Immature bird is brownish gray; has grayish bill with black base, no knob. **Status:** Accidental. Only one bird presumed wild has been recorded (on Hachijo I.) Introduced to park lakes, moats.

WHOOPER SWAN *Cygnus cygnus* <Ō-hakuchō > L 140cm. W 225cm. Entirely white but head often stained with orange. *Yellow area at base of the long bill comes to a point where it meets the black tip area beyond the nostril.* Immature birds are gray brown with darker head and neck; bill pink at base, black at tip. **Status:** Locally common winter visitor; lakes, marshes, large rivers, and bays in n. Japan.

WHISTLING SWAN *Cygnus columbianus* <Ko-hakuchō> L 120cm. Smaller, shorter necked, and with a stubbier bill than the Whooper. Two subspecies of this entirely white swan are seen in Japan. The bill of the common Eurasian subspecies *jankowskii* has an extensive yellow area at the base which is more rounded than the yellow on the Whooper's bill and ends behind the nostril. The rare American subspecies *columbianus* usually has only a small yellow spot at the base of the bill just below the eye. **Status:** Locally common winter visitor to Honshu, arriving earlier in fall and wintering farther south than the Whooper. American subspecies is a rare winter visitor. Habitat includes lakes, marshes, large rivers, and bays.

Swans

imm.

Mute Swan

Whooper Swan

imm.

Whistling Swan

imm.

form with black
on bill to forehead

subspecies *columbianus*

Geese

Family *Anatidae* in part (World: 14 species; Japan 9 species)   Large heavy-set waterfowl. Neck lengths are between those of swans and ducks. Highly vocal and gregarious. Flight fast and direct with powerful wingbeats. Migrate in long noisy lines or V's. Most are more terrestrial than ducks (Brant an exception), feeding on grasses, seeds, and aquatic plants in marshes, rice fields, rivers, and lakes as well as tidal mudflats, bays, and coastal waters. Sexes alike.

CANADA GOOSE *Branta canadensis* <Shijūkaragan> L 67cm. The *clear white chinstrap and neck ring* contrasting with the *black head and neck* are diagnostic. Back gray brown with buff barring; primaries dark brownish black; breast and belly barred lighter brown; upper and under tail coverts and ventral area white; tail dark. **Similar species:** Brant has black face and breast. **Status:** Rare winter visitor to lakes, marshes, and rice fields from central Honshu northward. Most often in mixed flocks with other geese.

BRANT [BRENT] *Branta bernicla* <Koku-gan> L 61cm. The smallest goose in Japan, just larger than a Mallard. *Black head, neck, and breast; white patch on side of neck.* The rear underparts are conspicuously white; upper tail coverts white; tail black but extremely short. **Similar species:** The larger Canada Goose has white cheek, pale breast. **Status:** Uncommon and local winter visitor to shallow saltwater bays and tidal mudflats; mainly in n. Japan.

SNOW GOOSE *Anser caerulescens* <Haku-gan> L 67cm. Adult birds are unmistakable; pure white except for *black primaries*. Bill and legs are pink. Immature birds are grayish white with a dark bill. **Similar species:** Swans are much larger with longer necks; no black primaries. **Status:** Rare winter visitor in mixed flocks with White-fronted. Marshes, rice stubble fields, and lakes; central Honshu northward.

Geese

Canada Goose

imm.

imm.

form without
white throat

Brant

imm.

imm.

Snow Goose

imm.

imm.

WHITE-FRONTED GOOSE *Anser albifrons* <Ma-ga n> L 72cm. Predominantly gray brown. *White patch surrounding base of bill* stands out against grayish-brown head and neck. *Strong irregular black markings on gray belly.* Bill pink or pinkish orange with white nail; feet and legs orange. **Immature:** Lacks white face patch and dark belly markings of adult. **Similar species:** See Lesser White-fronted Goose. Bean Goose has orange bill, black at tip and base; lacks face patch and belly markings; has darker neck. **Status:** Locally common winter visitor to marshes, rice fields, tidal flats, and salt water; mainly at Lake Izunuma, Miyagi Pref., and Katano, Ishikawa Pref.

LESSER WHITE-FRONTED GOOSE *Anser erythropus* <Karigane> L 58.5cm. Resembles a smaller version of White-fronted Goose but bill smaller and shorter; *white at base of bill extends to crown; tips of closed wings extend beyond tail;* fewer black blotches on belly. Both adult and immature have *yellowish eye-ring.* Immature lacks white forehead and dark belly markings. **Status:** Rare winter visitor to marshes and rice fields in Honshu. Usually mixed in with flocks of White-fronted Geese.

EMPEROR GOOSE *Anser canagicus* <Mikado-gan> L 67.5cm. A small goose with *distinctly scaled* bluish-gray plumage (feathers banded black with white margins), white tail, and dark under tail coverts. *White head and hindneck;* black throat; orange legs. **Immature:** Dark gray head; neck and breast not so distinctly marked; darker legs. **Status:** Accidental. A single individual in a flock of White-fronted Geese recorded in Miyagi Pref., 1964.

Geese

imm.

imm.

imm.

form with orange bill

White-fronted Goose

imm.

Lesser White-fronted Goose

Emperor Goose

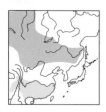

GRAYLAG GOOSE *Anser anser* <Haiiro-gan> L 84cm. A large gray goose with *pink legs and bill; pale forewings* contrast with dark flight feathers. Note pattern formed by gray rump, white upper tail coverts, and white-rimmed gray tail. **Similar species:** White-fronted Goose has orange legs, black belly markings, black tail. Bean Goose is darker with orange legs. **Status:** Rare winter visitor to marshes and rivers throughout Japan.

SWAN GOOSE *Anser cygnoides* <Sakatsura-gan> L 87cm. A large goose, grayish-brown above with lighter brown underparts and dark bars on flanks. *Long sloping black bill with white line at base.* The *buffy face and pale throat* contrast with the dark brown crown and hindneck. Orange legs. **Similar species:** No other gray goose in Japan has a clear pale throat and foreneck. **Status:** Rare winter visitor, Kyushu northward; marshes and rice fields.

BEAN GOOSE *Anser fabalis* <Hishikui> L 85cm. A large goose with a *uniformly dark brown head and neck;* paler grayish-brown back, breast, and belly; white rear underparts; *black bill with orange band;* orange legs. **Similar species:** Immature White-fronted Goose has a pink bill. See also Graylag Goose (pale forewings, pink legs and bill) and Swan Goose (pale foreneck and face). **Status:** Locally common winter visitor to marshes and rice stubble fields; mainly Lake Izunuma, Miyagi Pref.; Fukushimagata, Niigata Pref.; and Lake Biwa, Shiga Pref.

Geese

Graylag Goose

Swan Goose

Bean Goose

Feeding

Marsh Ducks

Geese

Swans

Ducks

Family *Anatidae* in part (World: 116 species; Japan: 36 species)   Waterfowl smaller than swans and geese, with shorter necks and legs. Sexes usually have quite different plumages, but immature males and males in eclipse plumage resemble females. Five groups in Japan.

Whistling Ducks

Long-legged ducks with an erect, goose-like posture, found mainly in warmer regions and the tropics. Sexes are similar.

INDIAN WHISTLING DUCK *Dendrocygna javanica* <Ryukyu-gamo> L 41cm. Small *long-legged* duck with *buffy neck* and cheek, dark *brown cap* and nape, and *rufous underparts* with buffy streaks on flanks. In flight, chestnut upper wing and upper tail coverts contrast with black flight feathers and tail. **Status:** Recent status uncertain. Probably extinct in Japan. Ponds with dense vegetation, mangrove swamps, and lagoons; Okinawa I. and the s. Ryuku Is.

Shelducks

Large ducks, midway in size between marsh ducks and geese, sharing characteristics of both. Sexes are not identical, but not as dissimilar as in marsh ducks.

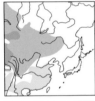

RUDDY SHELDUCK *Tadorna ferruginea* <Aka-tsukushi-gamo> L 63.5cm. A large, nearly goose-sized duck with an *orange-brown body and pale head.* The *extensive white on the wings contrasts strikingly* with the black primaries and orange body. Male has a narrow black ring around the neck. **Status:** Rare winter visitor to lake shores, river banks, and rice fields from Honshu southward.

COMMON SHELDUCK *Tadorna tadorna* <Tsukushi-gamo> L 62.5cm. A large duck with a greenish-black head, a *wide chestnut belt* encircling the white body, and a *broad black stripe down the center of the underparts.* Tail and wings white; tip of tail, scapulars, and flight feathers black; speculum green. Bill red, male's with knob in breeding season. **Status:** Locally common winter visitor to mudflats in Ariake Bay, Kyushu; rare visitor to tidal mudflats and watered rice fields near seacoast elsewhere.

CRESTED SHELDUCK *Tadorna cristata* <Kanmuri-tsukushi-gamo> L 64cm. Black crown with *black crest hanging over the nape;* finely barred dark gray back and underparts; chestnut scapulars and under tail coverts; white forewings; black flight feathers; green speculum. **Male:** Black crown extends to eye; black chin spot and breast; gray cheek and neck. **Female:** White breast, neck, and face; black spectacles. **Status:** Now uncertain. It was possibly a rare winter visitor to Japan in the 1800's.

Whistling Ducks
Shelducks

sexes similar

Indian Whistling Duck

♂ winter

♂ winter

♀

♂ summer

Ruddy Shelduck

♂ winter

imm.

♂ winter

♂ summer

♀

♂ winter

Common Shelduck

♂

♀

♂

Crested Shelduck

41

Marsh Ducks

Generally found on shallow water where they feed by dabbling on the surface or by upending and submerging the head and neck. Rarely dive. Often graze on land. Take flight by springing almost straight up. Sexes usually have different plumages, but immature and eclipse males resemble females. Both sexes usually have similar iridescent speculum on rear edge of wing.

MALLARD *Anas platyrhynchos* <Ma-gamo> L 64 cm. **Male:** The *iridescent green head, narrow white collar,* and *chestnut breast* mark this familiar duck. Back and wings gray; rump black with curled feathers; tail white; bill yellowish; legs orange. **Female:** Mottled brown; black patches on orange bill; orange feet. In flight both sexes show a *blue speculum bordered on both sides with white.* **Similar species:** Female Gadwall has orange panels on sides of finer brown bill; white secondaries often visible at rest. Female Pintail has longer neck, pointed tail, blue-gray bill. Spot-billed Duck is browner with paler head, distinctive bill. **Status:** Common winter visitor throughout. Some breed in north.

SPOT-BILLED DUCK *Anas poecilorhyncha* <Karugamo> L 60.5cm. Sexes alike. Large mottled brown duck with pale head and neck, dark brown cap and nape, dark *facial stripes through and below the eye, yellow-tipped black bill,* and orange legs. White tertiaries contrast with dark rump in flight. Speculum blue. From below the *white wing linings* contrast sharply with the dark body and flight feathers. **Similar species:** Female Mallard has browner head and paler, browner back. **Status:** Abundant resident of inland waters throughout Japan; population in Hokkaido winters in warmer areas.

(NORTHERN) SHOVELER *Anas clypeata* <Hashibiro-gamo> L 50cm. Diagnostic broad *dark spatulate bill,* which is longer than the head, is apparent even at a great distance and in flight. **Male:** Greenish-black head, black-and-white back, white breast, and *chestnut belly.* In flight the *pale blue wing coverts* above and the *white wing linings* below contrast with dark flight feathers. **Female:** Mottled brown body, dark stripe through eye, and gray-blue forewing. Both sexes have green speculum and orange legs. **Similar species:** Bill shape separates female from other brown ducks. **Status:** Common winter visitor to bays and freshwater marshes and lakes throughout Japan.

Marsh Ducks

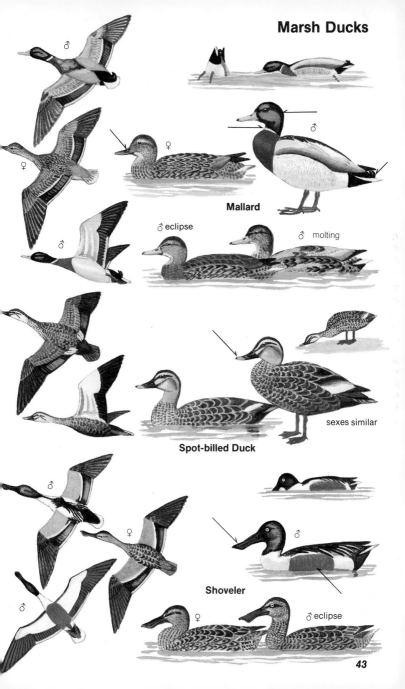

♂

♀

♀

Mallard

♂

♂ eclipse

♂ molting

Spot-billed Duck

sexes similar

♂

♀

♂

Shoveler

♂

♀

♂ eclipse

43

GREEN-WINGED TEAL [TEAL] *Anas crecca* <Kogamo> L 37.5cm. A small grayish duck. Both Eurasian and American subspecies occur in Japan. **Male:** Dark brown head with curving *iridescent dark green patch* (appears black except in sunlight); speckled buffy breast; black-bordered *yellow patch at stern.* At rest, Eurasian subspecies shows long *horizontal white stripe* on scapulars; American subspecies a *vertical white stripe* in front of the wing. **Female:** Speckled brown with dark line through eye. Both sexes have a *green speculum.* In flight entire wing appears dark except for white bars on either side of speculum. **Similar species:** Compare females of other teals and Garganey. **Status:** Eurasian subspecies a common winter visitor to freshwater ponds, lakes, and rivers. Breeds along mountain lakes in central and n. Honshu and Hokkaido. American subspecies *carolinensis* a rare winter visitor.

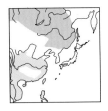

GARGANEY *Anas querquedula* <Shimaaji> L 38cm. A small duck the size of a teal. **Male:** At rest, shows *conspicuous broad white stripe curving over eye to nape and* long drooping black-and-white scapulars. In flight, *pale blue-gray forewing* contrasts with dark flight feathers; dark brown breast contrasts with white belly and pale sides. **Female:** Resembles female Green-winged Teal but has a *prominent eyebrow,* pale spot at base of bill, *grayish forewing,* and indistinct greenish speculum. **Similar species:** Compare female with females of the Green-winged and Baikal Teals. **Status:** An uncommon transient to freshwater ponds and marshes. A few birds breed in Hokkaido.

BAIKAL TEAL *Anas formosa* <Tomoe-gamo> L 40cm. **Male:** Unique *facial pattern of yellow, green, and black;* vertical white stripe in front of the wing; long drooping chestnut, black, and white striped scapulars form a fan over the flank. **Female:** Resembles female Green-winged Teal but has pronounced *white spot at base of bill* and *pale eyebrow.* **Similar species:** Compare female with Garganey and other female teals. **Status:** Uncommon winter visitor to inland lakes, paddy fields, and saltwater bays; but locally common. Number varies from year to year. Central Honshu southward.

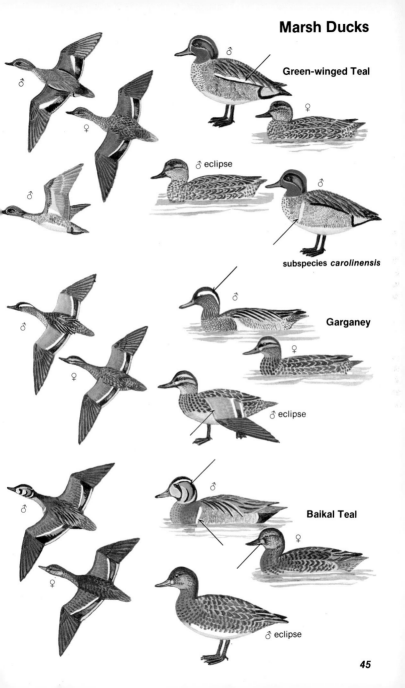

Marsh Ducks

Green-winged Teal

♂ eclipse

♂

subspecies *carolinensis*

Garganey

♂

♀

♂ eclipse

Baikal Teal

♂

♀

♂ eclipse

45

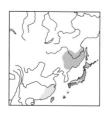

MANDARIN DUCK *Aix galericulata* <Oshidori>
L 45cm. The spectacular male is unmistakable. Long *orange whiskers;* red bill; glossy green crown; chestnut, green, and purple crest; broad buff eyebrow; purplish-chestnut breast; orange fan-shaped tertiaries always *raised like sails.* **Female:** *White spectacles* and white ring around base of bill; black bill. Male in eclipse resembles female but has a red bill. **Status:** A common local wanderer; some are resident. Summer visitor in Hokkaido. Wooded inland waters and city parks; breeds in holes in trees and nest boxes.

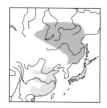

FALCATED TEAL *Anas falcata* <Yoshi-gamo> L 48cm. **Male:** *Long curving tertiary feathers droop over the tail;* iridescent brown head with *broad glossy dark green band curving to nape;* long sleek crest; white throat with black lower border; white spot above base of bill; *black bill* and legs. **Female:** Mottled brown; black bill; green speculum; no prominent distinguishing marks; no dark eyestripe; no light eyebrow. **Similar species:** Compare female with the female Green-winged Teal, Wigeon, and Gadwall. **Status:** Uncommon winter visitor, Honshu southward. Lakes, marshes, large rivers, and bays. A few breed in Hokkaido.

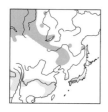

GADWALL *Anas strepera* <Okayoshi-gamo> L 50 cm. **Male:** Gray with *a conspicuous black stern,* gray tail, gray-brown head and neck, dark gray bill, yellowish-orange legs. In flight, shows white belly, *white speculum* contrasting with black stripe on underwing and black and chestnut stripes on upperwing. **Female:** Darkly mottled brown; white speculum; white belly; *orange-sided brown bill;* gray-brown tail. **Similar species:** Female Mallard has white tail; female Pintail lacks orange on bill and white speculum. **Status:** Uncommon winter visitor to freshwater lakes and rivers; Honshu southward. Some breed in Hokkaido.

Marsh Ducks

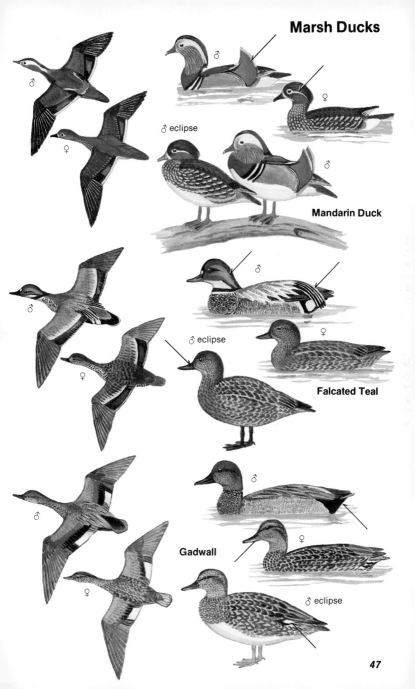

♂

♀

♂ eclipse

Mandarin Duck

♂ eclipse

♂

♀

♂

♀

Falcated Teal

♂

♀

Gadwall

♂

♀

♂ eclipse

PINTAIL *Anas acuta* <Onaga-gamo> L Male 75cm. Female 53cm. **Male:** Slender, long-necked duck with *long pointed central tail feathers* and a *conspicuous white line* running from the white foreneck up the side of the dark brown head. Brown hindneck; white breast and belly; black under tail coverts with cream band in front; black bill with bluish sides; gray legs; green speculum with buff border in front and white border behind. **Female:** Mottled brown with *shorter pointed tail,* long thin neck, dark bill. In flight, white border shows on rear edge of brown speculum. **Similar species:** Male Oldsquaw has long tail but entirely different color pattern. Compare also the female Mallard and Gadwall with the female Pintail. **Status:** Common winter visitor throughout Japan. Freshwater marshes, lakes, rivers, bays, and estuaries.

(EURASIAN) WIGEON *Anas penelope* <Hidori-ga mo> L 48.5cm. **Male:** *Buff crown and forehead on chestnut head;* bluish-gray bill with black tip; pinkish-brown breast; gray upperparts and sides; white wing coverts; black under tail coverts. At rest, *horizontal white line* shows along the flank. Juvenile male does not acquire white wing coverts until second winter. **Female:** Dark brown body, brown head, white belly, gray-brown upper wing coverts, white bars on both sides of dark speculum. **Similar species:** See American Wigeon and female Falcated Teal. **Status:** Common winter visitor to bays throughout Japan; also in fresh water.

AMERICAN WIGEON *Anas americana* <Amerika-hido ri> L 48cm. **Male:** In flight resembles Wigeon, but body is pinkish brown and head has *bright white crown, large green patch* from eye to hind neck, and buff cheek. **Female:** Like female Wigeon but slightly *grayish head.* **Similar species:** Compare female with female Falcated Teal. **Status:** Uncommon winter visitor mixed in with flocks of Wigeon; bays and lakes in Honshu and Kyushu.

Marsh Ducks

♂

♂

♀

♂ eclipse

Pintail

♂ form with green
eye stripe

♂

♀

♂ eclipse

♂

♀

♂ imm.

Wigeon

♂

American Wigeon

♂

♀

♂ eclipse

Bay Ducks

The diving ducks are divided here into this group and the sea ducks (description on pp 56, 58). Both bay ducks and sea ducks feed by diving from the surface and swimming underwater in search of small aquatic animals and plants. Diving ducks have smaller, more pointed wings than marsh ducks. They are swift fliers but must run along the surface for some distance before becoming airborne. Bay ducks winter in protected bays and seacoasts as well as in large lakes and river mouths. They breed in marshes and along lakeshores.

RED-CRESTED POCHARD *Netta rufina* <Akahashi-hajiro> L 56cm. **Male:** Red bill; *orange-chestnut head; black neck, breast,* and stern; white crescent on shoulder. In flight, white band across leading edge of upperwing; *large white oval patch on each flank;* black belly. **Female:** Dark brown cap over *whitish cheek,* black bill with orange tip. Both sexes have *white flight feathers* with narrow dark margins. **Similar species:** Compare female with female Smew and female Black Scoter. See Pochard. **Status:** Accidental; in winter to central Honshu (Fukui Pref.) and s. Ryukyu Is. Freshwater marshes and lakes.

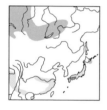

POCHARD *Aythya ferina* <Hoshi-hajiro> L 45cm. **Male:** *Reddish-brown head* with high crown and sloping forehead; dark bill with bluish-gray band; black breast and stern; *pale gray body;* reddish eyes; gray legs. In flight, pale gray band runs length of wing. **Female:** Brown head with pale eye-ring and pale area at base of bill, brown breast, darker body. **Similar species:** See Canvasback and female Ring-necked Duck. **Status:** Common winter visitor to marshes and lakes, Kyushu northward. Some breed in Hokkaido.

CANVASBACK *Aythya valisineria* <Ō-hoshi-hajiro> L 55cm. Both sexes resemble the Pochard but are larger with *longer black bills* and more sloping foreheads. **Male:** *Nearly white* upperparts. **Female:** Grayer than female Pochard with darker breast. **Status:** Accidental visitor to marshes, lakes, and bays in Hokkaido, Honshu, and Shikoku.

Bay Ducks

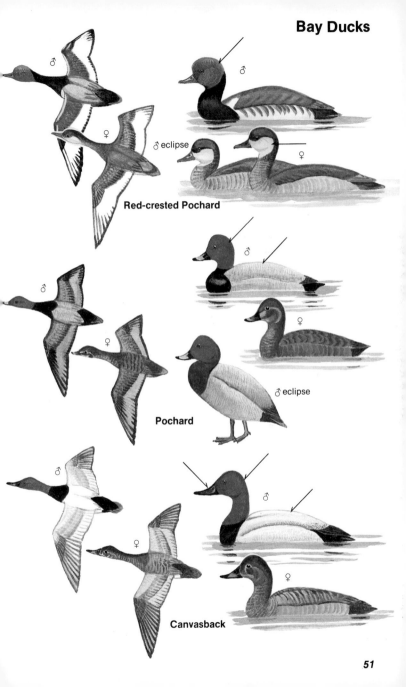

♂

♀

♂ eclipse

Red-crested Pochard

♂

♀

♂

♀

♂ eclipse

Pochard

♂

♀

♂

♀

Canvasback

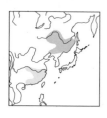

BAER'S POCHARD *Aythya baeri* <Aka-hajiro>
L 45cm. **Male:** *Black head glossed with green;* white
eye; reddish-brown breast; dark brown upperparts;
lighter brown flanks; white belly and under tail coverts.
Female: Brown head with *buffy patch* at base of bill;
dark eye. *Head and neck darker than breast.* In flight,
both sexes show a *white band across the flight feathers* contrasting with dark brown forewing. **Similar
species:** See White-eyed Pochard. **Status:** Rare winter
visitor to freshwater marshes, lakes, and ponds; Kyushu northward.

WHITE-EYED POCHARD [FERRUGINOUS DUCK]
Aythya nyroca <Mejiro-gamo> L 41cm. A small
dark duck resembling Baer's Pochard. Both sexes
show *white band across the flight feathers on upperwing.* **Male:** *Deep reddish-brown head, breast,and
flanks;* white eye; brown back; white under tail coverts.
Female: Duller brown; dark eye. **Similar species:**
Compare Baer's Pochard. **Status:** Accidental; one
record, Chiba Pref. Freshwater marshes and lakes.

COMMON GOLDENEYE *Bucephala clangula* <Hō
jiro-gamo> L 45cm. **Male:** Triangular, glossy greenish-black head with *white patch between eye and bill;*
yellow eye; blackish bill; white underparts; black
back, rump, and tail; outer scapulars predominately
white with black edges; orange legs. **Female:** Less
peaked brown head; black bill with *yellow band;* white
collar; grayish body. Immature male resembles female
but has cheek spot. In flight both sexes show *broad
white patches on upper wings;* in female, patch is
broken by two black lines. **Similar species:** Bufflehead
has white spot behind the eye. **Status:** Common winter visitor to lakes and rivers and along coasts; Kyushu northward.

BUFFLEHEAD *Bucephala albeola* <Hime-hajiro>
L 35.5cm. **Male:** Iridescent black head with a *large
white patch* beginning behind and below eye and
extending around back of head; small dark bill; white
neck, underparts, and flanks; black back and rump;
white outer scapulars; *white wing patches* like Common Goldeneye. **Female:** Dark grayish-brown above,
grayish below, large *white spot behind eye;* on wings
only the secondaries are white. **Similar species:** Common Goldeneye is much larger, has *white patch
between eye and bill.* At a distance female might be
confused with female Harlequin or Oldsquaw. **Status:**
Rare visitor to coastal waters in n. Japan. Usually
found with Goldeneyes.

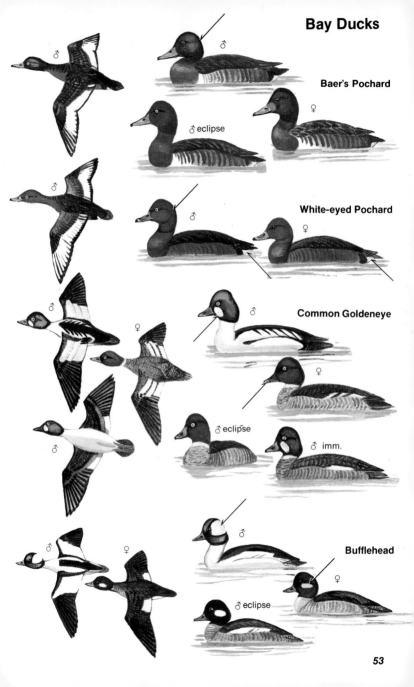

Bay Ducks

Baer's Pochard

♂

♂ eclipse

♀

White-eyed Pochard

♂

♀

Common Goldeneye

♂

♀

♂ eclipse

♂ imm.

♂

♀

Bufflehead

♂

♀

♂ eclipse

53

RING-NECKED DUCK *Aythya collaris* <Kubiwa-kinkuro> L 40cm. **Male:** All black above; *peaked head* glossed with purple, back and breast with green; flanks gray; bill dark *gray blue with black tip and two narrow bluish-white rings;* vertical white bar between black breast and gray flanks. **Female:** Dark brown above with *white spectacles* and whitish area behind base of bill and on chin. In flight both sexes show *gray stripe* across upper flight feathers. **Similar species:** Tufted Duck has tuft, lacks rings on bill, and has white sides and wing stripe. Greater Scaup has gray back and white wing stripe. Compare female with female Pochard. **Status:** Accidental. One female was recorded at a pond in Tokyo.

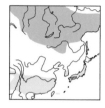

TUFTED DUCK *Aythya fuligula* <Kinkuro-hajiro> L 40cm. **Male:** The long *black crest* drooping from the purplish-black head and the *white belly and flanks* contrasting with the black breast, back, and stern are distinctive. **Female:** *Shorter crest;* dark brown head; body brown above the waterline; white belly. Sometimes has white patch at base of bill and on under tail coverts. Both sexes have a bright *white band* across the upper flight feathers; gray bill with black tip. **Similar species:** Greater Scaup has gray back, greenish gloss on head, and no crest. Ring-necked Duck has gray flanks, vertical white stripe, rings on bill, and no crest. **Status:** Common winter visitor to freshwater marshes, large rivers, and lakes throughout Japan. Some breed in Hokkaido.

GREATER SCAUP *Aythya marila* <Suzu-gamo> L 45cm **Male:** Black head and neck with *greenish gloss;* black breast and stern; *gray back;* white flanks and belly. Male in eclipse is browner with a little white at base of bill. **Female:** *White patch at base of bill;* brown upperparts. Both sexes show a *bright white bar* on upperwing in flight. Bill bluish gray with black tip. **Similar species:** See Ring-necked Duck and Tufted Duck. **Status:** Abundant winter visitor. Huge flocks in bays, estuaries, and large rivers throughout Japan.

Bay Ducks

Ring-necked Duck

♂

♀

Tufted Duck

♂

♀

♂ eclipse

♀ form with white on bill

♀ form with white on stern

Greater Scaup

♂

♀

♂ eclipse

♀

55

Sea Ducks

Generally heavy-bodied, short-necked diving birds found in rougher, more open water than bay ducks. All are expert divers. The oceanic species dive to the ocean floor in search of mollusks and crustaceans. Like bay ducks they run along the water surface for some distance before becoming airborne.

HARLEQUIN DUCK *Histrionicus histrionicus* <Shi nori-gamo> L 43cm. Short neck, narrow bill, and long tail. In the distance both sexes appear dark. Male is unmistakable; mostly dark blue with *chestnut flanks; boldly patterned with white* on head, breast, and back. Male in eclipse is blacker with more white pattern than female. **Female:** Dusky brown with *three white spots on head,* no wing patch. **Similar species:** See female Bufflehead (one face-spot) and female scoters. **Status:** Winter visitor to rocky outer seacoasts; common central Honshu northward; rare farther south. Some birds breed along rapid rivers in mountains of n. Honshu.

OLDSQUAW [LONG-TAILED DUCK] *Clangula hyemalis* <Kōri-gamo> L Male 60cm. Female 38cm. Both sexes have different summer and winter plumages; the latter is usually seen in Japan. White belly and dark unpatterned wings in all plumages. **Winter male:** *Long black central tail feathers;* white head and neck; *two-toned dark cheek;* black-and-white back; white flanks, belly, and under tail coverts; gray bill with orange band. **Summer male:** Head and neck black with large white face patch. **Winter female:** White head and neck, black crown and *cheek patch,* blackish-brown upperparts and breast. **Summer female:** Head grayer, foreneck darker. **Similar species:** Male Pintail has long tail but much longer neck and different plumage. **Status:** Winter visitor at sea, along coasts, and in bays. Common in Hokkaido; uncommon in n. Honshu.

BLACK SCOTER [COMMON SCOTER] *Melanitta nigra* <Kuro-gamo> L 48cm. **Male:** Plumage entirely black; *yellowish-orange knob* at base of black bill. **Female:** *Light cheeks and throat* contrast with dark brown cap and overall brown plumage; black bill with no knob. **Similar species:** Other male scoters have some white patches on head or wings; other females lack light cheeks and throat. **Status:** Common winter visitor to seacoasts and bays. Some may breed along freshwater lakes in Hokkaido: no nest records, but juveniles observed.

Sea Ducks

Harlequin Duck

♂

♂

♀

♂ imm.

♀

♂ eclipse

♂

♀

♂ summer

♀ summer

Oldsquaw

♂

♀

♂

♀

Black Scoter

STELLER'S EIDER *Polysticta stelleri* <Ko-kewata-gamo> L 46cm. **Male:** Appears mostly white and black on water; white head with small green crest on back of crown and on forehead; black collar extends down the white back. Distinctive in flight with *black line down back* and *buffy orange belly* contrasting with large white patches on forewing, black primaries, and blue speculum. **Female:** Dark brown with *white-bordered blue speculum* visible at rest and in flight. **Similar species:** Compare male with male Smew and Oldsquaw. **Status:** Locally uncommon winter visitor to Cape Nosappu in e. Hokkaido; one record n. Honshu.

KING EIDER *Somateria spectabilis* <Kewata-gamo> L 56cm. **Male:** Spectacular with *orange shield* on forehead above orange bill; squarish pearl-gray head with pale green cheeks and black stripes; black back and sides; *white patches on sides of black rump;* white foreparts; large white wing patches bordered with black. **Immature male:** Dark brown or black head with beginnings of orange shield; black upperparts and white breast. **Female:** Scaly brown plumage overall with lighter eye-ring and *white stripe* on upper wing. **Similar species:** Compare bill profiles of female eiders. **Status:** Accidental at sea and along rocky coasts. One record, a young male in Hokkaido.

WHITE-WINGED SCOTER [VELVET SCOTER] *Melanitta fusca* <Birōdo-kinkuro> L 55cm. **Male:** Black with *white spot beside the eye* and *black knob* on base of *orange bill.* **Female:** Dark brown overall with two round pale patches on face. Both sexes have *white secondaries,* sometimes visible at rest. **Similar species:** Other scoters in Japan lack white secondaries. **Status:** Common winter visitor to coasts and bays, Kyushu northward.

SURF SCOTER *Melanitta perspicillata* <Aranami-kinkuro> L 56cm. **Male:** Black plumage with *white patches on crown and nape; black, white, and orange-patterned large bill.* **Female:** Dusky brown plumage with *vague whitish patches on head and on nape.* No white on wings. **Similar species:** Other male scoters have darker heads. Female White-winged Scoter has white secondaries. Bill shape and whitish patch on neck distinguish female from female White-winged Scoter if absence of white secondaries cannot be ascertained. **Status:** Straggler to coasts and bays in n. Japan.

Sea Ducks

Steller's Eider
♂
♀

King Eider
♂
♀
♂ imm.

White-winged Scoter
♂
♀
♂ imm.
♂ imm.

Surf Scoter
♂
♀

59

Mergansers

Subfamily *Merginae* Fish-eating, diving ducks, all having long thin bills with serrated mandibles and slightly hooked tips. Conspicuous crests on all except male Common Merganser. Fast fliers with head, neck, and body held level. Mergansers require a running start to take off.

SMEW *Mergus albellus* <Miko-aisa> L 42cm. Differs significantly from other mergansers in shape, size, and bill. Distinctive in all plumages. **Male:** At rest appears *mostly white* with *black face mask,* black down center of back; at close range some black marks on nape and sides are visible. In flight, bold black-and-white pattern unlike that of any other duck. Small gray bill. **Female:** Chestnut cap and hindneck, *white cheek and throat,* indistinct black face mask; rest of upperparts gray. **Similar species:** Due to its habit of diving constantly, female at great distance may be confused with a grebe. Compare male to male Steller's Eider, female to female Red-crested Pochard and Black Scoter. **Status:** Uncommon winter visitor to marshes, lakes, and rivers; Kyushu northward. Some breed on wooded inland waters in Hokkaido.

RED-BREASTED MERGANSER *Mergus serrator* <Umi-aisa> L 55cm. Slim merganser with *long slender hooked red bill.* **Male:** Glossy greenish-black head with *conspicuous divided shaggy crest;* white collar; *rusty breast mottled black;* black back; grayish sides with double row of black and white stripes in front of wing. **Female:** Ashy brown with crested *reddish head blending into whitish throat and neck.* **Similar species:** Male Common Merganser is larger, lacks prominent crest, and has white breast. Female Common Merganser has sharp demarcation between white lower neck and reddish head. **Status:** Common winter visitor to coasts and bays, Kyushu northward.

COMMON MERGANSER [GOOSANDER] *Mergus merganser* <Kawa-aisa> L 65cm. **Male:** Greenish-black *head heavier and more rounded than* Red-breasted's and *lacking a shaggy crest;* black back; *white neck, breast,* and underparts tinged with peach; red bill. **Female:** Reddish head with crest; white chin spot; *sharp demarcation between red and white on neck.* **Similar species:** Red-breasted is smaller; male has crest; female lacks clear division between reddish head and white neck. **Status:** Common winter visitor to large lakes and marshes; central Honshu northward and n. Kyushu. Some breed in Hokkaido.

Mergansers

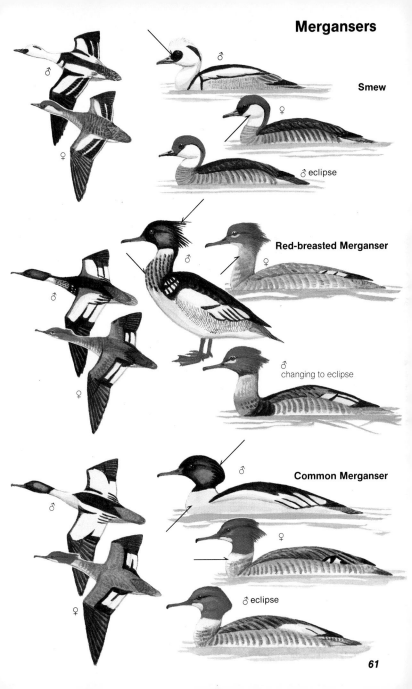

Smew

♂

♀

♂ eclipse

Red-breasted Merganser

♂

♀

♂

changing to eclipse

Common Merganser

♂

♀

♂

♂ eclipse

61

Auks (Alcids)

Family *Alcidae* (World: 20 species; Japan: 14 species) Small to medium-sized birds which inhabit the northern oceans. This group includes murres, murrelets, guillemots, puffins, and auklets. Generally have large heads, short tails, chunky bodies, and short legs. Plumage is mostly black and white. Fly rapidly with fast wingbeats; propel themselves underwater with their wings. Predominately pelagic; breed colonially on rocky islands and cliffs. Sexes alike.

THIN-BILLED MURRE [COMMON GUILLEMOT] *Uria aalge* <Umigarasu> L 43.5cm. *Long slender black bill.* **Summer:** Black head, throat, and upperparts; white line along rear edge of wing; white underparts; black underwings with white under wing coverts; brownish legs. **Winter:** White extends to throat and face; black stripe from eye across white cheek. **Similar species:** See Thick-billed Murre. **Status:** Locally common breeder on islands off Hokkaido. Uncommon winter visitor, central Honshu northward. Usually pelagic.

THICK-BILLED MURRE [BRUNNICH'S GUILLEMOT] *Uria lomvia* <Hashibuto-umigarasu> L 43.5cm. Resembles Thin-billed but *bill is thicker* with *white streak along base of upper mandible.* In winter black of crown extends below the eyes; white on bill less pronounced. **Status:** Uncommon winter visitor in pelagic waters off n. Japan; in mixed flocks with Thin-billed Murres.

SPECTACLED GUILLEMOT *Cepphus carbo* <Keima furi> L 37cm. *Conspicuous white spectacles* and bright *red feet.* **Summer:** Plumage dark except for white spectacles and white patches at base of black bill. **Winter:** Chin, throat, foreneck, and underparts white; white spectacles. **Similar species:** Pigeon Guillemot has white wing patch in summer and winter plumages; head black in summer, light and mottled in winter. **Status:** Locally common breeder along rocky coasts and cliffs, n. Japan. Winters along coasts farther south.

PIGEON GUILLEMOT *Cepphus columba* <Umibato> L 33cm. *White wing patch with double black bars,* black bill, red feet. **Summer:** Entire plumage sooty black except for wing patch. **Winter:** Upperparts dark brown; head, neck, and flanks whitish with brown bars. **Similar species:** Spectacled Guillemot lacks wing patches, has white spectacles. **Status:** Uncommon winter visitor to pelagic waters off n. Japan.

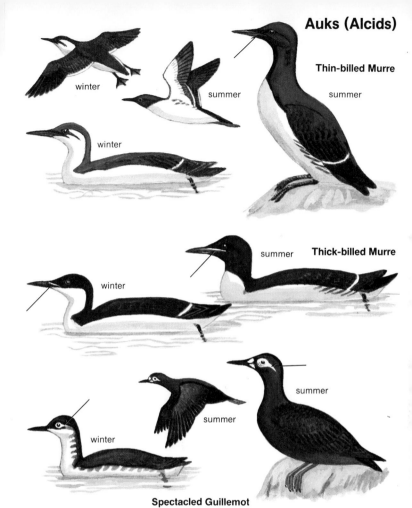

Auks (Alcids)

Thin-billed Murre

summer

winter

summer

winter

Thick-billed Murre

summer

winter

summer

winter

Spectacled Guillemot

Pigeon Guillemot

summer

winter

winter

MARBLED MURRELET *Brachyramphus marmoratus* <Madara-umisuzume> L 24.5cm. **Summer:** Dark brown above; *underparts whitish scaled with brown; long slender black bill;* white scapulars. **Winter:** Scaling absent; white below; white eye-ring. **Similar species:** Winter Ancient Murrelet lacks white scapulars. **Status:** Breeds in e.Hokkaido. Uncommon winter visitor mainly to coast of Hokkaido.

ANCIENT MURRELET *Synthliboramphus antiquus* <Umisuzume> L 25.5cm. Dark above, white below; black cap, gray back; *short bill, white eye-ring; white side of neck;* white under wing coverts. **Summer:** White stripe on each side of crown, white feathers on dark nape; pale bill. **Winter:** No crown stripe or white nape feathers; dark bill. **Similar species:** Japanese Murrelet has crest and black on side of neck. **Status:** Breeds on rocky cliffs in Hokkaido and n. Honshu. Common winter visitor, offshore waters throughout Japan.

JAPANESE MURRELET [CRESTED MURRELET] *Synthliboramphus wumizusume* <Kanmuri-umi suzume> L 24cm. Resembles Ancient but has *black crest* and *broad white stripes* on back of head which meet on nape in summer. Face, crown, center of nape black; upperparts slaty blue; underparts white. Crest shorter in winter. **Status:** Uncommon local breeder on isolated islets from central Honshu (Izu Is.) south. Offshore in winter.

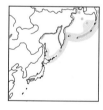

PARAKEET AUKLET *Aethia psittacula* <Umiōmu> L 23cm. Black above with white underparts; *stubby orange-red bill.* **Summer:** White plume behind eye; black throat and foreneck. **Winter:** Facial plume absent; bill darker; chin, throat, and foreneck white. **Similar species:** Least has white scapulars. Crested and Whiskered have dark breasts and sides above water line. **Status:** Pelagic rare winter visitor in waters off Hokkaido and Honshu.

LEAST AUKLET *Aethia pusilla* <Ko-umisuzume> L 15cm. Tiny; *white cheek; white scapulars* form white line on black back. **Summer:** Single white plume behind eye; *short red bill;* breast, underparts, and sides speckled. **Winter:** White stripe on scapulars; bill black; white underparts. **Similar species:** See Parakeet and other auklets. Ancient Murrelet lacks white scapulars; Marbled Murrelet has long pointed bill. **Status:** Uncommon winter visitor, mainly to pelagic waters off Hokkaido.

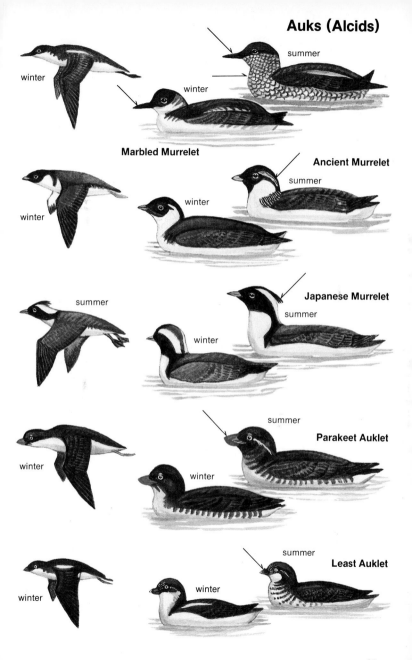

Auks (Alcids)

winter

summer

winter

Marbled Murrelet

winter

winter

summer

Ancient Murrelet

summer

winter

summer

Japanese Murrelet

winter

summer

winter

Parakeet Auklet

winter

summer

winter

Least Auklet

WHISKERED AUKLET *Aethia pygmaea* <Shirahige-umisuzume> L 17cm. A tiny auklet with *three white plumes* on each side of face; dark upperparts; lighter below. *Black crest* curls forward from forehead; three white plumes extend outward from face; *bright red bill* with white tip. **Immature:** No crest or plumes; bill black. **Similar species:** Crested, Parakeet, and Least Auklets have single facial lines. **Status:** Rare winter visitor to pelagic waters off n. Japan.

CRESTED AUKLET *Aethia cristatella* <Etorofu-umisuzume> L 24cm. Similar to Whiskered Auklet but larger, with *single white plume* behind eye. Bill bright orange in summer, paler in winter. Black crest shorter in winter. **Similar species:** See Whiskered Auklet. **Status:** Common winter visitor to pelagic waters off n. Japan.

RHINOCEROS AUKLET *Cerorhinca monocerata* <Utou> L 37.5cm. The largest auklet, puffin-sized but slender-billed; upperparts black; throat and flanks brownish gray; belly white; legs yellow. **Summer:** *Short horn projects from base of yellow bill;* two white facial plumes. **Winter:** Bill paler, horn and plumes absent. **Similar species:** Tufted and Horned Puffins have heavier bills. **Status:** Uncommon breeder on islands off Hokkaido and n. Honshu. Winters near breeding grounds, some to central Honshu.

TUFTED PUFFIN *Lunda cirrhata* <Etopirika> L 37.5cm. Large chunky alcid with *heavy triangular bill; dark body;* red legs. **Summer:** Face white; long *yellowish plumes* curve backward from eye; bright red bill, yellowish at base. **Winter:** Bill gray at base; no white on face; no plumes. **Similar species:** Horned Puffin has white underparts. **Status:** Uncommon breeder in e. Hokkaido. Winters in pelagic waters off n. Honshu and Hokkaido.

HORNED PUFFIN *Fratercula corniculata* <Tsunome dori> L 37.5cm. Large alcid with heavy *triangular bill.* Dark above with *clear white underparts* and orange legs. **Summer:** Face white; tiny erectile *horn* above eye; dark line behind eye; yellow bill with orange tip. **Winter:** Face grayer; bill dark with red tip. **Similar species:** Tufted Puffin has dark underparts and yellow tufts. **Status:** Uncommon winter visitor to pelagic waters off n. Japan. Single adults observed twice in summer at Kiritappu, Hokkaido in breeding colonies of Tufted Puffins.

Auks (Alcids)

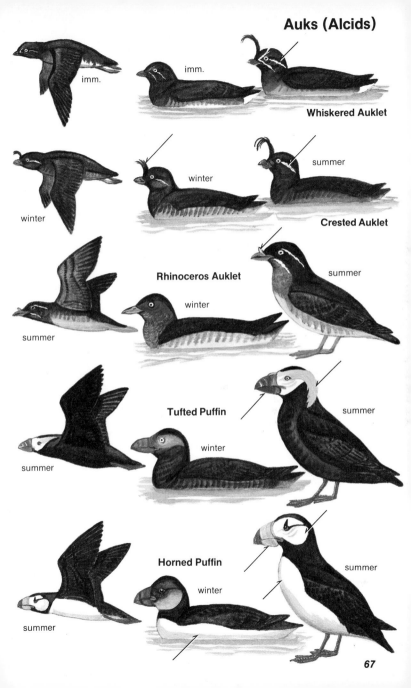

imm.

imm.

Whiskered Auklet

winter

winter

summer

Crested Auklet

Rhinoceros Auklet

summer

winter

summer

Tufted Puffin

summer

winter

summer

Horned Puffin

summer

winter

summer

67

Albatrosses

Family *Diomedeidae* (World: 13 species; Japan: 4 species) The largest seabirds. Most species inhabit southern oceans. Stoutly built with large heads, short tails, and strong hooked bills with tubular nostrils. Their long pointed wings are not well suited for flapping, but they can glide for enormous distances. Albatrosses can spend months over the oceans, alighting on the water only to feed. Most go to land only to breed. They nest on the ground in colonies, usually on remote islands. To take off they must run into the wind (on water or land) or drop off a cliff. Mainly white or sooty brown. In most species sexes are alike, but males are larger than females. Bill color and wing patterns give best clue to identity.

WANDERING ALBATROSS *Diomedea exulans* <Watari-ahōdori> L 120cm. W 300cm. The largest albatross. Requires 10 to 20 years to reach full adult plumage so is usually seen in some intermediate phase. **Adult:** Almost all plumage white, sometimes with *darker vermiculations* on the back; wings white with narrow black border on trailing edge and black tips to primaries; pinkish bill and feet. **Immature:** Brown body and upperwings, white face and throat. White areas increase as bird matures. Underwings are always white with black tips. **Similar species:** Adult Short-tailed has yellow head and neck and black patch on base of wings. **Status:** Accidental in Japan. Breeds in S. Hemisphere on islands in the Pacific south of 30° S.

SHORT-TAILED ALBATROSS *Diomedea albatrus* <Ahōdori> L 91.5cm. W 210cm. **Adult:** White body, *some yellow on head and neck.* Note upper surface pattern; black outer wing and *black tertiaries;* white inner wing and white back; white underwing with black margin. Tip of tail is black. *Bill and feet pink.* **Immature:** Dark brown; white patch on base of wings; white areas gradually increase with maturation. **Similar species:** Black-footed Albatross resembles immature Short-tailed but has *black feet and bill* and no white patches at base of wings. Immature Wandering Albatross resembles adult Short-tailed but black on upperwings not as sharply demarcated from white; back mottled. **Status:** A rare Japanese endemic breeder, breeds (winter) only on Torishima I. and the Senkaku Is. Seldom seen from ships on Pacific route.

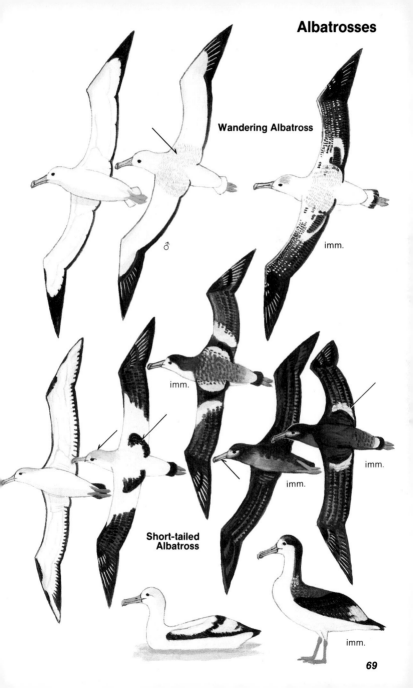

Albatrosses

Wandering Albatross

♂

imm.

imm.

Short-tailed Albatross

imm.

imm.

imm.

imm.

BLACK-FOOTED ALBATROSS *Diomedea nigripes* <Kuroashi-ahōdori> L 78.5cm. W 180cm. Sooty-brown plumage with whitish forehead and cheeks; pale streak stretches length of underwing. Young birds show white on upper tail coverts. *Black feet and black bill.* **Similar species:** Immature Short-tailed has white patches on the base of the wings, and bill and feet are pink. **Status:** Winter breeder on Torishima I., Ogasawara Is., and in the s. Ryukyu Is. A regular year-round visitor in the Pacific off Japan.

LAYSAN ALBATROSS *Diomedea immutabilis* <Ko-ahōdori> L 81cm. W 200cm. Head, neck, and body white. *Upperwings and back are uniformly black.* Underwing largely white outlined in black, with dark patches and occasional dark feathers. Tail white at the base, *black at the tip.* Flesh-colored feet and bill. **Similar species:** No other dark-backed albatross in Japanese waters has white head and white underparts. **Status:** Winter breeder locally in the Ogasawara Is. Regular year-round visitor in Pacific offshore waters.

Shearwaters

Family *Procellariidae* (World: About 60 species; Japan: 16 species) Mostly migratory, oceanic birds which come ashore only for breeding, usually in the Southern Hemisphere. From spring through fall they make long migrations into the Northern Hemisphere. Usually all-dark or dark with white underparts. They have long narrow wings, short tails, webbed feet, and bills which are always hooked at the tip with two unusual tubular nostrils along the culmen. Flight is rapid, alternating between rapid wingbeats and long glides, usually close to the surface of the water. Nest in colonies sometimes on open ground or ledges but most often in burrows or crevices in rocks.

(NORTHERN) FULMAR *Fulmarus glacialis* <Furuma-kamome> L 49.5cm. W 107cm. Stocky; thick-necked; short yellow bill; yellowish legs; short tail; broad short wings. Flies very fast alternately flapping and gliding. Swims with wing tips and tail lifted slightly. **Dark phase:** Gray plumage with *pale patch at base of primaries.* **Light phase** (rare in Japan): White head and underparts; gray back, wings, and tail. **Similar species:** Dark shearwaters are more slender with longer, narrower wings and darker bills. Prominent nasal tubes help distinguish the light phase from gulls. **Status:** Common winter visitor to seas around n. Japan. Many occur in summer off n. Hokkaido.

Albatrosses, Fulmars

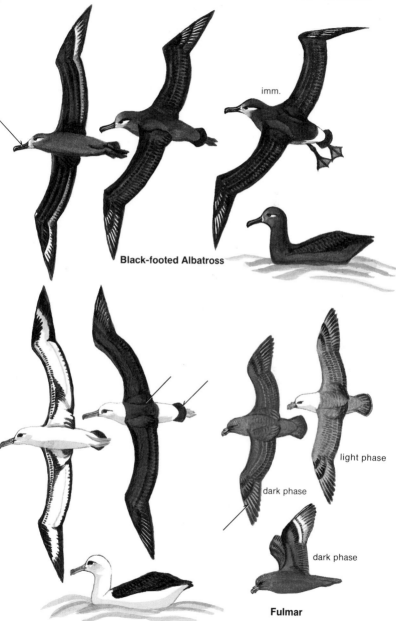

imm.

Black-footed Albatross

Laysan Albatross

light phase

dark phase

dark phase

Fulmar

71

KERMADEC PETREL *Pterodroma neglecta* <Ka wari-shirohara-mizunagidori> L 39cm. W 92cm. Entire plumage sooty brown with white patches near tip of underwings; bill black; legs flesh-colored. **Similar species:** Dark shearwaters lack the white patches on underwings. **Status:** Accidental; one record from Minami Daito I.

WHITE-NECKED PETREL *Pterodroma externa* <Ō-shirohara-mizunagidori> L 43cm. W 97cm. Like Bonin Petrel, but *white collar* separates black nape from gray back; underwing white with dark margin. **Similar species:** Stejneger's Petrel is much smaller, lacks white hind neck. **Status:** Accidental; one record in Nagoya (Aichi Pref.).

BONIN PETREL *Pterodroma hypoleuca* <Shirohara-mizunagidori> L 31cm. W 69cm. Short and stout. Black crown and nape; white forehead; dark patterned wings and back.*White underwing with distinct black diagonal stripe.* **Similar species:** Stejneger's Petrel lacks underwing stripe. See White-necked Petrel and Black-winged Petrel. **Status:** Breeds on Ogasawara Is. and Iwo Is. Rare elsewhere in Japanese waters.

STEJNEGER'S PETREL *Pterodroma longirostris* <Hime-shirohara-mizunagidori> L 25cm. W 71cm. Similar to Bonin Petrel but *underwing stripe is either absent or partial and indistinct.* **Similar species:** White-necked Petrel is much larger with white collar. **Status:** Rare migrant off Pacific coast.

HAWAIIAN PETREL *Pterodroma phaeopygia* <Hawai-shirohara-mizunagidori> L 42cm. W 92cm. Dark above with black cap and nape; white forehead, face, and underparts; white underwing with *thick dark margins;* black bill; yellowish feet. **Similar species:** White-necked Petrel has white collar, W-pattern on upper wing. **Status:** Accidental; one record from n. Honshu.

BLACK-WINGED PETREL *Pterodroma nigripennis* <Haguro-shirohara-mizunagidori> L 31cm. W 66 cm. *Gray crown* and upper body; black upperwings and tail; white cheeks and underparts; *dark patch on cheek;* white underwings with conspicuous black diagonal pattern. **Similar species:** See Bonin Petrel. **Status:** Accidental. One record; Hokkaido.

Petrels

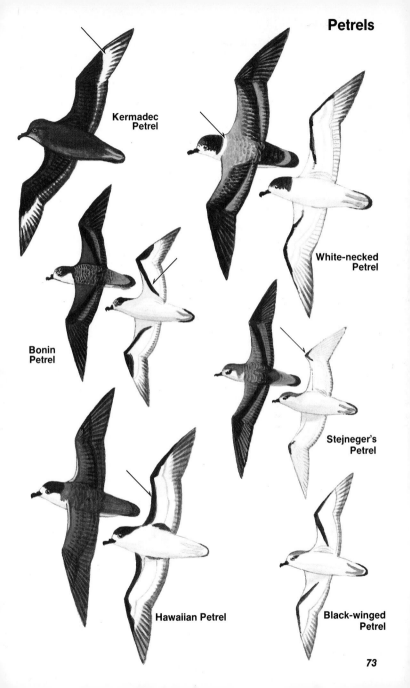

Kermadec Petrel

White-necked Petrel

Bonin Petrel

Stejneger's Petrel

Hawaiian Petrel

Black-winged Petrel

STREAKED SHEARWATER *Calonectris leucomelas*
<Ō-mizunagidori> L 48cm. W 122cm. Distinguished from other shearwaters by *pale head*. Streaks on head visible only at close range. Dark above with speckling on back; *white below;* white underwings with black flight feathers and black streaks on primary coverts; horn-colored bill, flesh-colored legs. **Status:** Abundant off the coast throughout Japan, frequently within sight of land. Breeds on coastal islands throughout Japan.

SOOTY SHEARWATER *Puffinus griseus* <Haiiro-mizunagidori> L 43cm. W 109cm. Uniformly sooty brown above, grayish brown below; *silvery wing linings* with dark margins; pale chin; dark bill and feet. **Similar species:** Short-tailed Shearwaters are smaller; fly faster; underwing not as silvery. **Status:** Common spring and summer visitor in the Pacific off Japan; often in mixed flocks with Short-tailed Shearwaters.

FLESH-FOOTED SHEARWATER [PALE-FOOTED SHEARWATER] *Puffinus carneipes* <Akaashi-mizunagidori> L 51cm. W 109cm. Large, heavily built with entire plumage dark brown; *long pink bill* conspicuous in flight; wings entirely dark above and below; short, round tail; slow, deliberate flight. **Similar species:** Sooty Shearwater is smaller with black bill and silvery underwing. Short-tailed Shearwater has black bill and feet, lighter underwing surface. **Status:** Common spring and summer visitor off the coast of Japan. Breeds in Australia and New Zealand.

SHORT-TAILED SHEARWATER [SLENDER-BILLED SHEARWATER] *Puffinus tenuirostris* <Hashiboso-mizunagidori> L 33cm. W 97cm. Sooty brown above, grayish brown below; short, rounded tail makes body look short behind the wings; throat varies from light gray to white; *underwing may vary from dark gray to whitish;* short, straight dark bill; dark legs. **Similar species:** Sooty Shearwater is larger, usually with whiter wing linings. Flesh-footed is larger with light bill and legs. Rare Christmas Shearwater is darker but difficult to separate in field. **Status:** Abundant spring transient and summer visitor in very large flocks.

Shearwaters

Streaked Shearwater

Sooty Shearwater

Flesh-footed Shearwater

Short-tailed Shearwater

form with white on underwing

AUDUBON'S SHEARWATER *Puffinus lherminieri*
<Seguro-mizunagidori> L 31cm. W 69cm. Small; black above and *white below*. Black bill is long and slender. Black cap; pale legs; short wings. Underwings have white linings with dark margins. Faster wingbeats than other shearwaters. **Similar species:** Bonin Petrel is larger with thicker bill, white forehead, and diagonal black stripe on underwing. **Status:** Breeds on Iwo Is. Uncommon at sea around Iwo Is. and Ogasawara Is.

WEDGE-TAILED SHEARWATER *Puffinus pacificus*
<Onaga-mizunagidori> L 39cm. W 97cm. The combination of *long wedge-shaped tail* and *flesh-colored feet* is distinctive. **Light phase:** Uniformly dark brown above, white below; *underwing white with dark margins*. Light bill with dark tip. **Dark phase:** Overall dark brown plumage; gray bill. **Similar species:** New Zealand Shearwater has pattern of light and dark gray on upperwings and back; white underwing. Streaked Shearwater is larger with shorter tail. **Status:** Breeds on Ogasawara Is. and Iwo Is. Uncommon elsewhere off the Japanese coast.

NEW ZEALAND SHEARWATER *Puffinus bulleri*
<Minami-onaga-mizunagidori> L 42cm. W 102cm. Slender, with white underparts, black cap, and a distinct dark *W-shaped pattern of dark gray against the light gray upperwing.* Bill uniformly dark. Relatively long tail is gray at base, black at tip. Flesh-colored feet. **Similar species:** See Wedge-tailed Shearwater and Bonin Petrel. **Status:** Accidental off Pacific coast of n. Honshu. Breeds in New Zealand.

CHRISTMAS SHEARWATER *Puffinus nativitatis*
<Ko-mizunagidori> L 36cm. W 82cm. Small, *entirely dark* shearwater with short rounded tail. *Sooty brown overall, including the underwing;* black bill, dark brown feet. **Similar species:** Slender-billed Shearwater usually has lighter underwing, but is difficult to distinguish in the field. Sooty Shearwater has silvery underwing. **Status:** Accidental off Pacific coast of Honshu. Breeds on Pacific tropical islands.

Shearwaters

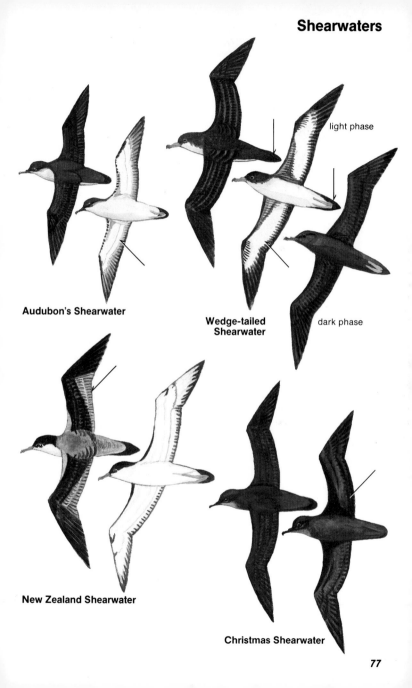

Audubon's Shearwater

Wedge-tailed
Shearwater

light phase

dark phase

New Zealand Shearwater

Christmas Shearwater

BULWER'S PETREL *Bulweria bulwerii* <Anadori> L 27cm. W 61cm. Sooty brown overall with a lighter band on secondaries; black bill; flesh-colored legs; *diagnostic long wedge-shaped tail.* Zigzags erratically over the ocean surface, swooping and gliding with occasional rapid wingbeats. **Similar species:** Dark-rumped storm petrels have quite different tails. Brown Noddy has white crown, lacks white wing stripe. **Status:** Common resident of Ogasawara Is. and Iwo Is. Sometimes observed off the Ryukyu Is.

Storm Petrels

Family *Hydrobatidae* (World: About 21 species; Japan: 7 species) The smallest seabirds; live at sea except when nesting. Flight is fluttery and erratic. Rarely alight on water, but hop and skip over the surface pattering their feet on the water. Long wings have pale stripe on wing coverts. For identification close attention should be paid to color of rump, shape of tail, and wing pattern.

WILSON'S STORM PETREL *Oceanites oceanicus* <Ashinaga-umitsubame> L 18cm. W 41cm. Sooty black above; *white rump; square tail; long legs with yellow-webbed feet extend beyond the tail.* Often follows ships. **Similar species:** Other white-rumped petrels have shorter legs, dark feet. **Status:** Straggler off the Pacific coast.

SOOTY STORM PETREL *Oceanodroma tristrami* <Ō suton-umitsubame> L 25.5cm. W 56cm. Largest storm petrel in Japan. Sooty brown; black bill and legs; *tail is deeply forked.* Glides and banks low over water; flutters occasionally. **Similar species:** Matsudaira's Storm Petrel is darker with white area at base of primaries. Swinhoe's Storm Petrel is smaller, tail is shorter and not as deeply forked, flight is more butterfly-like. **Status:** Uncommon breeder on the Izu Is. and Iwo Is. Common summer visitor off Pacific coast of Honshu.

MATSUDAIRA'S STORM PETREL *Oceanodroma matsudairae* <Kuro-umitsubame> L 22.5cm. W 56cm. Large and sooty brown; forked tail; *white area at base of primaries.* Gliding flight less erratic than in smaller species. **Similar species:** Swinhoe's Storm Petrel has obscure white patch at the base of primaries; butterfly-like flight. Sooty Storm Petrel lacks wing patch. **Status:** Winter breeder on Iwo Is. Rare spring visitor to Japanese waters.

Storm Petrels

Bulwer's Petrel

Wilson's Storm Petrel

Sooty Storm Petrel

Matsudaira's Storm Petrel

FORK-TAILED STORM PETREL *Oceanodroma furcata* <Haiiro-umitsubame> L 20cm. W 46cm. Only storm petrel with *gray plumage*. Head and upperparts pearl gray with black area around eye; underparts pale gray to white; throat and under tail coverts white; bill and legs black; tail deeply forked. **Similar species:** Phalaropes are the only other small pale birds which are seen at sea. **Status:** Uncommon visitor, mainly in winter, to n. Japanese waters.

LEACH'S STORM PETREL *Oceanodroma leucorhoa* <Koshijiro-umitsubame> L 20.5cm. W 48cm. Sooty above and below; *white rump bisected by indistinct gray line; deeply forked tail;* black bill and legs. Does not usually follow ships. **Similar species:** Band-rumped Storm Petrel lacks gray stripe on rump; tail less deeply forked. Wilson's Storm Petrel has rounded tail, long legs with yellow webbed feet. **Status:** Breeds on Daikoku I. in Hokkaido and Sanganjima I. in Iwate Pref. Offshore transient from Honshu southward.

BAND-RUMPED STORM PETREL [HARCOURT'S STORM PETREL] *Oceanodroma castro* <Kurokoshijiro-umitsubame> L 19cm. W 46cm. Sooty black; *white rump; some white on flanks and under tail coverts;* slightly forked tail; black bill and legs. **Similar species:** Leach's Storm Petrel has deeply forked tail and a gray line on white rump. Wilson's Storm Petrel has square tail, long legs, yellow-webbed feet. **Status:** Common summer visitor to the Pacific side of Honshu; breeds on Hidejima I. and Sanganjima I. in Iwate Pref.

SWINHOE'S STORM PETREL *Oceanodroma monorhis* <Hime-kuro-umitsubame> L 19cm. W 38.5cm. Small and blackish brown with a *dark rump*, obscure white patches on base of primaries (difficult to observe in the field), medium-forked tail, and black bill and legs. **Similar species:** Sooty Storm Petrel is larger with longer wings and longer, more deeply forked tail. Matsudaira's Storm Petrel is larger with white at base of primaries. **Status:** Common summer visitor off both coasts of Japan. Breeds in Honshu and Kyushu.

Storm Petrels

Fork-tailed Storm Petrel

Leach's Storm Petrel

Band-rumped Storm Petrel

Swinhoe's Storm Petrel

Tropicbirds

Family *Phaethontidae* (World: 3 species; Japan: 2 species) Mostly white, tern-like seabirds. Adults have extremely long central tail feathers. They fly high with steady wingbeats, hover, then dive for fish. Breed on oceanic islands in small flocks. Usually solitary at sea.

RED-TAILED TROPICBIRD *Phaethon rubricauda* <Akao-nettaichō> L 96cm. W 112cm. Two long *red central tail feathers,* almost all *white plumage,* and *coral red bill* are definitive. Blue legs, black feet. Summer plumage sometimes tinged with pink. **Immature:** Black barring on upperparts, *black bill,* and no long central tail feathers. **Status:** Breeds on Iwo Is. and Minami-torishima I. Rare straggler to main islands.

WHITE-TAILED TROPICBIRD *Phaethon lepturus* <Shirao-nettaichō> L 81cm. W 92cm. Two *long white central tail feathers; yellow bill;* black on primaries and across upperwing. **Immature:** *Yellow bill;* no long tail feathers. **Similar species:** See Red-tailed Tropicbird. **Status:** Rare visitor to southern waters (Ogasawara Is., Iwo Is., Minami-torishima I., Ryukyu Is.)

Frigatebirds

Family *Fregatidae* (World: 5 species; Japan: 2 species) Large soaring seabirds with hooked bills, long pointed wings, and deeply forked tails which they often open and close in flight. Males have inflatable red pouches. Non-migratory, they breed colonially on tropical oceanic islands. They almost never land on water. Sexes differ.

GREAT FRIGATEBIRD *Fregata minor* <Ō-gunkan dori> L 80—100cm. W 220cm. **Male:** Black plumage with brown band on median wing coverts; *red throat pouch* usually visible only when inflated. **Female:** Black with *gray throat;* white breast and upper belly; horn-colored bill; reddish or bluish legs. **Immature:** *Head, throat, breast, and upper belly whitish.* **Status:** Accidental. Oceanic islands and seacoasts; Honshu, Izu Is., Ogasawara Is., and Iwo Is.

LESSER FRIGATEBIRD *Fregata ariel* <Ko-gunkan dori> L 79cm. W 180cm. Similar to Great Frigatebird but male has *white patches on flanks;* female is browner with *black throat.* **Immature:** Buff-colored head and throat; *black breast band;* white upper belly. **Status:** Accidental; oceanic islands and seacoasts. More often around Japan than is Great Frigatebird.

Tropicbirds, Frigatebirds

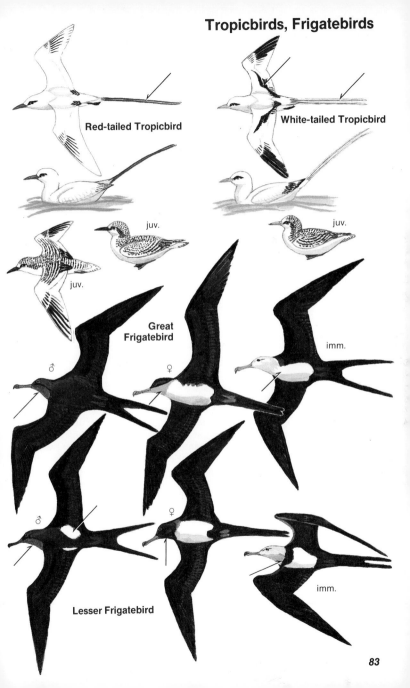

Red-tailed Tropicbird

White-tailed Tropicbird

juv.

juv.

juv.

Great
Frigatebird

♂

♀

imm.

♂

♀

imm.

Lesser Frigatebird

Pelicans

Family *Pelecanidae* (World: 6 species; Japan: 1 species) Huge seabirds, among the largest living birds. Distinctive appearance. Enormous pouched bill with hooked upper mandible, slightly crested head, long broad wings, short tail, short legs. Fly with neck pulled back on shoulders. Sexes alike.

SPOT-BILLED PELICAN *Pelecanus philippensis* <Haiiro-perikan> L 160cm. W 250cm. White plumage tinged with gray; from above, *black primaries and sooty-brown secondaries;* gray bill with orange pouch and *dark spots on upper mandible.* **Similar species:** Upperwing of White Pelican (*P. onocrotalus*), unverified in Japan, has black on primaries and secondaries. **Status:** Accidental in Japan. Seashores and large rivers.

Boobies

Family *Sulidae* (World: 9 species; Japan: 3 species) Large seabirds with cigar-shaped bodies, conical bills, long pointed wings, and wedge-shaped tails. Flight is rapid and direct. They dive for fish from great heights. Breed colonially usually on remote islands. Sexes alike.

BROWN BOOBY *Sula leucogaster* <Katsuodori> L 73cm. W 145cm. Dark brown plumage with *white belly, wing linings,* and under tail coverts; naked skin of face bluish in male, yellow in female; yellow bill and legs. **Immature:** Pattern on underside is same as in adult but light parts are mottled. **Similar species:** No other booby is entirely dark above. **Status:** Locally common resident on islands off Honshu and Kyushu and in the Ogasawara Is., Iwo Is., and Ryukyu Is.

MASKED BOOBY [BLUE-FACED BOOBY] *Sula dactylatra* <Aotsura-katsuodori> L 85cm. W 152 cm. Largest booby. White with *black tail,* black primaries, and black rear margin of wing; naked skin on face and throat bluish black; yellowish-orange bill; dark blue legs and feet. **Immature:** Dusky brown with white patches that increase in size with age; tail is always dark; breast is same color as belly. **Similar species:** Red-footed Booby has white tail, red feet, paler blue face mask. **Status:** Locally uncommon breeder on Senkaku Is. Accidental elsewhere.

RED-FOOTED BOOBY *Sula sula* <Akaashi-katsuodori> L 70cm. W 152cm. White with black primaries and secondaries; blue bill; blue naked skin on face; *white tail;* red legs and feet. **Immature:** Dusky above and below; red feet. **Status:** Locally uncommon breeder on Nakanoganjima I. in the s. Ryukyu Is. Accidental elsewhere.

Pelicans, Boobies

Spot-billed Pelican

♀ ♀ ♂

Brown Booby

imm.

Masked Booby

imm.

Red-footed Booby

Skuas and Jaegers

Family *Stercorariidae* (World: 4 species; Japan: 4 species) Dark, gull-sized predatory seabirds. Strong fast fliers, they pursue gulls and terns, harrying them until they disgorge their catch. Adults usually have long central tail feathers. *All have some white in primaries.* Pelagic except in breeding season. Sexes alike.

GREAT SKUA *Stercorarius skua* <Ō-tōzokukamome> L 58.5cm. Size of Herring Gull but with heavier body. Uniformly dark except for *conspicuous white patches* at base of primaries; *short tail* with central feathers projecting only slightly. Wings are broader and more rounded than those of jaegers. **Status:** Uncommon migrant; offshore waters, Kyushu northward.

LONG-TAILED JAEGER [LONG-TAILED SKUA] *Stercorarius longicaudus* <Shirohara-tōzokukamome> L 53cm. Slimmest jaeger. Distinctive *long thin* central tail feathers and white underbody *without breast band.* Black cap and gray back are separated by a more complete white and yellow collar than in other jaegers. Blue-gray legs. Dark phase (uniformly dark brown) occurs only rarely. **Immature:** Lacks central tail streamers; plumage grayer than immature Pomarine's. **Status:** Most pelagic of the skuas; uncommon migrant off Hokkaido, Honshu, and Izu Is.

POMARINE JAEGER [POMARINE SKUA] *Stercorarius pomarinus* <Tōzokukamome> L 51cm. Distinguished from other jaegers by *twisted central tail feathers* and *more white in primaries.* **Light phase:** Blackish upperparts and crown; *yellowish cheeks;* partial collar; white underparts with *dark breast band* and barred flanks. **Dark phase:** Uniformly dark brown with some white in primaries. **Immature:** Mottled dark brown and white with heavily barred underparts; no long tail feathers. **Status:** Uncommon migrant; offshore waters around Honshu and Hokkaido. Sometimes seen in winter.

PARASITIC JAEGER [ARCTIC SKUA] *Stercorarius parasiticus* <Kuro-tōzokukamome> L 46cm. Central tail feathers *straight and sharply pointed* in contrast to Pomarine's; *thicker and shorter* than Long-tailed's. Slender bill. Black legs. **Light phase:** Similar to Pomarine but breast band lighter. **Dark phase:** Uniformly blackish brown. **Status:** Uncommon pelagic migrant off Hokkaido, Honshu, Izu Is., and Ogasawara Is. May occur in summer off northern Hokkaido.

Skuas, Jaegers

Long-tailed Jaeger

Great Skua

imm.

light phase

light phase

dark phase

imm.

Pomarine Jaeger

light phase

dark phase

imm.

Parasitic Jaeger chasing
Black-legged Kittiwake

imm.

Parasitic Jaeger

87

Gulls

Family *Laridae*, Subfamily *Larinae* (World: 45 species; Japan:15 species) Medium-sized scavenging seabirds with stout bills. Mainly coastal. Buoyant fliers; frequently soar. Rarely dive below surface of water. Adults generally have white bodies and underwings, gray mantles, black on wing tips. Many small species have black heads in summer. Immature birds usually have mottled brown plumage and may be difficult to identify. Always gregarious. Sexes alike.

SLATY-BACKED GULL *Larus schistisagus* <Ō-seguro-kamome> L 61cm. W 135cm. A large white gull with *dark slaty-gray mantle* which contrasts little with black wing tips. Some white spots on wing tips. *Tail pure white.* Bill yellow with red spot on lower mandible. Legs flesh pink. **Immature:** Mottled brown with dark flight feathers, dark tail band, black bill, some white at base of tail. Indistinguishable from immature Herring Gull. **Status:** Abundant in winter along the coast and bays of northern Japan. Breeds in Hokkaido and northern Honshu.

HERRING GULL *Larus argentatus* <Seguro-kamome> L 60cm. W 135cm. Resembles Slaty-backed but has *pale gray mantle* and contrasting *black-tipped primaries with white spots.* **Immature:** Indistinguishable from immature Slaty-backed. **Similar species:** Glaucous and Glaucous-winged Gulls have paler upperparts and no black on primaries. **Status:** Common winter visitor to coast and occasionally to large rivers in Honshu and Hokkaido.

BLACK-TAILED GULL *Larus crassirostris* <Umineko> L 46.5cm. W 120cm. A medium-sized white gull with a broad *black subterminal band* across the white tail and *little contrast* between the dark mantle and black wing tips, which usually have no white spots. Yellow bill with *red tip and black ring;* yellow legs. **Immature:** Mottled dark brown with *pale forehead and throat.* Flesh-colored bill with black tip; flesh-pink legs. **Status:** Abundant resident along coast, Kyushu northward.

Gulls

imm.

imm.
first year

summer

winter

Slaty-backed Gull

imm.

winter

imm. first year

Herring Gull

summer

imm.
first year

imm.

Black-tailed Gull

GLAUCOUS-WINGED GULL *Larus glaucescens* <Washi-kamome> L 64cm. W 135cm. Large with white head, underparts, and tail; *pale gray mantle.* Resembles Herring Gull but *primaries are gray, not black.* Yellow bill has red spot on lower mandible. Flesh-pink legs. **Immature:** Mottled grayish-brown plumage, slightly darker primaries, black bill. Third-spring birds are much like adults but have black-tipped bills and retain brownish primaries. **Similar species:** Glaucous has whitish primaries. **Status:** Uncommon winter visitor to coasts and bays in northern Japan.

GLAUCOUS GULL *Larus hyperboreus* <Shiro-kamome> L 71cm. W 135cm. Large gull with *a pale gray mantle* and *whitish primaries.* Yellow bill has red spot on lower mandible. Flesh-pink legs. **Immature:** First-year birds are mottled pale brown and white. Second-spring birds are *almost entirely white* with some brown staining on upperparts. Bill is flesh colored with black tip. **Similar species:** Glaucous-winged has *dark or gray primaries.* Ivory Gull is much smaller than second-spring Glaucous and has *black feet and bill.* **Status:** Winter visitor to coasts and bays; common in northern Japan, uncommon elsewhere.

MEW GULL [COMMON GULL] *Larus canus* <Kamome> L 44.5cm. W 115cm. Medium sized, resembles a small Herring Gull but has *small unmarked yellow bill, greenish-yellow legs,* and dark eyes. **Immature:** Mottled grayish-brown upperparts, paler below. *Black subterminal band* on white tail. **Similar species:** Black-tailed is darker brown, has heavier bill. **Status:** Common in coastal areas in winter.

GREAT BLACK-HEADED GULL *Larus ichthyaetus* <Ō-zuguro-kamome> L 69cm. Large with white underparts and tail, gray mantle, *white primaries* with *subterminal black bars.* Yellow bill with black subterminal band and red tip. *Greenish-yellow legs.* **Summer:** Unmistakable with *black hood.* No other dark-hooded gull is near its size. **Winter:** Head is white with some dark streaking. Can be distinguished from Herring by larger size, wing pattern, and dark streaks on head. **Immature:** Mottled white head, dark brown mantle, white tail with black subterminal band, grayish bill and legs. **Status:** Accidental. One record (summer adult), at Ariake in Kyushu, 1982.

Gulls

imm. first year

winter

imm.

Glaucous-winged Gull

imm. first year

winter

imm.

Glaucous Gull

winter

imm.

imm. first year

Mew Gull

summer

winter

Great Black-headed Gull

second winter

second spring

Slaty-backed Gull

second winter

second spring

subadult

subadult

Slaty-backed Gull

second spring

Herring Gull

second spring

second spring

second spring

Glaucous-winged Gull

second spring

second winter

second spring

Glaucous Gull

first spring

first spring

Black-tailed Gull

SAUNDERS'S GULL *Larus saundersi* <Zuguro-kamome> L 32.5cm. Adults and immatures resemble Black-headed Gull but *bill is shorter and black;* legs red in summer, dark red in winter; white tips of primaries have *black dots.* In summer adult has black head; in winter head is white with a dark spot behind the eye. **Similar species:** See Black-headed Gull. **Status:** Uncommon winter visitor to mudflats of estuaries and coasts; Kyushu and Ryukyu Is.

BLACK-HEADED GULL *Larus ridibundus* <Yuri-kamome> L 40cm. W 93cm. *Pure white wedge on leading edge of primaries; black on underside of primaries.* Head is chocolate brown in summer with white eye-ring; in winter head is white with black spot behind eye. *Red bill and legs.* **Immature:** Like winter adult but has black bands on tail and wings; orange bill and legs. **Similar species:** Saunders's Gull has *black bill.* **Status:** Common winter visitor to both inland and coastal waters; uncommon in Ryukyu Is.

SABINE'S GULL *Larus sabini* <Kubiwa-kamome> L 33cm. Small with forked tail. Both adults and immatures have a distinctive pattern of *white and dark triangles on upper wings.* **Adult:** Back and upper wing coverts gray, tail white. Head turns from gray in summer to white with dusky markings in winter. Bill black with yellow tip. **Immature:** Back and wing coverts brown; slightly forked white tail with black terminal band. Bill black. **Similar species:** Immature Black-legged Kittiwake has diagonal black bands across upper wing coverts. **Status:** Accidental; only one record, from northern Honshu.

LITTLE GULL *Larus minutus* <Hime-kamome> L 28cm. The smallest gull in Japan. Short legs; tern-like posture; shows *dark underwings* in flight. **Summer:** Note the *jet black head,* deep red legs and bill. **Winter:** Head turns white with dark gray markings on crown and nape; bill black. **Immature:** W pattern on upper-wings similar to immature Black-legged Kittiwake and immature Ross's Gull but Little Gull has rounded tail and lacks black patch on nape. **Status:** Straggler to Hokkaido coast.

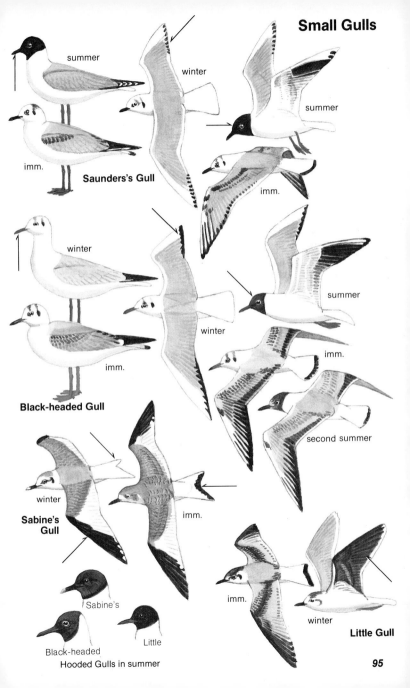

Small Gulls

summer

winter

summer

Saunders's Gull

imm.

imm.

winter

summer

winter

imm.

imm.

Black-headed Gull

second summer

Sabine's Gull

winter

imm.

Sabine's

Little

imm.

winter

Little Gull

Black-headed

Hooded Gulls in summer

95

BLACK-LEGGED KITTIWAKE *Larus tridactylus* <Mi tsuyubi-kamome> L 39cm. Note the *black wing tips* without white spots, yellow bill, and short *black legs*. Head white in summer, with gray nape in winter. **Immature:** Note the *black bands* across nape, on tail, and forming distinctive W on upperwings. **Similar species:** Adult Mew Gull has white spots on black wing tips. Immature Little Gull lacks black mark across nape. **Status:** Common winter visitor to off-shore waters, bays, and harbors north to central Honshu; uncommon in summer in northern Hokkaido.

RED-LEGGED KITTIWAKE *Larus brevirostris* <Aka ashi-mitsuyubi-kamome> L 38cm. Resembles Black-legged Kittiwake but has *bright red legs* and *darker underwings*. **Immature:** Like immature Black-legged except has *no diagonal black bands on upperwings and no band on tail*. **Status:** Straggler.

IVORY GULL *Larus eburneus* <Zōge-kamome> L 44cm. Small with white plumage, *black legs*, black bill with yellow tip. **Immature:** White plumage is *mottled with black;* narrow black terminal band on tail; black spots on edges of flight feathers; *black face mask*. **Status:** Rare straggler to coast. One record each from central Honshu and eastern Hokkaido.

ROSS'S GULL *Larus roseus* <Hime-kubiwa-kamome> L 30cm. Small, with a distinctive *wedge-shaped tail*. **Summer:** White or *rosy* head and neck, underparts, rump, and tail; pearl gray upperparts, dark under-wings; *narrow black collar*. **Winter:** No black collar; loses rosiness; head and neck tinged with gray. **Immature:** Some resemblance to Black-legged Kittiwake but *black-banded tail* is wedge shaped. **Status:** Rare winter straggler; only two records, from Hokkaido and northern Honshu.

Small Gulls

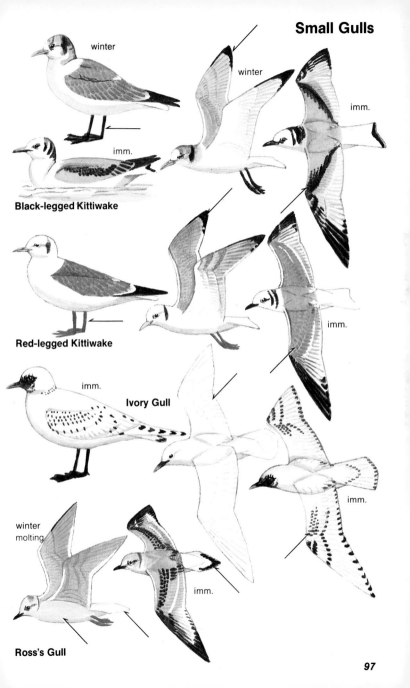

winter

winter

imm.

imm.

Black-legged Kittiwake

Red-legged Kittiwake

imm.

imm.

Ivory Gull

imm.

winter
molting

imm.

Ross's Gull

Terns

Family *Laridae,* Subfamily *Sterninae* (World: 42 species; Japan: 18 species) Slender, graceful birds found mostly on coastal or inland waters. Terns have long narrow wings and pointed bills. Most have black caps in summer and forked tails. Seldom soar but fly with regular wingbeats. Often hover with bills pointed toward the water. Sea terns dive head first for fish; marsh terns pick food from water surface. Unlike gulls, terns do not ordinarily swim. Colonial breeders. Sexes alike.

WHITE-WINGED BLACK TERN *Sterna leucoptera* <Hajiro-kurohara-ajisashi> L 23.5cm. **Summer:** Black head, back, and underparts; black wing linings; white wing coverts and tail; red bill and legs. **Winter:** White underparts; light gray back and upperwings; white head mottled with black on the crown; *black ear patch extends below the eye;* black bill. **Immature:** Similar to winter plumage but browner with *dark back.* **Similar species:** See Black Tern and Whiskered Tern. **Status:** Rare transient along coast and around inland waters.

BLACK TERN *Sterna nigra* <Hashiguro-kurohara-ajisashi> L 24cm. **Summer:** Black with dark gray upperwings and tail, white wing linings, black legs and bill. **Winter:** Like White-winged Black Tern except the *dark ear patch stops at the eye,* and it has a gray patch on the side of the breast in front of wing. **Immature:** Similar to winter plumage but browner with mottled back. **Similar species:** See White-winged Black Tern and Whiskered Tern. **Status:** Rare transient along coast and around inland waters.

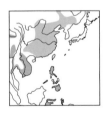

WHISKERED TERN *Sterna hybrida* <Kurohara-ajisashi> L 25cm. **Summer:** Dark with light gray wings and tail, *distinctive white band across cheek and side of neck,* black crown, black breast, red legs, and red bill with black tip. **Winter:** Resembles White-winged Black Tern but usually has less black on nape; black on nape often meets gray back. Bill is slightly longer than bill of White-winged Black Tern and Black Tern. **Immature:** Similar to winter plumage with brown mottling on back. **Similar species:** See White-winged Black Tern and Black Tern. **Status:** Rare transient to coasts and inland waters from Honshu southward.

Terns

winter

summer

White-winged Black Tern

juv.

summer

winter

winter

summer

Black Tern

juv.

summer

winter

winter

juv.

summer

Whiskered Tern

winter

99

CASPIAN TERN *Sterna caspia* <Oni-ajisashi> L 52.5cm. The largest tern in Japan. *Stout red bill; black on underside of primaries; shallow fork in tail.* The cap with its short crest is black in summer, streaked with white in winter. **Similar species:** Greater Crested has yellow bill, no black on underside of primaries. **Status:** Straggler in spring and fall.

GREATER CRESTED TERN *Sterna bergii* <Ō-aji sashi> L 45cm. A large tern with a *large yellow bill, white forehead, short black crest.* Crown is black in summer, streaked with white in winter; moderately forked tail; black feet. **Similar species:** Caspian has red bill, blackish underside of primaries. **Status:** Breeds in Ogasawara Is. and Ryukyu Is.; straggler to main islands of Japan. Coastal habitat.

GULL-BILLED TERN *Sterna nilotica* <Hashibuto-ajisashi> L 37.5cm. *Stout black bill,* shallow fork in tail. **Summer:** Black cap. **Winter:** White head with dark patch behind eye. **Similar species:** Common Tern is similar in summer but has deeply notched tail. **Status:** Straggler to mudflats on coasts and estuaries.

ALEUTIAN TERN *Sterna aleutica* <Koshijiro-ajisashi> L 33cm. Medium gray above with white underparts and deeply forked white tail. Note the *white forehead,* black cap, *black eyeline from bill to nape,* and black bill and feet. **Immature:** Barred mantle and browner head. **Similar species:** Common Tern in summer has no white on forehead; in winter forehead is streaked with white. Bridled and Spectacled Terns are similar but they do not have the white rump and tail and their distribution is quite different. **Status:** Straggler, Honshu northward.

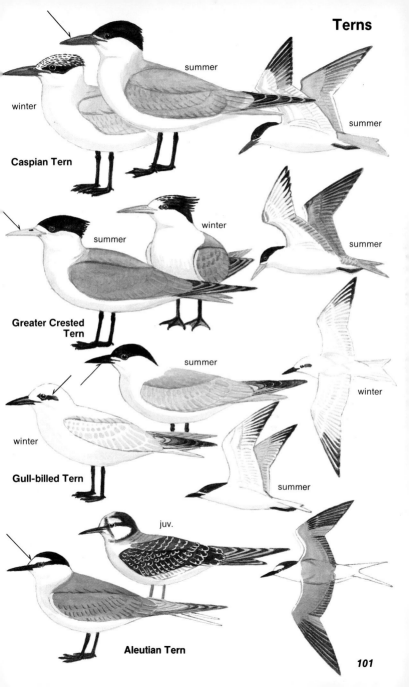

Terns

summer

winter

Caspian Tern

summer

summer

Greater Crested Tern

winter

summer

summer

winter

Gull-billed Tern

summer

juv.

Aleutian Tern

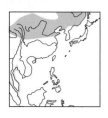

COMMON TERN *Sterna hirundo* <Ajisashi> L 35.5cm. **Summer:** Light to medium gray mantle; black cap and nape; white face, neck, and throat. *Breast and belly tinged with gray.* Deeply forked white tail; black bill and legs. Subspecies *minussensis,* which sometimes occurs in Japan, has red legs and red bill with black tip. **Winter:** Forehead and underparts are white. **Immature:** Like winter adult but with black patch on upper wing coverts. **Status:** Common spring and fall transient throughout Japan; coasts and estuaries.

ROSEATE TERN *Sterna dougallii* <Beni-ajisashi> L 31cm. At rest, *tail extends well beyond tips of folded wings.* **Summer:** Pale gray mantle is much lighter than in Common Tern; white underparts sometimes tinged with pink; long deeply forked, white tail; red bill with black tip; red legs. **Winter:** White forehead, black bill, and yellowish legs. **Similar species:** At rest, tail of Common Tern is about even with wing tips. Black-naped is lighter overall with different head pattern. **Status:** Locally common breeder in Ryukyu Is.

BLACK-NAPED TERN *Sterna sumatrana* <Eriguro-ajisashi> L 30cm. *White crown and black nape;* pale gray mantle; long deeply forked, white tail; black bill. **Status:** Locally common breeder from Osumi Is. southward, mainly in the Ryukyu Is.

LITTLE TERN *Sterna albifrons* <Ko-ajisashi> L 28cm. Distinguished from other terns by *small body size.* **Summer:** *Clear white forehead,* black cap and eye-stripe to base of bill, *yellow bill and feet.* **Winter:** *Bill and feet are dark,* white on forehead extends to crown, and eyestripe does not reach base of bill. **Similar species:** In summer Aleutian Tern has similar clear white forehead but legs and bill are black. **Status:** Common breeder; coastal and inland waters in warm regions from Honshu southward.

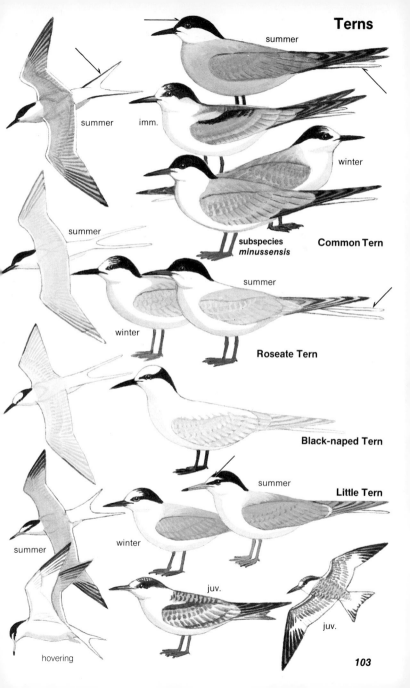

Terns

summer

summer

imm.

winter

subspecies
minussensis

Common Tern

summer

winter

summer

Roseate Tern

Black-naped Tern

summer

Little Tern

winter

juv.

summer

hovering

juv.

SPECTACLED TERN [GRAY-BACKED TERN] *Sterna lunata* <Nanyō-mamijiro-ajisashi> L 38cm. Resembles Bridled Tern; black crown, nape, and eyestripe; gray upperparts; deeply forked tail with white outer feathers; white underparts; black bill and legs. Slight difference in color is the only field mark. The Spectacled Tern is *grayer*. **Status:** Straggler to Iwo Islands and Minami-torishima Island.

BRIDLED TERN *Sterna anaethetus* <Mamijiro-ajisashi> L 35.5cm. Resembles Spectacled Tern. Slight difference in color is the only field mark. Bridled Tern is *browner*. **Status:** Locally uncommon breeder in southern Ryukyu Is. Straggler elsewhere in Japan.

SOOTY TERN *Sterna fuscata* <Seguro-ajisashi> L 40.5cm. Sharply contrasting *black above, white below;* white forehead and cheeks with black stripe through eye; black bill and legs; deeply forked tail. **Immature:** Blackish-brown overall with white barring on upperparts, light band across underwings, and light under tail coverts. **Status:** Locally common breeder in Minami-torishima Island, Ogasawara Islands, and Ryukyu Islands. Rare, main islands of Japan.

Terns

Spectacled Tern

Bridled Tern

Sooty Tern

imm.

imm.

BLUE NODDY *Anous cerulea* <Haiiro-ajisashi> L 25cm. A small *blue-gray* tern with paler head, neck, and underparts; white tips on secondaries; black bill; black legs and feet; yellow webs. **Status:** Accidental. Only old records from Iwo Islands and Minami-torishima Island.

BROWN NODDY [COMMON NODDY] *Anous stolidus* <Kuro-ajisashi> L 39cm. Dark brown, light cap, *wedge-shaped tail with a shallow notch,* black bill, dark legs. **Similar species:** See Black Noddy. **Status:** Locally common breeder in Ogasawara Islands Minami-torishima Islands, and Ryukyu Islands. Accidental elsewhere in Japan.

BLACK NODDY [WHITE-CAPPED NODDY] *Anous tenuirostris* <Hime-kuro-ajisashi> L 36cm. Resembles the Brown Noddy but is *smaller, bill is thinner and longer,* cap is whiter, and plumage is darker. **Status:** Accidental to the Iwo Islands, Minami-torishima Island, and Ryukyu Islands.

WHITE NODDY [FAIRY TERN] *Anous albus* <Shiro-ajisashi> L 27.5cm. Unmistakable. *Snowy white overall* with black eye-ring. Black bill is blue at base; legs vary from black to pale blue; feet have yellow webs. **Similar species:** Check possibility of an albino Black or Blue Noddy which would have red eyes, pink bill and legs. **Status:** Accidental.

Terns

Blue Noddy

Brown Noddy

Black Noddy

White Noddy

Herons and Bitterns

Family *Ardeidae* (World: About 60 species; Japan: 19 species) Medium to large wading birds. Necks and legs are long in herons and egrets, shorter in bitterns. Feed at water's edge; roost in trees or reedbeds; breed colonially in trees. Fly with necks pulled back, legs stretched out beyond tails, broad wings beating slowly. When alarmed, bitterns freeze in a typical concealing posture with bills pointed upward.

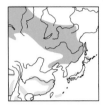

(EURASIAN) BITTERN *Botaurus stellaris* <Sankano-goi> L 70cm. W 120cm. Black crown; yellowish-brown upperparts mottled with black; dark yellow bill; yellowish-green legs. Primarily crepuscular. **Voice:** Deep *boo* in breeding season. **Similar species:** Japanese and Malay Night Herons are smaller with reddish-brown upperparts, no distinct black markings. Immature Black-crowned Night Heron has darker upperparts and yellow legs. **Status:** Uncommon winter visitor, Honshu southward; some may breed in Hokkaido. Large reedbeds.

CHINESE LITTLE BITTERN *Ixobrychus sinensis* <Yoshi-goi> L 36.5cm. Brown upperparts, paler below; greenish-yellow legs. In flight, distinct pattern of black flight feathers, buffy wing coverts, and brown back. **Male:** Black crown. **Female:** Buffy stripes on underparts. **Juvenile:** Whitish underparts, dark streaks above and below. **Voice:** *Ou-ou* in breeding season. **Similar species:** Schrenck's Little Bittern has chestnut upperparts; no sharp contrasting pattern on upperwings. **Status:** Common summer visitor, Honshu northward; reedbeds and rice fields.

SCHRENCK'S LITTLE BITTERN *Ixobrychus eurhythmus* <Ō-yoshi-goi> L 40cm. Dark chestnut upperparts; greenish-yellow legs. **Male:** One dark stripe down foreneck. **Female:** White spots on brown back; dark streaks on buffy underparts. **Juvenile:** Resembles female; yellow tinge on upperparts. **Similar species:** Cinnamon Bittern has rufous flight feathers; male has dark rufous upperparts. **Status:** Uncommon summer visitor, Honshu northward. Reedbeds and grasslands.

CINNAMON BITTERN *Ixobrychus cinnamomeus* <Ryukyu-yoshi-goi> L 40cm. Diagnostic rufous flight feathers in all plumages. Yellowish-green legs. **Male:** Uniformly rufous upperparts, paler underparts. **Female:** Browner upperparts with buffy spots; dark streaks on paler underparts. **Similar species:** See Schrenck's. Japanese Night Heron has dark green legs. Malay Night Heron has green legs and blue lores. **Status:** Common resident, Amami Is. southward; marshes, wet rice fields, reedbeds.

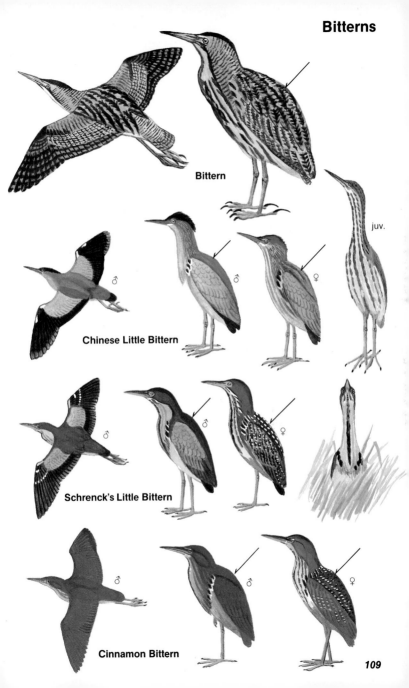

Bitterns

Bittern

Chinese Little Bittern ♂ ♀ juv.

Schrenck's Little Bittern ♂ ♀

Cinnamon Bittern ♂ ♀

109

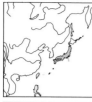

JAPANESE NIGHT HERON *Gorsakius goisagi* <Mizo-goi> L 49cm. *Upperparts reddish brown;* head and neck chestnut, crown darker; underparts paler; bill short; *lore greenish yellow,* blue in summer; legs dark green. **Voice:** Deep *buo-buo* at night in breeding season. **Similar species:** Malay Night Heron has black crown; white tips on primaries. **Status:** Uncommon summer visitor, Honshu south to Kyushu; low mountain forests. Some winter in s. Ryukyu Is. Nocturnal.

BLACK BITTERN *Ixobrychus flavicollis* <Takasago-kuro-sagi> L 61cm. Upperparts blackish; *underparts and side of neck buffy with black stripes;* legs black; bill dark. Female and immature are browner than male. **Similar species:** Green-backed Heron has no black stripes. **Status:** Accidental; Awashima I. (Niigata Pref.). Reedbeds and swamps.

MALAY NIGHT HERON *Gorsakius melanolophus* <Zuguro-mizo-goi> L 47cm. Resembles Japanese Night Heron but *crown is black* and *primaries have white tips. Lore is blue.* **Immature:** White spots on black crown; *finely speckled* pale gray-brown plumage. **Voice:** Similar to Japanese Night Heron's. **Status:** Uncommon resident in s. Ryukyu Is. Subtropical jungles; feeds in wet rice fields at night.

RUFOUS NIGHT HERON *Nycticorax caledonicus* <Hashibuto-goi> L 60cm. Upperparts reddish brown; crown black with white plumes; bill blackish; legs greenish yellow. **Similar species:** See Japanese and Malay Night Herons. **Status:** Subspecies *crassirostris,* Ogasawara Is.; extinct in Japan since 1889. Other subspecies inhabit South Pacific islands.

BLACK-CROWNED NIGHT HERON [NIGHT HERON] *Nycticorax nycticorax* <Goi-sagi> L 57.5cm. *Head and back black; wings gray;* underparts whitish; bill black; legs yellow; long white plumes on head in summer. **Immature:** Dark brown, spotted and streaked with buff; eye changes from yellow to red in first winter. **Voice:** *Quock.* **Similar species:** Green-backed Heron has sharper bill; upperparts entirely greenish gray. **Status:** Common resident, Honshu to Kyushu. Nocturnal.

GREEN-BACKED HERON *Butorides striatus* <Sasa-goi> L 52cm. Head black; *upperparts greenish gray, feathers bordered with white;* underparts paler gray; bill black; legs pale yellow. **Immature:** Upperparts dark brown with white spots on wings. **Voice:** *Qewee.* **Status:** Common summer visitor, Honshu to Kyushu; some winter from s. Kyushu south.

Bitterns, Night Herons

Japanese Night Heron

Black Bittern ♂

Rufous Night Heron

imm.

Malay Night Heron

juv.

Black-crowned Night Heron

summer

juv.

Green-backed Heron

imm.

111

CHINESE POND HERON *Ardeola bacchus* <Aka gashira-sagi> L 45cm. At rest, posture resembles a bittern's. In flight, *dark back and white wings diagnostic.* Yellow bill with black tip; yellowish-orange legs. **Summer:** *Chestnut head, crest, and neck; black back.* **Winter:** Buffy head and underparts with dark stripes; brown back. **Status:** Rare migrant throughout Japan; marshes, rice fields. In 1981 bred in Kyushu (Kumamoto Pref.).

CATTLE EGRET *Bubulcus ibis* <Ama-sagi> L 50.5 cm. Small with *short yellow bill,* black legs. **Summer:** *Buffy orange on head, neck, and back;* yellow lores are reddish only during breeding season. **Winter:** White with little or no buffy tinge. **Similar species:** Little Egret has black bill. Intermediate Egret has longer bill and neck. **Status:** Common summer visitor, Honshu to Kyushu; some winter from Kyushu south. Marshes and meadows.

CHINESE EGRET *Egretta eulophotes* <Kara-shira-sagi> L 65cm. White plumage. **Summer:** *Bushy crest on nape;* plumes on breast and back; *yellow bill;* blue lores; black legs; yellow or yellowish-green feet. **Winter:** Brownish bill with yellow base; yellowish-green lores; greenish-brown legs. **Similar species:** Little Egret has black bill. Eastern Reef Heron has thicker and longer bill, less color difference between legs and feet. **Status:** Rare migrant or winter visitor to tidal mudflats and marshes throughout Japan.

LITTLE EGRET *Egretta garzetta* <Ko-sagi> L 61cm. Most common white egret in Japan. Black bill, black legs, *yellow feet,* greenish-gray lores. **Summer:** *Long plumes droop from nape; upturned plumes* on back; lores reddish during breeding season. **Similar species:** Great and Intermediate Egrets have black feet. Chinese Egret has yellow bill. **Status:** Common resident Honshu to Kyushu; in winter some migrate to Ryukyu Is. and southward. Marshes, wet rice fields, and tidal mudflats.

INTERMEDIATE EGRET [PLUMED EGRET] *Egretta intermedia* <Chū-sagi> L 68.5cm. White plumage; shorter bill than in Little or Great; *black feet* and legs; yellow lores. **Summer:** Plumes on breast and back; black bill; reddish lores only during breeding season. **Winter:** Yellow bill may have brown tip. **Similar species:** See Little and Great Egrets. **Status:** Uncommon summer visitor, Honshu to Kyushu; some winter from s. Kyushu south. Marshes, meadows, wet rice fields.

Pond Herons, Egrets

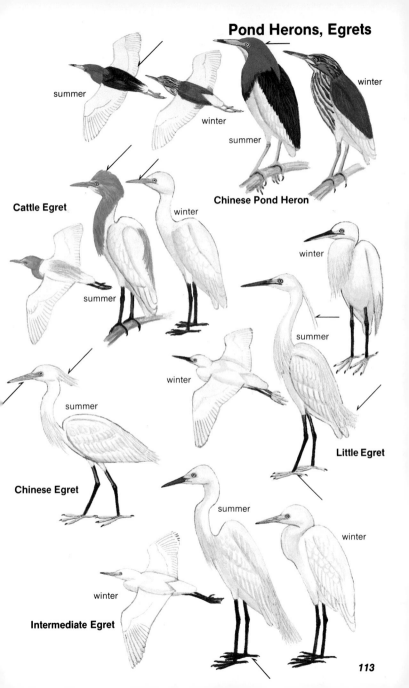

summer

winter

Chinese Pond Heron

summer

winter

Cattle Egret

summer

winter

winter

summer

Little Egret

summer

winter

Chinese Egret

summer

winter

Intermediate Egret

winter

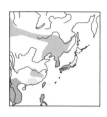

GREAT EGRET [GREAT WHITE EGRET] *Egretta alba* <Dai-sagi> L 90cm. W 160cm. Largest white egret in Japan with longest bill, neck, and legs. All plumage white. Black legs and feet, grayish upper legs. Of the white egrets Great has slowest wingbeats, and in flight outstretched legs extend farther beyond the tail. **Summer:** White plumes on breast and back; *black bill; bluish-green lores* tinged reddish only during breeding season. **Winter:** *Yellow bill;* greenish-yellow lores. **Similar species:** Little Egret has smaller body, yellow feet. Intermediate Egret has smaller body, shorter bill. **Status:** Uncommon summer visitor from Honshu south to Kyushu; some winter from Honshu southward. Wet rice fields, marshes, tidal mudflats.

EASTERN REEF HERON *Egretta sacra* <Kuro-sagi> L 62.5cm. Greenish-yellow legs; yellow feet; crest in summer. **Dark phase:** Diagnostic *slaty black plumage;* some have white on throat; dark bill. **White phase:** All plumage white; *yellow bill;* greenish-yellow lores. **Similar species:** Little Egret is about the same size but has a black bill. Chinese Egret has shorter thinner bill; in summer bushy crest; distinct difference in color of feet and legs. **Status:** Common resident, Honshu southward; rocky coasts. On main islands most birds are dark phase. From Osumi Is. southward about half are white phase. Intermediate phase rare in Japan.

GRAY HERON *Ardea cinerea* <Ao-sagi> L 93cm W 160cm. Largest member of heron family in Japan. Gray plumage with *black crest, black stripes on foreneck,* and black flight feathers. Yellow bill; yellowish-brown legs. In flight distinct contrast between black flight feathers and gray back and wing coverts. Flight is slow on long broad *bowed* wings. **Immature:** Duller gray; no black crest. **Similar species:** See Purple Heron (brownish tinge). Cranes and storks fly with necks outstretched. **Status:** Locally common resident, Kyushu northward. In winter some in colder areas migrate south; found from Honshu southward. Marshes and tidal mudflats.

Egrets, Herons

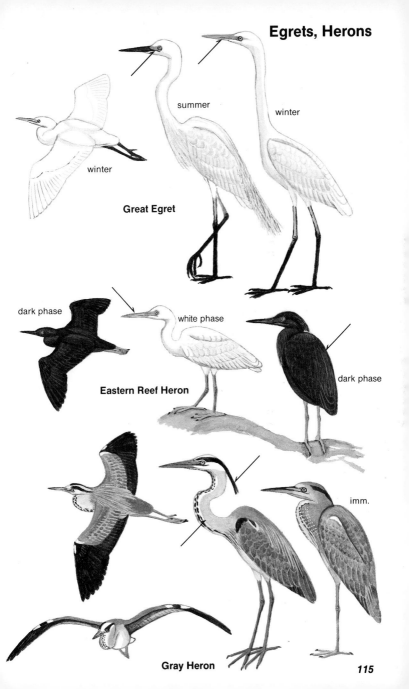

winter

summer

winter

Great Egret

dark phase

white phase

Eastern Reef Heron

dark phase

imm.

Gray Heron

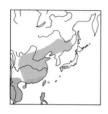

PURPLE HERON *Ardea purpurea* <Murasaki-sagi>
L 78.5cm. Large heron, smaller than Gray Heron and
Great Egret. Characteristic reddish tint and long toes.
Legs and bill are brownish yellow. When alarmed,
hides behind weeds with neck straight. **Immature:** All
plumage browner and duller; no crest. **Similar species:** Gray Heron is *gray;* neck and bill are thicker;
sharper contrast on upperwings in flight. **Status:**
Uncommon resident in southern Ryukyu Is. In other
areas rare migrant or winter visitor. Marshes, wet rice
fields, lakes.

Storks
Family *Ciconiidae* (World: 17 species; Japan: 2 species) Large
wading birds with long necks and legs and long thick bills. The *Ciconia*
species, which are found in Japan, are voiceless. Clatter mandibles together
to make *kata-kata-kata* sound in display. Fly with necks and legs outstretched, legs extending beyond tails; slow strong wingbeats. Feed in large
marshes and rice fields; nest in trees in nests of loosely stacked twigs.

WHITE STORK *Ciconia ciconia* <Kōnotori> L 112cm.
Large and white with black flight feathers. Thick black
bill; pink legs. **Similar species:** Japanese Crane has
red crown and black neck; in the wings, only the
secondaries are black. Siberian White Crane has red
face; only the primaries are black; shows no black
plumage at rest. Cranes have loud voices and do not
perch in trees. **Status:** Widely distributed throughout
Japan 100 years ago. Last breeding record was 1959,
in central Honshu. Now rare migrant or winter visitor
throughout, but mainly Ryukyu Is.

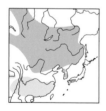

BLACK STORK *Ciconia nigra* <Nabe-kō> L 99cm.
Smaller than White Stork. Glossy black plumage with
white underparts; *red bill and legs.* Large size, black
plumage, and red bill are diagnostic. **Juvenile:** Plumage more brownish without gloss; buffy spots on
neck; bill and legs grayish green. **Status:** Accidental
winter visitor, Honshu southward. Only 4 records in
last decade.

Herons, Storks

Purple Heron

imm.

White Stork

juv.

Black Stork

Ibises and Spoonbills
Family *Threskiornithidae*
(World: 28 species; Japan: 4 species) Medium to large wading birds with a variable amount of bare skin around the base of the bill. Long bills are decurved in ibises and flat and spatulate at the tip in spoonbills. Flight is direct. Unlike herons and egrets, they fly with necks extended. Feed in large marshes, wet rice fields, and tidal mudflats.

JAPANESE CRESTED IBIS *Nipponia nippon* <Toki> L 76.5cm. Characteristic long decurved black bill with red tip; bushy crest; naked red face; red legs. White plumage with pale salmon-pink tinge. In flight, underwings are beautiful salmon pink, *Toki* color in Japanese; feet do not extend beyond tail. **Summer:** Gray head, crest, and back. **Similar species:** Oriental Ibis has black face and legs. Egrets and herons fly with necks pulled back. **Status:** In 1981 all 5 wild birds were captured on Sado for cage breeding. In 1986, 1 male and 1 female are still alive in cage on Sado. In 1985, 21 birds were found in China.

ORIENTAL IBIS *Threskiornis melanocephalus* <Kurotoki> L 68cm. Long decurved black bill; naked black head and upper neck; black legs, longer than in Japanese Crested Ibis; white plumage. In flight, feet extend beyond tail. **Summer:** Gray plumes on the back. **Immature:** Face covered with dark gray feathers; some black on tips of outer primaries. **Similar species:** See Japanese Crested Ibis. **Status:** Rare winter visitor, central Honshu southward. Few records in Hokkaido or in summer.

SPOONBILL *Platalea leucorodia* <Herasagi> L 86cm. Black spatulate bill with *yellow tip.* White plumage with crest. Heavier build than egrets. Black lores. When feeding, sweeps bill from side to side in shallow water. **Summer:** Crest and breast are yellow. **Immature:** Brown bill; black on wing tips. **Similar species:** See Black-faced Spoonbill. **Status:** Rare winter visitor, Honshu southward.

BLACK-FACED SPOONBILL *Platalea minor* <Kuro tsura-herasagi> L 73.5cm. Similar to Spoonbill, but larger area of black skin on face extends to forehead and surrounds eye. *Black* spatulate bill. Feeds in same manner as Spoonbill. **Summer:** Crest and breast are yellow. **Immature:** Bill dark pinkish gray; wings have black on tips. **Similar species:** White egrets are more slender with shorter pointed bills; fly with slower wingbeats and necks pulled back. **Status:** Rare winter visitor, Honshu southward.

Ibises, Spoonbills

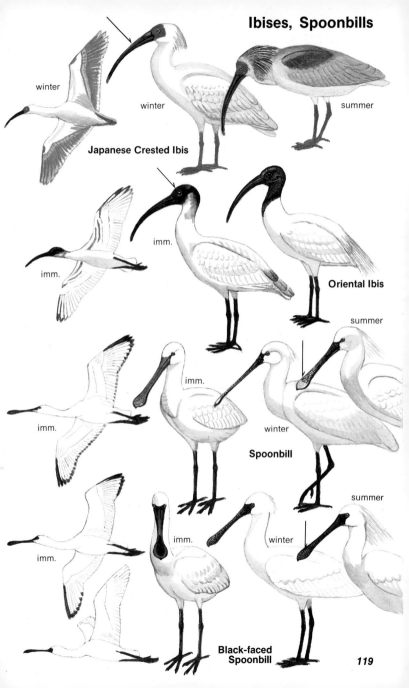

winter

winter

summer

Japanese Crested Ibis

imm.

imm.

Oriental Ibis

imm.

imm.

winter

summer

Spoonbill

imm.

imm.

winter

summer

Black-faced Spoonbill

Cranes

Family *Gruidae* (World: 13 species; Japan: 7 species) Tall, elegant wading birds with long bills, necks, and legs. Long tertiaries droop over the tail. Fly slowly in long lines or in V formation with necks and legs outstretched. Do not perch in trees. Both sexes perform picturesque courtship dancing display. Loud trumpet-like calls. Arasaki, in Kyushu, is the main wintering area for Hooded and White-naped Cranes. Only the Japanese Crane breeds in Japan. Found in open fields.

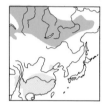

COMMON CRANE *Grus grus* <Kuro-zuru> L 114cm. Gray with red crown; black face, throat, and nape; *curving white stripe* on side of head and neck; blackish-brown primaries. **Similar species:** White-naped has white head, red face, darker underparts, and reddish legs. Hooded has much darker underparts; little contrast between dark primaries and wing coverts; head and neck much whiter. **Status:** Regular in winter in small numbers at Arasaki; usually in flocks of Hooded Cranes. Accidental elsewhere.

HOODED CRANE *Grus monacha* <Nabe-zuru> L 96.5cm. *White head and neck, black forehead,* red crown; body slate gray. **Immature:** Lacks black forehead and red crown; face tinged with brown; body much darker. **Similar species:** White-naped has red face, dark stripe on side of neck, more contrast in wings, and reddish legs. Sandhill has generally paler plumage and stronger contrast between primaries and wing coverts. **Status:** Locally abundant winter visitor. Over 4,000 birds recorded regularly at Arasaki, Kagoshima Pref. **Hybrid of Hooded and Common Crane:** Since the early 1970's hybrids of Hooded and Common Cranes have wintered at Arasaki. These birds have diluted characteristics of both species. Intermediate body color; *some* contrast in wings; head is like that of Hooded but with black on throat and breast. Second generation hybrids are now coming to Arasaki. Hybrids among cranes are extremely rare.

SANDHILL CRANE *Grus canadensis* <Kanada-zuru> L 100cm. *Red forehead and crown, white chin and throat,* dark gray body tinged with brown. Immature is brown. **Similar species:** Resembles Common and Demoiselle in flight but less contrast between dark primaries and pale wing coverts. **Status:** Accidental, winter; usually found in flocks of other cranes.

DEMOISELLE CRANE *Anthropoides virgo* <Anehazuru> L 97.5cm. Gray with black on face and crown, *white ear tufts,* black throat and foreneck with long black feathers hanging over breast. Bill much smaller than in other cranes. **Similar species:** See Common, Hooded, and Sandhill Cranes. **Status:** Accidental; only a few records in the last ten years.

Cranes

Gray Heron

imm.

Common Crane

Hooded Crane

imm.

hybrid of Hooded and
Common Crane

Sandhill Crane

Demoiselle Crane

121

JAPANESE CRANE [RED-CROWNED CRANE] *Grus japonensis* <Tanchō> L 140cm. W 240cm. The largest crane in Japan. *White; black forehead, throat, and neck* with white nape and *red crown;* white primaries, *black secondaries.* Tail is white, but at rest it is completely covered by the long drooping black tertiaries. **Immature:** Brownish head and neck, white body tinged with chestnut, blackish-brown secondaries and tertiaries. **Similar species:** Siberian White Crane has *black primaries* and *white secondaries;* red face. Smaller White Stork has long, stout, black bill; *black primaries and secondaries.* **Status:** Locally common resident in Kushiro-Nemuro area of eastern Hokkaido. Straggler elsewhere.

SIBERIAN WHITE CRANE *Grus leucogeranus* <Sode guro-zuru> L 135cm. A large white crane, nearly as large as Japanese Crane. Unmistakable *white body, red face, long reddish-brown bill* (longer than bill of other cranes), and dark red legs. White tertiaries droop over tail. In flight, *black primaries* contrasting with *white body and wings* are diagnostic. **Immature:** Some chestnut plumage on head, neck, back, and tip of wing coverts. Wing pattern in flight similar to adult's. **Similar species:** Japanese Crane has *white primaries, black secondaries.* White Stork is slightly smaller and has *black primaries and secondaries.* **Status:** Straggler.

WHITE-NAPED CRANE *Grus vipio* <Mana-zuru> L 127cm. A large crane, slightly smaller than Japanese and Siberian White Cranes. Conspicuous *red face;* white head, neck, and nape; *dark gray stripe* on side of neck. Elongated tertiaries cover the tail. Body and belly are generally dark gray, paler toward the rear. *Primaries and secondaries black, wing coverts whitish.* Reddish legs. **Similar species:** Common Crane has black head, face, and neck. Hooded has much darker body and black legs. **Status:** Locally abundant winter visitor only to Arasaki, Kagoshima Pref., Kyushu. Rare elsewhere.

Cranes

imm.

Japanese Crane

imm.

imm.

Siberian White Crane

White-naped Crane

123

Rails, Gallinules, and Coots

Family *Rallidae*

(World: About 130 species; Japan: 11 species) Rails, gallinules, and coots are small to medium-sized marsh birds with small heads, stout bodies, short rounded wings, short tails, and long toes. Flight is weak with legs dangling. Nests among reeds or on the ground. Chicks are generally dark and resemble baby chickens. Rails are especially shy and skulking, usually staying hidden in dense vegetation. Sexes usually similar.

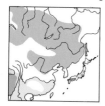

(EUROPEAN) COOT *Fulica atra* <Ō-ban> L 39cm. Almost totally black marsh bird slightly larger than Common Gallinule. Unmistakable *white bill and frontal shield;* in flight, tips of secondaries show a *narrow white edge.* Green legs with large toes. **Juvenile:** Dusky gray with white throat and upper breast. **Similar species:** Common Gallinule has red bill and shield, white flank stripe and under tail coverts. See Watercock. **Status:** Uncommon. Breeds mainly from central Honshu northward. Some new breeding records from western Honshu and northern Kyushu. Winters from central Honshu southward.

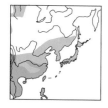

COMMON GALLINULE [MOORHEN] *Gallinula chloropus* <Ban> L 32.5cm. A duck-like marsh bird with bright red frontal shield, *yellow-tipped red bill, white flank stripe,* and *white under tail coverts.* When swimming pumps head and neck back and forth and keeps short tail cocked. **Juvenile:** Brown with paler face and underparts; white chin and throat; bill and small shield are greenish brown. **Similar species:** Coot is larger and has white bill and frontal shield. See Watercock. **Status:** Common resident Honshu southward; breeds in Hokkaido.

Coots, Gallinules

juv.

Coot

alarmed

juv.

Common Gallinule

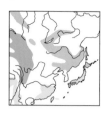

WATER RAIL *Rallus aquaticus* <Kuina> L 29cm.
Long reddish bill; olive-brown upperparts; slate-gray face, throat, foreneck, and breast; *black-and-white barred* flanks and under tail coverts. **Voice:** *Bee bee.*
Similar species: Ruddy Crake is smaller, has much more reddish brown on neck and breast, and is a *summer* visitor. Baillon's Crake is similar in color, but is smaller. **Status:** Common throughout. Breeds in northern parts of Japan; winters in warmer regions.

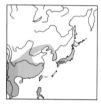

RUDDY CRAKE *Porzana fusca* <Hi-kuina> L 22.5cm.
Small rail about the size of a Gray Starling. Upperparts generally brown; throat white; *underparts reddish brown or wine red;* lower belly and flanks *barred brown and white;* legs red. **Voice:** Short, sharp, accelerating *kyo kyo kyo kyo kyo,* most often heard at dawn or dusk. **Similar species:** Baillon's Crake is much smaller and is streaked with black and white on the back. Banded Crake has similar plumage but has black legs, is much larger, and occurs only in the southern Ryukyu Is. **Status:** Common summer visitor; breeds throughout Japan. Resident in Ryukyu Is.

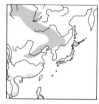

BAILLON'S CRAKE *Porzana pusilla* <Hime-kuina> L 19.5cm. Small, olive brown with dark streaks, conspicuous *white spots on the back,* and *boldly barred sides; short bill is dark olive.* **Similar species:** Swinhoe's Yellow Rail shows *white secondaries* in flight; is smaller with darker back; is a winter visitor. **Status:** Uncommon summer visitor throughout Japan. Occasional winter records from warmer regions.

SWINHOE'S YELLOW RAIL *Porzana exquisita* <Shima-kuina> L 12.5cm. The smallest rail in Japan. Upperparts brown with black streaks *finely barred with white;* chin and throat white; flanks and under tail coverts distinctly barred brown and white; tail short and cocked. In flight, *white secondaries* are conspicuous. **Similar species:** See Baillon's Crake. **Status:** Uncommon winter visitor in small numbers from central Honshu southward; transient in northern Japan.

ASHY CRAKE *Poliolimnas cinereus* <Mamijiro-kuina> L 20cm. A small rail about the size of Baillon's. Brown upperparts; gray underparts; *white stripes above and below dark eyestripe;* white belly; *no barring on buffy flanks;* short pointed tail slightly cocked. **Status:** Believed extinct. Records from the Iwo Is. until 1911.

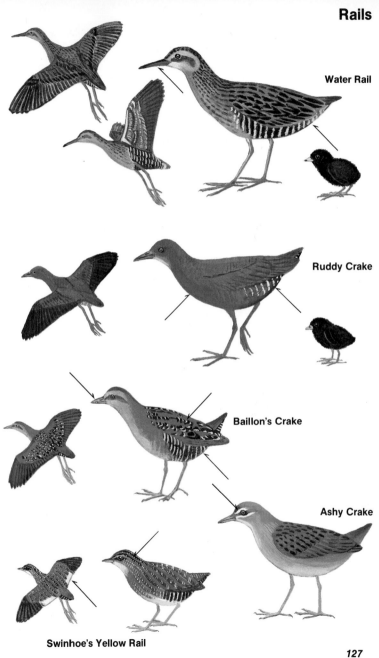

Rails

Water Rail

Ruddy Crake

Baillon's Crake

Ashy Crake

Swinhoe's Yellow Rail

127

OKINAWA RAIL *Rallus okinawae* <Yanbaru-kuina> L 30cm. A newly discovered rail with a *large bright red bill, red legs and feet,* and extremely short wings. Upperparts generally olive brown; breast and belly black with distinct white bars; eye blood-red; face black with a conspicuous white line from behind the eye down the cheek onto the neck. *Runs very fast* to hide; *most likely flightless.* Feeds mainly on insects and lizards. **Similar species:** Ruddy Crake also has red legs but is much smaller and has a greenish-brown bill. **Status:** Rare resident, northern Okinawa I. *only.* Officially identified as a new species in 1981. Exact population unknown. Prefers dense habitat near grassy and swampy areas.

BANDED CRAKE *Rallina eurizonoides* <Ō-kuina> L 26cm. Upperparts olive brown; face, neck, and breast reddish brown; chin and throat white; *belly, flanks, and under tail coverts boldly barred black and white;* legs black. Runs fast to escape from danger. **Similar species:** Ruddy Crake is smaller with red legs. Water Rail is larger, has streaked back and no reddish plumage. **Status:** Common resident in Ryukyu Is. Usually nests in trees.

WATERCOCK *Gallicrex cinerea* <Tsuru-kuina> L 33cm. **Summer male:** Brilliant *red frontal shield;* bright yellow bill; *red legs;* blackish upperparts with gray edges to feathers; slate-gray belly and flanks with white feather edges; buffy under tail coverts. **Female and winter male:** Paler upperparts mottled with gray; whitish throat; brown bill; yellowish shield; dull *greenish legs.* Active at dawn and dusk; rarely flies. **Similar species:** Common Gallinule is slightly smaller; frontal shield is red year-round; has white streaks on flanks and white under tail coverts. Coot has white frontal shield and is seen more often in open water. **Status:** Uncommon resident in Ryukyu Islands. Rare transient elsewhere.

WHITE-BREASTED WATERHEN *Amaurornis phoenicurus* <Shirohara-kuina> L 32.5cm. Slaty upperparts. *Conspicuous white face, breast, and belly; chestnut under tail coverts;* green bill with red base; yellow legs. **Similar species:** Immature Coot has paler upperparts; underparts are not as white. **Status:** Uncommon resident in Ryukyu Is. Accidental from Kyushu northward. Occasionally observed in open areas and away from water.

Rails

Okinawa Rail

Banded Crake

♂ summer   ♂ winter

Watercock

♀

White-breasted
Waterhen

Bustards

Family *Otidae* (World: 24 species; Japan: 2 species.) Medium to large-sized terrestrial birds with long thick necks, stout bodies, broad wings, and strong legs. Very shy. Flight powerful; walk stately.

GREAT BUSTARD *Otis tarda* <Nogan> L Male 100cm. Female 75cm. A large terrestrial bird easily identified by *very large size, stout body,* and *long thick neck and legs.* Male has chestnut band on breast and long white moustache. Female is smaller; lacks breast band and moustache. In flight white coverts contrast strikingly with black wing tips. **Status:** Straggler in winter; several records, throughout Japan.

LITTLE BUSTARD *Otis tetrax* <Hime-nogan> L 43cm. Summer male has slaty gray cheeks and throat and *black neck with characteristic white marks.* Flight feathers mostly white. Female and winter male lack gray, black, and white on face and neck. **Status:** Accidental. Only one record, from Kyushu.

Waders

Small to medium-sized wading birds with pointed wings. Most migrate through Japan in spring and fall, but a few winter here as well. In most cases sexes are similar. Prefer sandy beaches, mudflats, rice fields, marshlands, and rivers.

Jacanas

Family *Jacanidae* (World: 7 species; Japan: 1 species) Marsh birds with extremely long toes which enable them to walk on floating vegetation. They take high steps and can run swiftly. They are good swimmers and divers and sometimes submerge to hide.

PHEASANT-TAILED JACANA *Hydrophasianus chirurgus* <Renkaku> L 55cm in summer. *Long tail streamers,* white wings with black tips, and long toes. **Summer:** White head and foreneck; *yellow nape* bordered in black; blackish-brown body and tail. **Winter:** Short tail; white underparts; white eyebrow; yellow stripe on side of neck; dark line from eye down the neck to breast band. **Status:** Straggler; marshes and lotus ponds, central Honshu south.

Oystercatchers

Family *Haematopodidae* (World: 4 species; Japan: 1 species) Large chunky shorebirds with long thick red bills, used to open shellfish and bivalves.

OYSTERCATCHER *Haematopus ostralegus* <Miya kodori> L 45cm. Large black-and-white shorebird. Black head and neck, *long red bill, and pink feet* are diagnostic. In flight, the broad white wingbar and black bar on the white tail are distinctive. **Status:** Rare transient; some winter.

Bustards, Jacanas, Oystercatchers

♀

♂

♀

Great Bustard

♂

♀ summer

♀

Little Bustard

summer

summer

winter

Pheasant-tailed Jacana

imm.

Oystercatcher

131

Plovers

Family *Charadriidae* (World: 60 species; Japan: 12 species) Plovers are small to medium-sized shorebirds with characteristic large heads, large eyes, short necks, and short bills. They usually have three forward toes. Different plumage in summer and winter. Carnivorous feeders generally found on mudflats or wet grasslands, they run quickly in an upright posture. Birds in this group do not feed and move at the same time. In most species sexes are similar.

RINGED PLOVER *Charadrius hiaticula* <Hajiro-kochidori> L 19cm. Brown upperparts; white underparts; white collar. Similar to Little Ringed Plover but is larger; *lacks white line between black on forehead and grayish-brown crown; white wing bar* shows in flight. Yellow legs. **Summer:** Black face mask and breast band. Black bill has *orange* base. **Winter:** Brown face mask and breast band; black bill. **Status:** Uncommon transient or winter visitor.

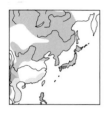

LITTLE RINGED PLOVER *Charadrius dubius* <Kochidori> L 16cm. Smallest plover. Note the *yellow legs* and *yellow eye-ring;* white underparts; white collar; black-and-white facial pattern with white line separating gray-brown crown from black band across forehead; black breast band. **Immature:** Duller in color; pattern less distinct; black is replaced by brown. **Similar species:** Long-billed Ringed Plover is larger with a longer bill, pale legs, and a brownish facial pattern. See Ringed Plover. **Status:** Common summer visitor; some winter in southwestern Japan.

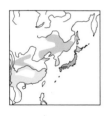

LONG-BILLED RINGED PLOVER *Charadrius placidus* <Ikaru-chidori> L 20.5cm. Larger than Little Ringed Plover, with *longer bill.* Eyestripe is grayish brown, not black; yellow legs are pale; in flight, wing bar is faint and indistinct. **Similar species:** Ringed Plover has orange on bill and black eyestripe in summer; more distinct wing bar. **Status:** Common resident; prefers riverbeds and cut rice stubble fields.

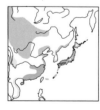

SNOWY PLOVER [KENTISH PLOVER] *Charadrius alexandrinus* <Shiro-chidori> L 17.5cm. Small plover with white forehead and white line above eye; interrupted breast band or a dark patch at side of breast; *black legs* and bill; white wing bar shows in flight. Male in summer has black mark between *rufous crown* and white forehead; black patch on side of breast. Male in winter, female, and immature have brown crown and patch on side of breast. **Status:** Common resident; forms large flocks in winter. Prefers sandy beaches and mudflats of estuaries.

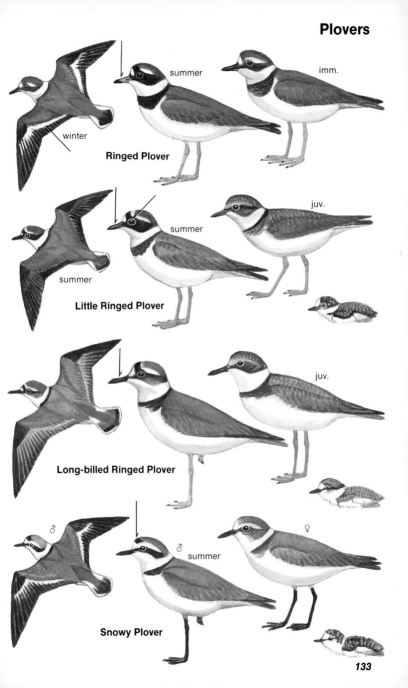

Plovers

Ringed Plover
winter
summer
imm.

Little Ringed Plover
summer
summer
juv.

Long-billed Ringed Plover
juv.

Snowy Plover
♂
♂ summer
♀

133

MONGOLIAN PLOVER *Charadrius mongolus* <Me dai-chidori> L 19.5cm. Larger than Snowy Plover. Short black bill; dark legs. **Summer:** *Broad rufous band across breast;* rufous on front and sides of crown and on sides of neck; white throat and forehead bordered with black. **Winter:** Upperparts brownish gray; underparts white with narrow brown breast band; white forehead and eyebrow; no rufous. **Similar species:** Greater Sand Plover is larger with longer heavier bill, yellow legs. **Status:** Common transient on beaches and mudflats.

GREATER SAND PLOVER *Charadrius leschenaultii* <Ōmedai-chidori> L 21.5cm. Resembles Mongolian Plover in color but is slightly larger and taller; longer heavier black bill not wider at tip; *legs longer and yellowish.* **Summer:** Rufous breast band, with *no black border,* is narrower and fainter than in Mongolian Plover. **Winter:** Whiter; gray brown across breast; no rufous. **Status:** Uncommon transient; found in flocks of Mongolian Plovers.

CASPIAN PLOVER *Charadrius asiaticus* <Ō-chidori> L 22.5cm. Smaller than Lesser Golden Plover. *Long yellowish-orange legs;* thin black bill; brown crown and upperparts; white belly. **Summer:** White face; *chestnut breast* with black across lower breast. **Winter:** White eyebrows; pale brown breast; plain back. **Similar species:** Greater Sand Plover in winter has a distinct band on breast. Lesser Golden Plover in winter is similar size but legs are black. **Status:** Straggler on arable land near coast and along inland rivers and lakes.

DOTTEREL *Eudromias morinellus* <Kobashi-chidori> L 21cm. Blackish-brown crown; *broad whitish eyebrows meet at nape;* faint *white band on breast;* gray-brown upperparts with rufous edges to feathers visible at close range; black bill; yellow legs. **Summer:** Chestnut underparts and grayish-brown breast divided by white band are diagnostic. **Winter:** Paler and browner with indistinct breast band; no chestnut on underparts. **Juvenile:** Similar to winter adult, but has buff fringes on the upperparts. **Similar species:** Lesser Golden Plover is larger with black legs and yellowish upperparts. **Status:** Straggler in fall; mudflats, rice fields, and sandy grassland near coast.

Plovers

winter

summer

winter

changing to winter

juv.

Mongolian Plover

winter

summer

winter

Greater Sand Plover

summer

summer

winter

Caspian Plover

juv.

summer

juv.

Dotterel

135

LESSER GOLDEN PLOVER *Pluvialis dominica*
<Munaguro> L 24cm. Heavy body with golden-brown back, *dark rump*, black bill and legs. In flight upper surface appears golden with a faint wing bar. **Summer:** Back finely patterned with *golden yellow and black*. Underparts from eyeline to belly are black. Diagnostic *white band* across forehead and down sides separates patterned crown and back from black underparts. **Winter:** Yellowish-brown breast. **Voice:** *Kyobie, kyobyo.* **Similar species:** Black-bellied Plover has white rump; in summer plumage, black underparts do not extend as far back toward the tail. **Status:** Common transient on mudflats, rice fields, and other arable land. Some winter on the Ogasawara and Ryukyu Islands.

BLACK-BELLIED PLOVER [GRAY PLOVER] *Pluvialis squatarola* <Daizen> L 29.5cm. Mottled black-and-white back. In flight whitish underwing with *black axillars* is diagnostic; white wing bar and *white rump* are distinctive. **Summer:** Underparts black from eyeline to belly. **Winter:** Grayish with faint speckling on breast. **Voice:** Whistle-like long rising inflective *pyuieh.* **Similar species:** Great Knot has a longer bill and shorter legs; different feeding habits. Lesser Golden Plover has dark rump; black underparts extend farther back toward tail. **Status:** Common transient on mudflats and shallow water along coasts and estuaries; rarely found inland. Some winter, Honshu southward.

(NORTHERN) LAPWING *Vanellus vanellus* <Tageri> L 31.5cm. *Long thin crest;* upperparts dark iridescent green with *white tips to primaries;* underwings black with white lining and base of secondaries; belly white; tail white with black subterminal band; bill black; legs dark orange. In flight unmistakable pattern on underside. **Summer:** Longer crest and *black throat.* **Winter:** Shorter crest and *white throat.* **Voice:** *Miao,* like a kitten. **Status:** Uncommon or locally common winter visitor on open rice fields. A few recent breeding records, central Honshu.

GRAY-HEADED LAPWING *Microsarcops cinereus* <Keri> L 35.5cm. Large with *long yellow legs. Yellow bill* with black tip. Gray head, neck, and breast; black band on lower breast; white belly; brown back. Inconspicuous on the ground, but striking pattern in flight, legs extending beyond tail. **Status:** Uncommon breeder; rice fields and grasslands in northern and central Honshu. In winter, populations from snowy regions migrate southward.

Plovers, Lapwings

molting

summer

juv.

Lesser Golden Plover

juv.

juv.

summer

juv.

Black-bellied Plover

juv.

winter

juv.

winter

Lapwing

Gray-headed Lapwing

Sandpipers

Family *Scolopacidae* (World: About 80 species; Japan: 50 species) Sandpipers are small to large-sized shorebirds with long bills and long legs. Move about in rice fields or on mudflats with heads down, feeding chiefly on small invertebrates. Feeding and moving at the same time is characteristic. Sexes are similar but plumage is different in summer and winter.

RUFOUS-NECKED STINT [RED-NECKED STINT] *Calidris ruficollis* <Tōnen> L 15cm. Small with short stout black bill, *black legs.* In flight shows narrow white wing bar. **Summer:** *Rufous face, neck, and upper breast;* black, brown, and rufous mottling on upperparts. **Winter:** Rufous is lost; upperparts grayish brown. **Similar species:** Dunlin is larger with longer decurved bill. See Little Stint. **Status:** Common transient.

TEMMINCK'S STINT *Calidris temminckii* <Ojiro-tō nen> L 14.5cm. Small sandpiper with black bill and *yellowish-green legs.* **Winter:** *Uniformly dark gray* back and breast; most often seen in this plumage. In flight, white wing bar and white band on sides of tail are distinctive. **Voice:** *Chiriri chiriri.* **Similar species:** Long-toed Stint has a white V-shaped line on back. **Status:** Uncommon transient; some winter. Small flocks; shallow inland waters.

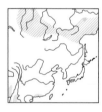

LONG-TOED STINT *Calidris subminuta* <Hibari-shigi> L 15cm. Thin black bill; long olive-yellow legs and toes; white eyebrow; *white V* on brownish back; black streaks on upperparts; *finely streaked breast;* upright stance. **Summer:** Neck, breast, and upperparts are tinged with rufous. **Voice:** *Puriri* or *kuriri.* **Similar species:** See Least Sandpiper. Sharp-tailed is larger; Baird's lacks V on back, and folded wings extend past the tail. **Status:** Uncommon transient; shallow inland waters.

LITTLE STINT *Calidris minuta* <Yōroppa-tōnen> L 13.5cm. Similar to Rufous-necked Stint, but can be distinguished by the rather fine bill proportionally wider at the tip and the high degree of activity during feeding. **Similar species:** Difficult to distinguish from Rufous-necked Stint in the field. In the hand, smaller wing/tarsus ratio. **Status:** Straggler; mudflats. One record from Sagami River estuary in Kanagawa Pref.

LEAST SANDPIPER *Calidris minutilla* <Amerika-hibari-shigi> L 14.5cm. Smaller than Long-toed Sandpiper; *slight bill;* yellowish or greenish legs; no rufous coloring; *sharp clear edge* where finely and densely streaked breast meets white belly. **Status:** Accidental; mudflats. Records from Kanagawa and Kagoshima Prefs.

Small Sandpipers

winter

juv.

summer

Rufous-necked Stint

winter

winter

summer

Temminck's Stint

winter

summer

Long-toed Stint

juv.

winter

Little Stint

juv.

Least Sandpiper

BAIRD'S SANDPIPER *Calidris bairdii* <Hime-uzura-shigi> L 15.5cm. Buffy sandpiper, can be difficult to identify. At rest, *wings extend well beyond the tail;* back appears *scaly* with distinct white and buff fringes and black shafts; buffy wash on breast in all plumages; straight black bill; *black legs.* **Status:** Straggler in fall; sandy mudflats.

PECTORAL SANDPIPER *Calidris melanotos* <Ameri ka-uzura-shigi> L 22cm. Dark brown crown; streaked back; erect posture; longer neck than smaller sandpipers. Distinguishing *sharp, abrupt ending of the breast streaks where they meet the white belly.* Dark bill; greenish-yellow legs. **Similar species:** Sharp-tailed Sandpiper has rufous crown and buffier breast. **Status:** Rare.

SHARP-TAILED SANDPIPER *Calidris acuminata* <Uzura-shigi> L 21.5cm. Brownish sandpiper with olive-yellow legs; slightly larger than a Dunlin. **Summer:** Distinctive *rufous crown. Dense dark spots* on face, breast, and sides. **Winter:** Indistinct spots on breast. In flight, faint wing bar; legs do not extend beyond the tail. **Similar species:** Buff-breasted Sandpiper has a thinner bill and fewer spots on breast; crown not rufous. Ruff is larger and has long legs which extend beyond the tail in flight. Pectoral Sandpiper is not as brown, and breast streaks end abruptly at white belly. **Status:** Common transient; shallow inland waters, rice fields.

BROAD-BILLED SANDPIPER *Limicola falcinellus* <Kiriai> L 17cm. Longish *black bill slightly decurved* and distinctly broad from base to tip; *forked white eyebrow;* mottled rufous-and-black back with distinct shaft streaks, pale fringes, and a white V in the center; white wing bar shows in flight; black legs. **Status:** Uncommon transient in flocks of Dunlins and Rufous-necked Stints.

ROCK SANDPIPER *Calidris ptilocnemis* <Chishima-shigi> L 21cm. Dunlin-sized sandpiper with yellow legs and *black-tipped yellow bill.* **Summer:** A few dark splotches on face, side, and upper breast. Large *black patch* on lower breast; fringes on back turn rufous. **Winter:** Slaty gray crown, neck, and back with white fringes; dense *slaty gray spots* on breast and sides; white eyebrow and belly. **Similar species:** Dunlin has longer black bill and black legs; paler in winter; in summer black patch is lower on belly. **Status:** Uncommon winter visitor to Chiba Pref.; rare winter visitor elsewhere. Rocky coast.

Small Sandpipers

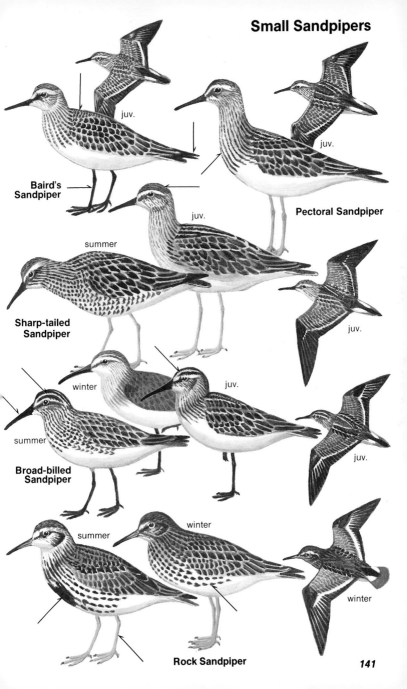

Baird's Sandpiper

juv.

Pectoral Sandpiper

juv.

juv.

Sharp-tailed Sandpiper

summer

juv.

juv.

Broad-billed Sandpiper

winter

summer

juv.

juv.

summer

winter

Rock Sandpiper

winter

DUNLIN *Calidris alpina* <Hama-shigi> L 21cm. Slightly decurved long black bill. **Summer:** Large *black patch* on belly; rufous and black mottling on crown and back; black streaks on white breast. **Winter:** Upperparts gray; underparts white with grayish streaking on neck and breast. **Juvenile:** Underparts white with *brown spots* on breast and flanks. **Similar species:** Sanderling has shorter, stouter bill; white underparts; black shoulder. Broad-billed Sandpiper has forked eyebrow and white V on dark back. **Status:** Common transient and winter visitor to mudflats of estuaries; often in large flocks.

CURLEW SANDPIPER *Calidris ferruginea* <Saru hama-shigi> L 21.5cm. Long tapering decurved black bill; long black legs; *white rump.* White wing bar shows in flight. **Summer:** Unmistakable *chestnut-red* head, breast, and belly. **Winter:** White eyebrow; white belly; grayish wash on neck and breast. **Juvenile:** Mottled upperparts; buffy breast with faint streaks; white belly. **Similar species:** Dunlin in winter is slightly smaller with shorter bill and legs and *no white on rump.* **Status:** Uncommon transient; mudflats, beaches, and estuaries.

SANDERLING *Crocethia alba* <Miyubi-shigi> L 19cm. Slightly smaller than Dunlin with short, stout black bill and short black legs. In flight the *white wing bar* is distinct. **Summer:** *Rufous and black* mottling on face, breast, and back; white belly. **Winter:** White underparts; pale gray upperparts; *black shoulder.* **Similar species:** Rufous-necked Stint in summer is smaller with rufous face and breast. Spoon-billed Sandpiper has characteristic bill. **Status:** Common transient; winters locally. Prefers sandy beaches; often at water's edge.

WESTERN SANDPIPER *Calidris mauri* <Hime-hama-shigi> L 16cm. Almost the same size as Rufous-necked Stint. Black bill droops slightly at the tip; is usually longer than bill of other small sandpipers. Black legs. **Summer:** Rufous crown and nape; upperparts black with rufous edges to feathers; fine black streaks on gray neck and breast. **Winter:** Grayish-brown upperparts often with *rufous shoulder;* pale gray streaks on breast. **Status:** Straggler; mudflats of estuaries.

Small Sandpipers

Dunlin
summer
winter
juv.
winter

Curlew Sandpiper
winter
summer
juv.
juv.

Sanderling
winter
summer
juv.
winter

Western Sandpiper
summer
winter
winter

143

GREAT KNOT *Calidris tenuirostris* <Oba-shigi> L 28.5cm. Chunky with *dense dark spots on breast and sides.* Holds long body *more horizontally* than other sandpipers. Distinct *white rump* and wing bar. Black bill; greenish-black legs. **Summer:** Dark gray back with light tips; *large chestnut spots* and black mottling on shoulders; broad dark breast band. **Winter:** Heavy black streaks on buffy breast; black shaft streaks and white edges on back; no rufous on shoulder. **Similar species:** Black-bellied Plover is larger with a shorter bill and black axillars. Red Knot in winter has uniformly gray back and finer streaking on face and breast. **Voice:** Whistling *pyuee*. **Status:** Common transient on mudflats. Often found feeding in compact flocks with all birds moving together in the same direction.

RED KNOT [KNOT] *Calidris canutus* <Ko-oba-shigi> L 24.5cm. Smaller than Great Knot; shorter bill is about the same length as the head; legs yellowish olive. **Summer:** *Rufous face and breast;* back mottled with rufous, black, and gray. **Winter:** *Uniformly gray back,* but fine black shaft streaks and edges are distinct at close range. **Similar species:** Curlew Sandpiper has rufous breast but is smaller with a long decurved bill. See Great Knot. **Status:** Uncommon transient on mudflats.

SPOON- BILLED SANDPIPER *Eurynorhynchus pygmeus* <Hera-shigi> L 15cm. Resembles Rufous-necked Stint but has a *unique spatulate bill.* Clear contrast between white belly and mottled dark upperparts. Black legs. **Summer:** Black streaks on rufous breast. **Winter:** Black crown; mottled black-and-white back; broad black eyeline; white forehead. **Similar species:** Color in winter similar to color of juvenile Sanderling, but Sanderling is larger with black on shoulders. Winter Rufous-necked Stint has a lighter cap and brown on upperparts. *It is essential to see the bill.* **Status:** Rare; mainly fall, in flocks of Rufous-necked Stints.

BUFF-BREASTED SANDPIPER *Tryngites subruficollis* <Komon-shigi> L 20cm. *Buff* sandpiper with short black bill, small head, long neck, long orange legs, and white eye-ring. Upright posture. In flight, upperwing is uniform; *white underwing and buffy body* are distinct. When disturbed it prefers to run rather than fly. When flushed, twists and turns like a snipe. **Similar species:** No other sandpiper is entirely buffy below. **Status:** Straggler on short grass fields, rice stubble fields.

Sandpipers

juv.

summer

juv.

Great Knot

juv.

winter

juv.

summer

Red Knot

juv.

summer

juv.

Spoon-billed Sandpiper

juv.

juv.

Buff-breasted Sandpiper

RUFF [REEVE] *Philomachus pugnax* <Erimaki-shigi> L Male (Ruff) 32cm. Female (Reeve) 25cm. Relatively tall shorebird with short, slightly decurved bill and black eyestripe. Pale margins on the dark feathers give back a *scaly* appearance. Feathers often bristle up. In flight *white oval patch* shows on each side of the tail; yellow-orange to red legs extend slightly beyond the tail; white wing bar is narrow but clear. **Male:** In summer has unique *ruff and ear tufts* which are in widely variable combinations of colors (see illustration). In winter has white underparts with breast streaked gray. **Female:** Similar to winter male. **Juvenile:** Like winter plumage but breast washed buff. **Similar species:** Greenshank and Redshank have longer bills and gray or blackish upperparts (Ruff is more brownish); the white rump is not divided. Black-tailed Godwit is larger, with longer bill and legs, black-and-white pattern on wings and tail. Sharp-tailed Sandpiper has rufous crown and relatively short legs which do not extend beyond tail in flight. **Status:** Uncommon transient; rice fields and marshes; mainly in juvenile plumage.

Pratincoles
Family *Glareolidae* (World: 8 species; Japan: 1 species) Pratincoles are medium-sized waders with short stubby bills, short legs, long pointed wings, and deeply forked tails. They prefer riverbanks and dry grassland such as reclaimed land. Feed in the air on insects.

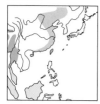

INDIAN PRATINCOLE *Glareola maldivarum* <Tsu bame-chidori> L 26.5cm. Upright posture with tail pointed downward; looks somewhat like a large long-legged swallow. **Summer:** *Creamy throat bordered with black; white rump;* black forked tail; white belly; dark underwings with *chestnut under wing coverts.* **Winter:** Duller throat patch with indistinct border. Folded wings extend beyond tail. Flight swallow-like or tern-like with slow wingbeats. **Status:** Uncommon transient; breeds locally in western Japan.

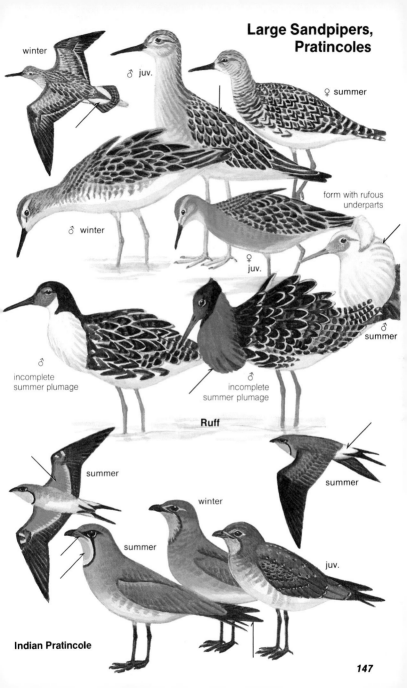

Large Sandpipers, Pratincoles

winter

♂ juv.

♀ summer

♂ winter

form with rufous underparts

♀ juv.

♂ summer

♂ incomplete summer plumage

♂ incomplete summer plumage

Ruff

summer

summer

summer

winter

juv.

Indian Pratincole

147

Sandpipers Family *Scolopacidae* (continued)

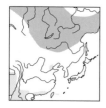

WOOD SANDPIPER *Tringa glareola* <Takabu-shigi> L 21.5cm. Brownish-gray back with *conspicuous white spots* especially in summer. *White eyebrow, rump, and underwing;* white tail has dark brown bars. Long dark yellow legs; black bill. In flight feet extend beyond tail. **Voice:** Alert *pipipit.* **Similar species:** Green Sandpiper is larger and darker with darker legs, less clear eyebrow, more conspicuous white rump, and dark underwings. **Status:** Common transient; mainly in freshwater marshes.

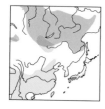

GREEN SANDPIPER *Tringa ochropus* <Kusa-shigi> L 24cm. *Dark* above with small white spots, dark streaking on breast, white belly, white rump and tail with dark bars on tip. *White eye-ring* and faint eyebrow; dark bill; dark greenish legs. Distinguished from all other sandpipers by *dark underwings.* **Voice:** A *tsui tsui tsui* when flushed. **Similar species:** Common Sandpiper is chunkier with shorter legs and a white wing bar in flight. White curves around bend of wing. No white on rump. See Wood Sandpiper. **Status:** Fairly common transient; some winter from central Honshu to Kyushu. Freshwater marshes and along rivers; solitary or in small flocks.

MARSH SANDPIPER *Tringa stagnatilis* <Ko-aoashi-shigi> L 24.5cm. Long slender straight black bill; *long legs are pale olive green;* small head; slim body; delicate appearance. In flight, long legs extend beyond the tail; white on tail, rump, and lower back forms a *distinct wedge.* **Summer:** Blackish-brown spots on breast. **Winter:** White underparts and pale gray back. **Voice:** *Pyu* or *pi pi pi.* **Similar species:** Greenshank is chunky and has a stouter, slightly upturned bill. Different call, *tchoo tchoo tchoo.* **Status:** Uncommon transient often found among Wood Sandpipers in freshwater marshes.

Large Sandpipers

juv.

summer

Wood Sandpiper

winter

summer

Green Sandpiper

changing to
first winter
plumage

summer

Marsh Sandpiper

149

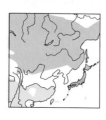

COMMON SANDPIPER *Tringa hypoleucos* <Iso-shigi> L 20cm. Dark olive-brown crown and back; white eyebrow and belly; streaked face and breast; *white on lower breast curves around bend of wing.* Constantly bobs the tail up and down in teetering motion. In flight, distinctive *white wing bar* but *no white on rump;* shallow wingbeats; olive-yellow legs do not extend beyond tail. **Status:** Common; breeds along riverbanks and lake shores in Honshu and Hokkaido; winters from Honshu southward.

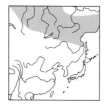

TEREK SANDPIPER *Xenus cinereus* <Sorihashi-shigi> L 23cm. Proportionally *short orange-yellow legs* and *long upturned black bill* with yellow base; in flight, *white edge on secondaries;* legs do not extend beyond tail. **Summer:** Brownish-gray back with black lines on scapulars. **Winter:** Uniformly gray back. **Similar species:** Gray-tailed Tattler is slightly larger and has a straight bill, pale yellowish legs, and a dark underwing. **Status:** Common transient on mudflats of estuaries. Very active, feeds while moving.

RUDDY TURNSTONE *Arenaria interpres* <Kyōjo-shigi> L 22cm. Chunky, with characteristic facial, breast, and wing pattern; short *orange legs;* short slightly upturned black bill. **Summer:** Mottled rufous and black on back. **Winter:** No rufous on back; pattern on face and breast is duller. **Similar species:** Great Knot has longer straight bill and black legs. **Status:** Common transient on mudflats, sandy beaches, rocky coasts, and shallow inland water. Often in small flocks.

STILT SANDPIPER *Micropalama himantopus* <Ashi naga-shigi> L 22cm. Long decurved black bill; *long olive-yellow legs* extend beyond tail. **Summer:** White eyebrow, *rusty cheek,* barred breast and belly. **Winter:** No rust on cheek; underparts white with faint streaking. *Dark trailing edges of wings; white rump.* **Similar species:** Marsh Sandpiper in winter plumage is similar but it has a straight bill and a white wedge on tail and lower back. **Status:** Accidental, from North America; mudflats, shallow pools, and marshes.

Sandpipers

Common Sandpiper

juv.

calling
in breeding season

summer

Terek Sandpiper

winter

summer

♂ summer

♂ summer

Ruddy Turnstone

juv.

♀ summer

winter

summer

Stilt Sandpiper

winter

(reduced)

SPOTTED REDSHANK *Tringa erythropus* <Tsuru-shigi> L 32.5cm. Medium-sized and slender with white rump and lower back; heavy barring on upper tail coverts; white underwing. Long tapered *straight bill is black with red base* to lower mandible; *orange-red legs.* **Summer:** *Black with white spots on back,* white scaling on belly. **Winter:** Gray back and white belly, with fine streaks on side of neck, faint barring on sides; *white eyebrow.* **Juvenile:** Brownish-gray with heavy barring on neck and underparts; white eyebrow. **Similar species:** Redshank is smaller; has white secondaries, shorter bill and legs; in winter is brownish and lacks complete white eyebrow. Greenshank has white underparts, rump, and tail; slightly upturned bill with thick base. **Status:** Common transient; freshwater marshes, mudflats, and rice fields.

REDSHANK *Tringa totanus* <Akaashi-shigi> L 27.5cm. Slightly smaller than Spotted Redshank with proportionally shorter legs and bill; *diagnostic white secondaries;* white underwing; white rump; *white line from base of bill to eye;* brown bars on white tail; bill red at base, black at tip; *reddish-orange legs.* **Similar species:** Greenshank has long upturned bill, whitish underparts, white rump and tail, and greenish legs. Gray-tailed Tattler is smaller with shorter yellowish legs, uniformly gray upperwing and rump, and dark underwing. **Status:** Uncommon transient; some breed in eastern Hokkaido. Mudflats, rice fields, brackish marshes.

GREATER YELLOWLEGS *Tringa melanoleuca* <Ō-kiashi-shigi> L 35cm. Slightly larger than Greenshank, *long yellow legs* and long slightly upturned *thick bill.* Whitish rump does not extend up lower back; no wing bar. **Summer:** Dark bars on breast and flanks. **Winter:** White underparts with brown streaks on breast. **Similar species:** Greenshank has paler underparts and a wedge-shaped white patch at base of tail. Gray-tailed Tattler has uniformly gray rump. Lesser Yellowlegs is smaller, more slender, and has thinner bill. **Status:** Accidental.

LESSER YELLOWLEGS *Tringa flavipes* <Ko-kiashi-shigi> L 25cm. Slender, straight *black bill; long, bright yellow legs;* square white patch on rump. **Similar species:** Greater Yellowlegs is larger; has a thick slightly upturned bill. Wood Sandpiper has a proportionally shorter bill, olive-yellow legs, less distinctive eyebrows. **Status:** Accidental; mudflats.

Large Sandpipers

winter

juv.

summer

Spotted Redshank

winter

summer

summer

Redshank

Lesser Yellowlegs

juv.

summer

Greater Yellowlegs

GREENSHANK *Tringa nebularia* <Aoashi-shigi> L 35cm. Medium-sized; appears *whitish; long stout bill slightly upturned;* white on tail and rump extends up back; in flight *grayish-green to yellowish-green legs* extend beyond the tail; unmarked wings; barring on white wing lining is difficult to see. **Summer:** Black streaks on white head, neck, breast, and flanks; some brownish tone and black markings on upperparts. **Winter:** Upperparts gray; underparts white with indistinct streaks on breast. **Voice:** Characteristic three-note whistle, *tchoo tchoo tchoo* or *kyo kyo kyo.* **Similar species:** Marsh Sandpiper is small and slim with a delicate straight bill and different call, *pyu* or *pi pi pi.* **Status:** Common transient on mudflats and rice fields.

SPOTTED GREENSHANK [NORDMANN'S GREEN-SHANK] *Tringa guttifer* <Karafuto-aoashi-shigi> L 31cm. Resembles Greenshank but with *shorter yellowish legs;* pure white underwings and axillars; stouter, nearly *straight bill is thicker* and yellowish on the basal half; feet do not extend as far beyond the tail; upperparts are darker in summer, paler in winter. **Similar species:** Gray-tailed Tattler has dark underwing, black straight bill, gray rump. Terek Sandpiper is smaller with upturned bill; white edges on secondaries. **Status:** Rare transient on mudflats.

GRAY-TAILED TATTLER [ASIAN WANDERING TATTLER] *Tringa brevipes* <Kiashi-shigi> L 25cm. White eyebrow, dark eyeline, *straight black bill, unmarked dark gray upperparts,* shorter *yellow legs,* laterally long body. **Summer:** Narrow gray wavy barring on breast and sides; *white on center of belly* and under tail coverts. **Winter:** White underparts with pale gray breast and flanks. **Voice:** Whistled *pyuee pyuee.* **Similar species:** Wandering Tattler has completely barred underparts. Terek Sandpiper has an upturned bill and black scapulars. **Status:** Common transient; rice fields, mudflats, rivers, rocky coasts.

(AMERICAN) WANDERING TATTLER *Tringa incana* <Meriken-kiashi-shigi> L 28cm. Resembles Gray-tailed Tattler, but in summer underparts (including under tail coverts) are entirely covered with *dense broader wavy barring.* **Voice:** Continuous *pi pi pi.* **Similar species:** Gray-tailed Tattler has white on belly and under tail coverts; different call, whistled *pyuee.* **Status:** Uncommon transient; beaches and rocky coasts.

Large Sandpipers

Greenshank

summer

winter

winter

winter

winter

Spotted Greenshank

summer

winter

Gray-tailed Tattler

summer

juv.

summer

Wandering Tattler

summer

summer

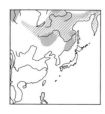

BLACK-TAILED GODWIT *Limosa limosa* <Oguro-shigi> L 38.5cm. Large, with long black legs. *Long straight bill* is flesh colored on basal half and dark at tip. *Distinctive black-and-white pattern in flight* with *broad white wing bar* and *black band on tip of white tail;* white underwings; legs extend beyond tail. **Summer:** Chestnut head, neck, and breast; white belly; *black barring on sides of breast and belly.* **Winter:** Grayish-brown with pale brown neck and breast; *no mottling on grayish underparts.* **Similar species:** Bar-tailed Godwit has upturned bill, shorter legs, gray underwings, and different pattern in flight. In summer has rufous underparts and no black barring on sides. **Status:** Common transient; mudflats, rice fields, freshwater marshes.

BAR-TAILED GODWIT *Limosa lapponica* <Ō-sori hashi-shigi> L 41cm. Tapering, *slightly upturned bill* with pinkish or orange base; *narrowly barred tail;* gray underwing. **Summer:** Rufous face, neck, breast, and belly. **Winter:** Pale grayish brown. **Similar species:** Black-tailed Godwit has longer legs and straight bill, white belly and barred flanks in summer, and white under tail coverts in winter. Whimbrel has a decurved bill and a white median line on head. **Status:** Common transient; mudflats and rice fields.

ASIATIC DOWITCHER *Limnodromus semipalmatus* <Shiberia-ōhashi-shigi> L 33cm. Same size as Greenshank. Long legs and *straight black bill* slightly swollen at tip. In flight, legs extend beyond tail; *rump and secondaries pale* with faint barring on rump. **Summer:** *Rufous head and underparts* with some whitish on belly. **Winter:** Pale brown breast. **Similar species:** Bar-tailed Godwit has tapered, upturned bill not swollen at tip; basal half is flesh colored. Black-tailed Godwit has broad white wing bar and black-and-white tail; basal half of bill is flesh colored. **Status:** Rare; mudflats.

Godwits, Dowitchers

summer

winter

winter

Black-tailed Godwit

juv.

winter

juv.

summer

winter

Bar-tailed Godwit

juv.

summer

winter

Asiatic Dowitcher

LONG-BILLED DOWITCHER *Limnodromus scolopaceus* <Ōhashi-shigi> L 29cm. Slightly larger than Gray-tailed Tattler, with olive-yellow legs. *Long straight black bill* with pale base is twice the length of the head. In flight, *distinct white wedge up lower back; white across trailing edge of secondaries.* **Summer:** *Rufous underparts* with dense black bars on belly. **Winter:** White eyebrow and dark upperparts; pale gray underparts with darker barring on side; black-and-white striped under tail coverts. **Similar species:** Gray-tailed Tattler has shorter bill and dark rump. Asiatic Dowitcher has black legs, barring on rump, and an entirely black bill. **Status:** Uncommon winter visitor or transient. Shallow inland waters and estuaries.

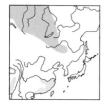

(EURASIAN) CURLEW *Numenius arquata* <Dai shaku-shigi> L 60cm. Large with *an extremely long decurved bill*. *White rump* extends in wedge up lower back; white belly, under tail coverts, and *wing lining*. **Voice:** Mellow whistled *curlee* or a strong *hoiieen*. **Similar species:** Australian Curlew has a brownish rump. Whimbrel is smaller with a shorter bill, white eyebrow and median stripe, different call. **Status:** Uncommon transient; locally common winter visitor, Ariake Bay in Kyushu. Often in large flocks in winter on vast mudflats.

AUSTRALIAN CURLEW *Numenius madagascariensis* <Hōroku-shigi> L 61.5cm. Large with *extremely long decurved bill; dark lower back and rump;* brownish underparts, under tail coverts, and underwings. **Similar species:** Curlew has white rump, under tail coverts, and underwing. Whimbrel is darker brown and smaller with white rump, median line, and eyebrow. **Status:** Uncommon but locally common transient in small numbers. Often seen in flocks of Curlews on vast mudflats.

Dowitchers, Curlews

juv.

winter

winter

summer

Long-billed Dowitcher

Curlew

Australian Curlew

SLENDER-BILLED CURLEW *Numenius tenuirostris* <Shirohara-chūshaku-shigi> L 41cm. Resembles Whimbrel but is *paler;* has no dark cap with median crown stripe; tapered bill is finer at tip. White lower back and rump; white tail barred on tip; white underparts with *heart-shaped black spots* on breast and flanks; whitish underwings. **Status:** Accidental; two specimens.

BRISTLE-THIGHED CURLEW *Numenius tahitiensis* <Harimomo-chūshaku> L 44.5cm. Resembles Whimbrel but is more cinnamon in color; distinct *cinnamon upper tail coverts;* only a few brown bars on tail; *speckled back.* **Voice:** Different from Whimbrel, a clear *kuieyo kuit* or *pyupee.* **Status:** Rare transient; grassy fields near beaches or on mudflats.

WHIMBREL *Numenius phaeopus* <Chūshaku-shigi> L 41cm. Dark brown upperparts with pale rump and long decurved bill. *Dark cap* with *white median stripe; white eyebrows.* **Voice:** Short mellow whistle repeated rapidly 6 or 7 times. **Similar species:** Bristle-thighed Curlew has unbarred cinnamon rump. Little Whimbrel is smaller with a shorter bill, yellowish-brown upperparts and rump; but take care to distinguish Little Whimbrel from immature Whimbrel which is smaller than adult with a shorter bill. Immature Whimbrel is larger with a thicker bill. **Status:** Common transient on mudflats, arable land, and rocky shores.

LITTLE WHIMBREL *Numenius minutus* <Koshaku-shigi> L 31cm. *Smallest* curlew. *Short slender slightly decurved bill; buffy plumage* with buffy eyebrow and crown stripe and *buffy back and rump.* **Voice:** *Pyu ryu.* **Similar species:** Whimbrel has darker upperparts without buffy coloration, a paler rump, a longer thicker bill, and a different call. Ruff has a scaly back with pale feather margins; shorter, almost straight bill; legs are usually a different color. **Status:** Uncommon transient; mudflats or arable land near coast.

Curlews

Slender-billed Curlew

Bristle-thighed Curlew

Whimbrel

Little Whimbrel

161

COMMON SNIPE *Gallinago gallinago* <Ta-shigi> L 27cm. Black and creamy stripes on the face; broad creamy stripes on the back. In flight shows *white trailing edge on upper side of secondaries* and whitish wing lining. When flushed characteristic rolling erratic flight. **Summer:** Darker contrasting mottling on back; reddish face and breast. **Winter:** Brownish unmarked coverts. **Voice:** *Jett.* **Similar species:** See Pintail Snipe, Latham's Snipe, and Swinhoe's Snipe. Field identification of these species is usually impossible even for experts. **Status:** Common transient or winter visitor; rice stubble fields, riverbanks, and marshes.

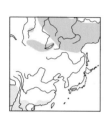

PINTAIL SNIPE *Gallinago stenura* <Hario-shigi> L· 25cm. Resembles Common Snipe; usually difficult to separate from it. Characteristics to look for include fine speckling on more yellowish-brown plumage, narrower and *fainter* white lines on back, much *narrower fainter white tips* on trailing edge of secondaries, *darker underwing*, narrower wing, and different call. **Voice:** Two notes, *jeht, jeht.* **Similar species:** Latham's Snipe is larger; Swinhoe's Snipe has chunkier proportions; probably indistinguishable in the field. **Status:** Uncommon but easily confused with other snipes. Same habitat as the Common Snipe.

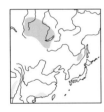

SWINHOE'S SNIPE *Gallinago megala* <Chūji-shigi> L 27cm. Resembles Latham's Snipe in color and proportions, but is slightly smaller. Probably impossible to distinguish in the field since it doesn't breed in Japan so can't be identified by voice in display flight. In hand, difference in number of tail feathers. **Status:** Transient in spring and fall throughout Japan. Number uncertain because of difficulty in identification.

LATHAM'S SNIPE *Gallinago hardwickii* <Ōji-shigi> L 30cm. Larger than Common Snipe and proportionally chunkier, paler *yellowish-brown plumage;* finely streaked dark underwing; shows *no white trailing edge on secondaries.* **Voice:** In breeding season flies around singing *ji, ji, ji, zubiyahk, zubiyahk, zubiyahk* then dives with *ga, ga, ga,* or *zazazah* sound. **Similar species:** Outside of breeding season difficult to distinguish in the field and even in the hand from Pintail and Swinhoe's. **Status:** Common breeder on grasslands, central Honshu northward. During migration, throughout Japan; rice stubble fields, marshes, riverbanks.

Snipes

Common Snipe

Pintail Snipe

Swinhoe's Snipe

display flight

Latham's Snipe

163

SOLITARY SNIPE *Gallinago solitaria* <Ao-shigi> L 30cm. Resembles Common Snipe but is *larger;* plumage is *brownish,*not yellowish. Face and stripes on back are *white* instead of creamy; no white on underwing and on trailing edges of secondaries. **Status:** Uncommon winter visitor to mountain streams and upper reaches of rivers; mainly central Honshu northward.

JACK SNIPE *Lymnocryptes minimus* <Ko-shigi> L 20cm. Distinguished from other snipes by *small size, shorter bill,* dark center of crown, *forked eyebrow,* dark brown unmarked *wedge-shaped tail.* Silent when flushed; usually drops into cover quickly. **Status:** Rare transient or winter visitor; rice stubble fields, lotus ponds, marshes.

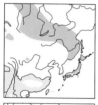

(EUROPEAN) WOODCOCK *Scolopax rusticola* <Yama-shigi> L 34cm. Well camouflaged, chunky, long-billed snipe-like bird, usually seen only when flushed from cover. Broad, *rounded wings; transverse bars on head.* Nocturnal; stays on the ground during the day. **Voice:** *Chikit chikit, boo boo* during display flight at dawn and dusk. **Similar species:** See Amami Woodcock. **Status:** Uncommon breeder in Hokkaido and north-central Honshu; winters in warmer regions. Secondary deciduous and bamboo forests.

AMAMI WOODCOCK *Scolopax mira* <Amami-yama-shigi> L 36cm. Probably indistinguishable in the field from the Woodcock. Plumage is more olive brown. Found *only* on Amami-Oshima I. **Status:** Common local resident Amami-Oshima I. in ever-green forests and sugar cane fields.

Painted Snipes

Family *Rostratulidae* (World: 2 species; Japan: 1 species) Waders with a snipe-like appearance. Decurved bill is shorter than in snipes. Female more brightly colored than male which incubates eggs and raises young. Polyandrous.

PAINTED SNIPE *Rostratula benghalensis* <Tama-shigi> L 23.5cm. Yellowish crown stripe; *white mark through eye; white on underparts* curves up over shoulder onto back; blackish-brown mark on each side of breast; *slightly decurved bill.* Trailing legs in flight. **Female:** Throat and foreneck rich chestnut; fine black bars on upperwings. **Male:** Yellow spots on upperwings; large buffy V on back. **Voice:** At night *koh koh koh, uh uh.* Silent when flushed. **Similar species:** Distinguished from the other snipes by brighter coloring, rounded wings, slow flight. **Status:** Uncommon resident, central and southwest Honshu and Kyushu.

Snipes, Woodcocks, Painted Snipes

Solitary Snipe

Jack Snipe

Woodcock

Amami Woodcock

♀
♂
♀

Painted Snipe

Common Snipe   Painted Snipe ♂

165

Stilts
Family *Recurvirostridae* (World: 7 species; Japan: 2 species)
Graceful black-and-white shorebirds with extremely long legs, small heads, long thin bills, and long pointed wings.

BLACK-WINGED STILT *Himantopus himantopus* <Seitaka-shigi> L 31cm. Extremely *long pink legs,* black mantle and wing, and white underparts are diagnostic. Young birds have brownish crown, nape, and back. **Status:** Uncommon transient or winter visitor. A few breeding records from Aichi and Chiba Prefectures in central Honshu. Shallow inland water; occasionally on mudflats.

AVOCET *Recurvirostra avocetta* <Sorihashi-seitaka-shigi> L 43cm. Long tapering *upturned black bill;* white plumage with bold *black-and-white pattern on wings* visible both in flight and at rest; black cap and hindneck; lead-blue legs. When feeding, swings bill from side to side. **Status:** Winter straggler; brackish pools, salt lagoons, mudflats.

Phalaropes
Family *Phalaropodidae* (World: 3 species; Japan: 2 species) Small swimming shorebirds with lobed toes. Often spin in circles in shallow water to stir up food such as plankton or aquatic insects. Highly pelagic, on passage travel in large flocks; occasionally on coast, tidal mudflats, pools, or inland lakes. Females have brighter plumage in summer. Sex roles are reversed.

NORTHERN PHALAROPE [RED-NECKED PHALA-ROPE] *Phalaropus lobatus* <Akaeri-hireashi-shigi> L 19cm. Tapering, *needle-like black bill;* small head; slender neck. In flight shows white bar down dark wing. **Summer:** Black cap, white throat, and *reddish side of neck.* **Winter:** Face and neck white; *black eyeline, cap,* and nape; *blackish upperparts* with white feather edges. **Similar species:** Winter Red Phalarope has stout blackish bill usually with some yellow on base; gray upperparts. Sanderling lacks black eyeline, never swims. **Status:** Common transient; pelagic but often seen after storms along the coast and on inland waters.

RED PHALAROPE [GRAY PHALAROPE] *Phalaropus fulicarius* <Haiiro-hireashi-shigi> L 22cm. Black bill with yellowish base is shorter and stouter than that of Northern Phalarope. **Summer:** Black crown and nape, *reddish underparts,* white face. **Winter:** *Gray mantle,* white face with dark eyeline. **Similar species:** See Northern Phalarope. Sanderling in winter plumage is whitish with black shoulders and black legs. **Status:** Uncommon highly pelagic transient; rare on coasts and inland waters after stormy weather.

Stilts, Avocets, Phalaropes

♀

juv.

♂ summer

Black-winged Stilt

Avocet

♂ summer

imm.

juv.

♂ summer

♀ summer

changing to first winter plumage

juv.

Northern Phalarope

winter

♂ summer

♀ summer

♀ winter

Red Phalarope

Hawks, Eagles, and Vultures

Family *Accipitridae* (World: about 210 species; Japan: 22 species) Diurnal birds of prey with hooked bills. Most species take live prey, but some eat carrion. Sexes are often alike, but the female is larger. Large species often soar on thermals. Medium and small species are skillful fliers in forests and marshes. Some hover and dive for prey. All have good eyesight and powerful beaks and claws.

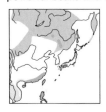

OSPREY *Pandion haliaetus* <Misago> L Male 54cm. Female 64cm. W 160cm. White crown, broad *black eyestripe, clear white belly,* dark upperparts, *long* narrow white wings with *black wrist marks* and dark flight feathers, short tail. In flight has characteristic crook in wings. Often hovers, then plunges feet first for fish. Lives exclusively on fish. **Status:** Common throughout Japan. Breeds Kyushu northward; summer visitor to Hokkaido. Seacoasts, lakes, and large rivers.

WHITE-TAILED EAGLE *Haliaeetus albicilla* <Ojiro-washi> L Male 80cm. Female 95cm. W 182—230cm. A large sea eagle slightly smaller than Steller's Sea-Eagle. Adult's *pure white tail* is shorter than Steller's and not as obviously wedge shaped. Head usually paler brown than body. *Bill and legs pale yellow.* Wingbeats sluggish. **Immature:** Head and tail dark brown, blackish bill. Feeds mainly on fish and birds. **Similar species:** See Steller's and Golden Eagles. Bill is smaller and paler than in Steller's. Trailing edge of wing is *straight,* not curved. **Status:** Locally common winter visitor mainly to northern Japan.

STELLER'S SEA-EAGLE *Haliaeetus pelagicus* <Ō-washi> L Male 88cm. Female 102cm. W 220—245cm. A large eagle with *huge bright orange-yellow bill* and *long white wedge-shaped tail.* Forehead, rump, upper tail coverts, thighs, and under tail coverts are also white. Larger than Golden Eagle and White-tailed Eagle. Adult has prominent *white* lesser and median wing coverts which immature lacks. Feeds mainly on fish and birds. **Similar species:** Immature resembles White-tailed Eagle, but bill is much larger and trailing edge of wing is *curved,* not straight. **Status:** Locally uncommon winter visitor; abundant on Shiretoko Peninsula in Hokkaido.

Ospreys, Sea-Eagles

Osprey

hovering

(reduced)

imm.

imm.

White-tailed Eagle

(reduced)

imm.

imm.

Steller's Sea-Eagle

GOLDEN EAGLE *Aquila chrysaetos* <Inu-washi> L 85cm. W 190cm. Large; blackish-brown plumage; *diagnostic golden feathers on nape and wing coverts;* long slightly rounded tail. **Immature:** Darker than adult with *white at base of flight feathers and base of tail:* In flight, primaries are spread and up-turned. Often seen soaring quite high. Takes most of prey on ground. **Similar species:** Immature White-tailed Eagle has broader wings, shorter white wedge-shaped tail. **Status:** Uncommon resident in Honshu; rocky mountainous areas. Nests on rocky ledges, occasionally in trees.

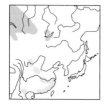

IMPERIAL EAGLE *Aquila heliaca* <Katashiro-washi> L 82cm. W 175—185cm. A large eagle, slightly smaller than Golden Eagle. Dark brown plumage with *pale crown and nape;* a few prominent pure *white feathers on scapulars;* blackish-brown bill, yellow cere; yellow feet. Silhouette similar to Golden's but tail shorter, wings held more horizontal-ly. **Immature:** Light brown with *streaked undersides.* Sluggish behavior; prefers open fields, plains, and swamps. **Similar species:** Adult resembles adult Golden Eagle, but shows paler inner primaries on underside in flight. **Status:** Accidental winter visitor; about 10 records in Japan.

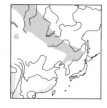

SPOTTED EAGLE *Aquila clanga* <Karafuto-washi> L 70cm. W 160—182cm. Smaller than Golden Eagle, with *glossy dark brown plumage,* slightly paler below. A *little white* is visible on upper tail coverts. Tail rather short and rounded. Head small with dark brown bill. **Immature:** Pale spots on back and wing coverts. Wing coverts have whitish tips and are darker than in immature Imperial Eagle. Flight resembles a buzzard's. Wings proportionally broader than Golden's; droop slightly from carpal joint when gliding. Feeble wingbeats. **Status:** Accidental; recorded only in 1952, 1968, and 1973.

Eagles

Golden Eagle

imm.

Imperial Eagle

juv.

juv.

juv.

Spotted Eagle

juv.

juv.

171

HODGSON'S HAWK-EAGLE *Spizaetus nipalensis* <Kuma-taka> L Male 72cm. Female 80cm. W 140—165cm. A large hawk. Crown, *short crest*, and nape are boldly streaked with black. In flight, black bars on *broad wings* and *long tail* conspicuous. Flies with flattened wings; slow wingbeats. **Status:** Uncommon resident in mountainous areas at elevations from 500m. to 1,500m.

CRESTED SERPENT-EAGLE *Spilornis cheela* <Kan muri-washi> L 55cm. A small eagle about the size of a buzzard, with *prominent crown* and crest mottled with black and white. In flight, *short broad wings* with widely spread primaries are held in a V. Unmistakable *black-and-white pattern* clearly visible on underside. Blackish-brown tail has *broad white bar* and white tip. Immature looks much whiter. Feeds on snakes, frogs, and other small prey. **Status:** Locally common resident in southern Ryukyu Is. where breeding was confirmed in 1981.

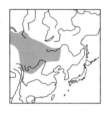

(EUROPEAN) BLACK VULTURE *Aegypius monachus* <Kuro-hagewashi> L 102—112cm. W 234—274cm. A huge vulture with *uniform sooty-brown plumage* that looks black at a distance; blackish down on head; *bare skin of head* and neck bluish-gray; long, broad wings with primaries spread wide in flight; slightly wedge-shaped tail. In its normal range is usually rather solitary; found in mountainous regions. Feeds on carrion. **Status:** Accidental; only a few records in Japan. This species is different from Black Vulture, *Coragyps atratus*, of North America.

Eagles, Vultures

Hodgson's Hawk-Eagle

imm.

Crested Serpent-Eagle

imm.

imm.

imm.

Black Vulture

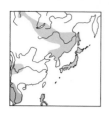

HONEY BUZZARD *Pernis apivorus* <Hachikuma> L 58.5cm. W 128cm. A *long-necked,* medium-sized hawk. *Variable plumage, barring on underwings,* dark tail bands, dark upperparts, *white throat with black center stripe.* When gliding, wings held horizontally or droop very slightly with upturned tips. Hovers only briefly in a characteristic manner with wings held high. Feeds on larvae of bees, sometimes mice, frogs, and snakes. **Similar species:** Gray-faced Buzzard-Eagle is smaller, has a *shorter neck* and a less pronounced curve to trailing edges of wings. **Status:** Common summer visitor to mountains up to 1,500m., central Honshu northward. Migrates in flocks along regular routes in early October. Cape Irago-zaki in Aichi Pref. and Cape Sata-misaki in Kagoshima Pref. are best locations for observing migration.

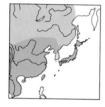

BLACK KITE *Milvus migrans* <Tobi> L Male 58.5cm. Female 68.5cm. W 150cm. A large brown hawk with *long forked tail* and *prominent pale patches at base of primaries.* When tail is spread wide it may look straight or rounded on the end. **Immature:** Streaked with buff. Rides thermals and soars high; glides in circles with wings held horizontally. Wingbeats are slow, usually followed by long glides. Feeds mainly on carrion and dead fish. **Status:** Common resident throughout Japan, but straggler in Ryukyu Is. Locally abundant on seacoasts, large rivers, and lakes.

GRAY-FACED BUZZARD-EAGLE *Butastur indicus* <Sashiba> L 49cm. W 102.5—115cm. A *reddish-brown* hawk. Gray cheeks, creamy eyebrow, *white throat with central black stripe,* brown tail with dark bands, pale underwings with brown bars, under-parts *barred horizontally.* **Immature:** *Underparts are barred vertically.* Soars in circles with flat wings; faster wingbeats and gliding speed than Black Kite's. **Similar species:** Honey Buzzard is larger and more heavily built with *longer neck.* Goshawk has broader wings. **Status:** Common summer visitor, Honshu southward to Kyushu. Migrates in large flocks along same routes in early October as Honey Buzzard.

Honey Buzzards, Kites

two color phases

Honey Buzzard

display flight

Black Kite

juv.

juv.

dark phase

Gray-faced Buzzard-Eagle

ROUGH-LEGGED BUZZARD [ROUGH-LEGGED HAWK] *Buteo lagopus* <Keashi-nosuri> L 55cm. Whitish head and upper breast streaked with brown; *dark brown lower breast and belly;* whitish underwings with conspicuous *dark carpal patches* and dark tips to primaries; brown upperwings with *white patch at base of primaries;* white tail with *black terminal band;* whitish *feathered legs.* Hovers frequently holding wings in a slight V. Feeds mainly on rodents and snakes. **Similar species:** Common Buzzard lacks white wing patch and white tail with dark band. **Status:** Uncommon winter visitor to northern Japan.

UPLAND BUZZARD *Buteo hemilasius* <Ō-nosuri> L 60cm. Similar to Common Buzzard but slightly larger and generally paler. Whitish-brown underparts and head are particularly pale; *brown thighs;* broad wings have distinct dark carpal patches; tail is pale brown below, *whitish above* with several fine brown bars which may not be visible in flight; *dark brown rump.* **Similar species:** See Common Buzzard and Rough-legged Buzzard. **Status:** Straggler in winter to Kyushu and Tsushima Island.

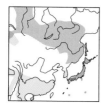

COMMON BUZZARD *Buteo buteo* <Nosuri> L 54cm. W 122-137cm. *Broad wings* brown above, pale below with distinct *black carpal patches* and black tips to primaries; *rounded tail;* and *short neck* are the best field marks. Brown head; pale breast with dark streaks; dark brown upper belly and flanks; pale brown lower belly, *thighs,* and under tail coverts. Plumage is variable. In flight, wings held in a slight V, with the tips slightly forward. Flight often laborious. Soars high, hovers frequently, and dives for small rodents, snakes, lizards. **Similar species:** See Upland Buzzard. **Status:** Common resident throughout Japan. Winters in warmer regions.

Buzzards

hovering **Rough-legged Buzzard**

Upland Buzzard

hovering **Common Buzzard**

177

NORTHERN HARRIER [HEN HARRIER] *Circus cyaneus* <Haiiro-chūhi> L Male 43cm. Female 53cm. W 98.5—123.5cm. *White rump* always conspicuous. **Male:** *Primaries black* above and below; rest of *plumage gray* except for white belly, under tail coverts, and underwings. **Female:** Upperparts dark brown, crown and throat pale brown, belly streaked with brown. Glides very low over marshes and swamps with *wings held in a shallow V.* Feeds on frogs, mice, and small birds. **Similar species:** Female is similar to female Pied Harrier but has browner upperparts and darker underparts. **Status:** Uncommon winter visitor throughout Japan.

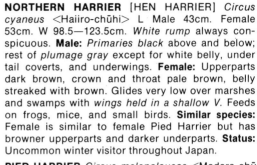

PIED HARRIER *Circus melanoleucos* <Madara-chū hi> L 45cm. Slightly smaller than Marsh Harrier. **Male:** Silvery gray upperparts with *unmistakable pattern* formed by white lesser wing coverts and black head, back, median wing coverts, and primaries. White underparts. **Female:** Head and upperparts dark brown; underparts white, streaked with dark reddish brown. **Similar species:** Male Northern Harrier *lacks the black head and the black-and-white pattern* on the upper surface. Female Pied has more gray in wings and paler underparts than female Northern and lacks conspicuous white rump. **Status:** Accidental transient; only a few records.

MARSH HARRIER *Circus aeruginosus* <Chūhi> L Male 48cm. Female 58cm. W 113—137cm. Common harrier found over marshy and swampy areas. Small head, long rounded wings, long tail. **Male:** *Variable.* Gray head and upperparts streaked with black; dark back; white lower breast, belly, and flanks; gray tail. Some males have black heads and black across upperwings, similar to Pied Harrier. **Female:** Evenly dark brown except for much *paler brown head, breast,* and under wing coverts. Glides low over marshes, swamps, and reedbeds with *wings held in V.* **Similar species:** Male Northern Harrier has *more black on wing tips* and *no black on head.* Females of other harriers have *barred wings.* **Status:** Common winter visitor. Some breed in Honshu and Hokkaido.

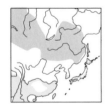

Harriers

♂

♂

♀

♂

♀

Northern Harrier

♂

♂

♀

juv.

♀

♂

Pied Harrier

♂

♂

two color
phases

♀

♂

♀

imm.

Marsh Harrier

179

(NORTHERN) GOSHAWK *Accipiter gentilis* <Ō-taka> L Male 50cm. Female 56cm. W 105—130cm. Medium-sized with *conspicuous broad white stripe over eye. Blue-gray back;* pale gray, closely barred breast; short, broad rounded wings; finely barred whitish underwings; long tail with dark bars. **Immature:** Brown above; buffy underparts vertically streaked with dark brown. Much whiter Siberian race (subspecies *albidus*) has been recorded twice in Hokkaido. Typical flight, few rapid wingbeats followed by a glide. **Similar species:** Hodgson's Hawk-Eagle is much larger with slower wingbeats. Sparrow Hawk is much smaller; female's back is paler; male's underparts are reddish brown. **Status:** Uncommon resident, Honshu and Hokkaido; woodlands. Throughout Japan in fall and winter.

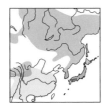

(EUROPEAN) SPARROW HAWK *Accipiter nisus* <Hai-taka> L Male 32cm. Female 39cm. W 62—76cm. *Small* hawk, similar to Goshawk but with *less prominent white eyebrow.* **Male:** Slaty-blue upperparts; *rufous cheeks;* light underparts finely barred with *rufous;* underwings finely barred with dark brown; long tail with dark bars. **Female:** Slaty-brown upperparts; white underparts closely barred with dark brown. Wingbeats rapid and stiff; wings held straight while gliding; seldom soars or dives. **Similar species:** Goshawk is larger, lacks rufous on face and underparts, and has slower wingbeats. Japanese Lesser Sparrow Hawk is smaller with darker back and no distinct white eyebrow. **Status:** Uncommon breeder in Hokkaido and northern Honshu. Throughout Japan in fall and winter.

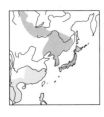

JAPANESE LESSER SPARROW HAWK *Accipiter gularis* <Tsumi> L Male 27cm. Female 30cm. W 51—63cm. Smallest accipiter in Japan. Chin and throat white; long tail has broad dark bands; distinct dark bands on underside of wings. **Male:** *Pale rufous breast and belly,* sometimes with white barring. **Female:** White underparts with broad gray-brown bars. **Similar species:** See other accipiters. Wingbeats and flight faster than Goshawk's and Sparrow Hawk's. Chinese Sparrow Hawk has black wing tips. **Status:** Uncommon breeder throughout Japan. Those in northern Japan winter in warmer regions. Resident in Ryukyu Is.

CHINESE SPARROW HAWK *Accipiter soloensis* <Akahara-daka> L 30cm. Small accipiter. *White underwings with black-tipped primaries, pale rufous wash on breast and belly* diagnostic. **Similar species:** See Japanese Lesser Sparrow Hawk. **Status:** Locally common transient in Ryukyu Is.

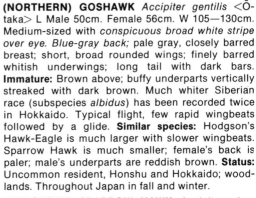

subspecies *albidus*

Accipiters

Goshawk

juv.

juv.

Sparrow
Hawk

juv.

♂

♀

juv.

Japanese Lesser
Sparrow Hawk

juv.

♂

♀

juv.

Chinese
Sparrow Hawk

juv.

juv.

Falcons

Family *Falconidae* (World: About 60 species; Japan: 7 species.) Small to medium-sized streamlined birds of prey with long pointed wings, long tapered tails. Direct powerful flight with rapid but shallow wingbeats. Feed mainly on birds.

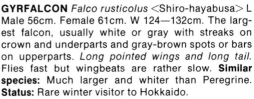

GYRFALCON *Falco rusticolus* <Shiro-hayabusa> L Male 56cm. Female 61cm. W 124—132cm. The largest falcon, usually white or gray with streaks on crown and underparts and gray-brown spots or bars on upperparts. *Long pointed wings and long tail.* Flies fast but wingbeats are rather slow. **Similar species:** Much larger and whiter than Peregrine. **Status:** Rare winter visitor to Hokkaido.

PEREGRINE FALCON *Falco peregrinus* <Haya busa> L Male 38cm. Female 51cm. W 84—120cm. *Heavy black moustaches* are best field mark. Shows great contrast between dark upperparts and light underparts which are narrowly barred in adult, streaked in immature. Swoops on prey almost vertically at terrific speed with wings partly folded. **Similar species:** Gyrfalcon is much larger, generally much paler, and moustaches not clear. Hobby is smaller, wings are longer and *more pointed*, with thighs and under tail coverts *chestnut*. **Status:** Common winter visitor and uncommon breeder throughout Japan.

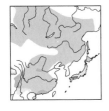

HOBBY *Falco subbuteo* <Chigo-hayabusa> L 30cm. W 69—76cm. Similar to Peregrine only *much smaller; moustaches narrower;* longer wings are narrower and more pointed; tail slightly shorter; breast and belly heavily streaked, not barred; *thighs and under tail coverts chestnut.* When perched, wings are longer than tail. **Juvenile:** Browner upperparts, heavier streaks on underparts, and no chestnut on thighs and under tail coverts. **Similar species:** See Peregrine Falcon. Kestrel has longer tail with black tip, narrower wing, is paler on underside, and does not fly as fast. Merlin is smaller with longer tail, less distinct moustache, and less pointed wings. **Status:** Uncommon local breeder, central Honshu northward; winters in warmer regions.

Falcons

light phase

Gyrfalcon

intermediate phase

light phase

imm.

Peregrine Falcon

juv.

imm.

Hobby

juv.

183

MERLIN *Falco columbarius* <Ko-chōgenbō> L Male 28cm. Female 31cm. W 61—66cm. A small fast falcon of open areas. Pointed wings, slate-gray tail with broad black subterminal band and white tip. **Male:** *Slate-blue above,* pale buffy-orange below with black streaks. **Female:** Brown above, whitish below with *dark brown streaks.* **Similar species:** Hobby is slightly larger; tail is shorter *without black terminal band.* Eurasian Kestrel has longer tail, paler underparts, chestnut back, and it hovers more frequently and flies more buoyantly. **Status:** Uncommon winter visitor throughout Japan.

(EURASIAN) KESTREL *Falco tinnunculus* <Chōgen bō> L Male 30cm. Female 33cm. W 69—74cm. A small falcon distinguished by *pointed wings, slim tail, and frequent hovering.* **Male:** *Spotted chestnut upperparts;* warm buff underparts with *scattered black spots;* gray head and rump; gray tail with black subterminal band and white tip. **Female:** *Rusty barred upperparts and tail.* **Similar species:** See Merlin and Lesser Kestrel. **Status:** Uncommon breeder, central and northern Honshu; common winter visitor throughout.

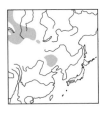

LESSER KESTREL *Falco naumanni* <Hime-chōgen bō> L Male 28cm. Female 31cm. W 61—66cm. Similar to Kestrel, but slightly smaller, more *brightly colored.* **Male:** *Unspotted bright chestnut upperparts and bluer head and tail than Kestrel.* From above, secondaries show large slate-blue patches. **Female and immature:** Very similar to Kestrel and almost indistinguishable except for *white claws* (black in Kestrel) visible only at close range. **Similar species:** Kestrel male has black spots on wings; lacks the slate-blue patches on secondaries. **Status:** Accidental. Only one record from Tsushima I.

AMUR RED-FOOTED FALCON *Falco amurensis* <Akaashi-chōgenbō> L Male 25cm. Female 30cm. W 69—76cm. A small falcon about the size of a Kestrel with *white under wing coverts, reddish-orange cere and feet,* long wings and tail. **Male:** Dark slaty gray with rusty lower belly and under tail coverts, pure white under wing coverts. **Female:** Distinguished by gray upperparts and the contrast between the boldly barred flight feathers and the pale wing linings. With light rufous wash on underparts closely resembles female Kestrel but has *short dark moustache stripes.* Female Kestrel *lacks the red feet and cere,* dark moustache. **Status:** Straggler, Tsushima I. and Goto Is.

Falcons

Merlin

Kestrel

♀ hovering

Lesser Kestrel

♂ hovering

Amur Red-footed Falcon

185

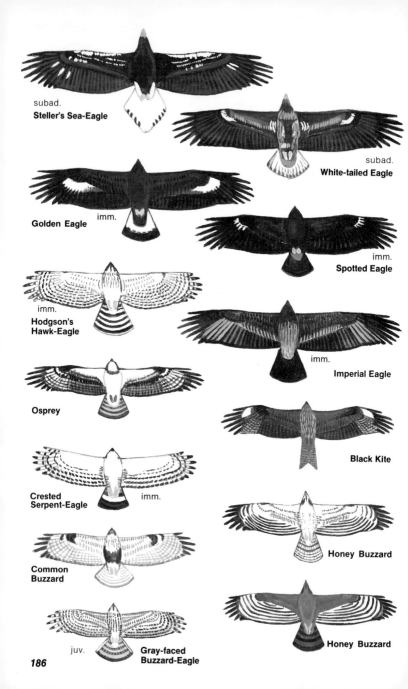

subad.
Steller's Sea-Eagle

subad.
White-tailed Eagle

Golden Eagle imm.

imm.
Spotted Eagle

imm.
Hodgson's Hawk-Eagle

imm.
Imperial Eagle

Osprey

Black Kite

Crested Serpent-Eagle imm.

Honey Buzzard

Common Buzzard

juv. **Gray-faced Buzzard-Eagle**

Honey Buzzard

186

Birds of Prey, overhead

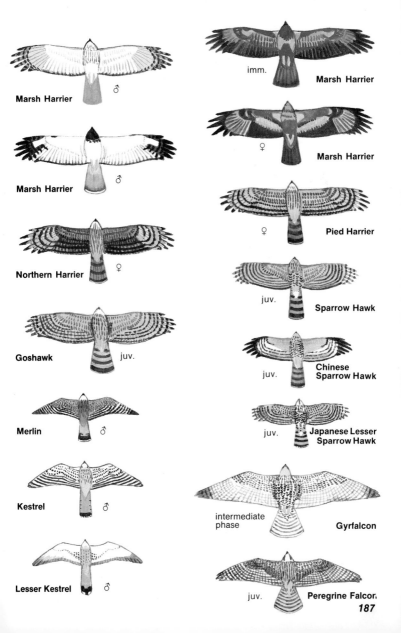

Marsh Harrier ♂

Marsh Harrier ♂

Northern Harrier ♀

Goshawk juv.

Merlin ♂

Kestrel ♂

Lesser Kestrel ♂

imm. Marsh Harrier

♀ Marsh Harrier

♀ Pied Harrier

juv. Sparrow Hawk

juv. Chinese Sparrow Hawk

juv. Japanese Lesser Sparrow Hawk

intermediate phase Gyrfalcon

juv. Peregrine Falcon

Owls and Barn Owls
Families *Strigidae* and *Tytonidae*
(*Strigidae*—owls: World: About 130 species; Japan: 11 species. *Tytonidae*—barn owls: World: 10 species; Japan: 1 species) Nocturnal birds of prey, generally characterized by large forward-facing eyes in large heads, flat facial discs, hooked bills, long powerful claws, and heavily feathered legs. Their flight is noiseless on broad rounded wings. Sexes usually similar.

SNOWY OWL *Nyctea scandiaca* <Shiro-fukurō> L 60cm. *Large white* owl with *yellow eyes* and no ear tufts. Variable number of brown flecks or bars but few on adult male. Female generally has more markings and is larger than male. Dark bill and white feathered legs. **Voice:** Usually silent in winter, but utters a loud *krow-ow* in flight or a repeated *rick* when breeding. **Status:** Rare winter visitor to Hokkaido; straggler to Honshu. One record in summer (Mt. Taisetsu, Hokkaido, 1977). Open country and along seacoasts.

EAGLE OWL *Bubo bubo* <Washi-mimizuku> L 66cm. *Huge, rust-colored* owl with large *orange eyes,* and *long, prominent ear tufts. Tawny upperparts* mottled with dark brown; brown underparts with *darker brown streaks, broader on breast.* Black bill; tawny *feathered legs and toes;* short tail. **Voice:** A brief deep *ooo-hu* may be followed by quiet chuckling sounds. **Status:** Accidental. Hokkaido, Goto Is., Izu Is., Amami Is.; woodland areas.

BLAKISTON'S FISH-OWL *Ketupa blakistoni* <Shima-fukurō> L 71cm. *Largest* Japanese owl. *Grayish brown* with dark brown facial disc; *long broad ear tufts;* dark brown bars, spots, and streaks; dark bill; *yellow eyes.* Pale *legs are feathered, but toes are not.* **Voice:** Short deep *boo boo, uoo.* **Similar species:** Eagle Owl has darker plumage with broader streaks on breast, orange eyes. **Status:** Uncommon resident; Hokkaido. Forests along rivers.

Owls

Snowy Owl

Eagle Owl

Blakiston's Fish-Owl

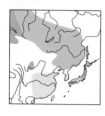

LONG-EARED OWL *Asio otus* <Torafu-zuku> L 38cm. Medium-sized owl with long ear tufts; rufous facial disc bordered with black; mottled gray-brown and buff plumage *streaked with black; orange-yellow eyes*, black bill. Long wings and deep wingbeats. **Voice:** Low moaning *boo-boo-boo* only during breeding season. **Status:** Uncommon breeder in forests; central Honshu northward. Winters from central Honshu southward; lowland groves. Occasionally winters in small parties.

SHORT-EARED OWL *Asio flammeus* <Komimizuku> L 38.5cm. A ground owl. Tawny color; grayer facial disc with black around eyes; *short scarcely visible ear tufts;* streaked underparts. Long wings with buffy patch at base of primaries; *dark patch* at carpal joint, conspicuous in flight. Usually silent in winter. **Status:** Uncommon winter visitor throughout Japan. Open grassland near rivers and marshes.

URAL OWL *Strix uralensis* <Fukurō> L 50cm. *Pale gray plumage* heavily streaked with dark brown; a large round head with *no ear tufts;* pale gray facial disc; dark brown eyes; boldly barred broad wings and tail. **Voice:** Irregular and harsh *gro ho ko.* **Status:** Common resident, Kyushu northward; woodlands.

GRASS OWL *Tyto capensis* <Minami-menfukurō> L 35cm. Only barn owl (*Tytonidae* family) to occur in Japan. Whitish *heart-shaped facial disc;* dark brown upperparts with rufous-buff spots; dark brown wings with rufous patch at base of primaries; buff underparts with blackish spots; light-colored tail barred with black; long white feathered legs; yellowish bill. **Status:** Accidental; one reported in 1975, southern Ryukyu Is.

Owls

Long-eared Owl

Short-eared Owl

Grass Owl

Ural Owl

191

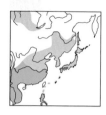

SCOPS OWL *Otus scops* <Konoha-zuku> L 20cm. Smallest owl in Japan. The small size, feathered legs but unfeathered toes, and *yellow eyes* help distinguish this owl from the Collared Scops Owl. Streaked and barred brownish-gray plumage; relatively long ear tufts (erect when alarmed); dark bill. There is a rufous phase with reddish-brown plumage. **Voice:** Soft monotonous, toad-like *pew-pew-pew.* **Status:** Uncommon resident; Honshu, in mountain forests; Hokkaido, in lowland forests. Common in evergreen woods on the Ryukyu Is. Some winter in warmer areas.

COLLARED SCOPS OWL *Otus bakkamoena* <Ō-konoha-zuku> L 24cm. Resembles Scops Owl but is slightly larger; has a *grayish collar on the nape; orange eyes; feathered toes.* **Voice:** Weak cat-like *mew.* **Status:** Uncommon resident throughout Japan. Breeds in mountain forests (also lowlands in north) and winters in warmer areas. Sometimes occurs in woods near human habitation.

BOREAL OWL [TENGMALM'S OWL] *Aegolius funereus* <Kinme-fukurō> L 25cm. Large round head with *no ear tufts;* pale facial disc with a black border; *yellow eyes and bill;* brown upperparts with *white spots;* whitish underparts with dark brown streaks; feathered legs and feet. **Voice:** High and musical, a rapid *poo-poo-poo.* **Status:** Accidental, Hokkaido and Honshu.

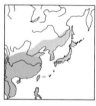

BROWN HAWK-OWL *Ninox scutulata* <Aoba-zuku> L 29cm. Slender. *Chocolate-brown upperparts and face* with no prominent facial disc and no ear tufts; white around yellow bill; white underparts with bold brown streaks; long brown tail with black bars; feathered legs; yellow toes. **Voice:** *Hoho hoho.* **Status:** Common summer visitor throughout Japan. Woodlands at high and low elevations, parks and gardens with tall trees.

Owls

Scops Owl

rufous phase

Collared Scops Owl

Boreal Owl

Brown Hawk-Owl

193

Ptarmigans and Grouse
Family *Tetraonidae*

(World: 19 species; Japan: 2 species) Fowl-like, plump birds of the Northern Hemisphere, adapted to many different environments. They are primarily ground dwelling, but some are partly tree dwelling. They have short stout bills and legs, short rounded wings. They walk more than fly, but flight is strong and swift. They are well camouflaged and in keeping with their generally far northern range, in winter they grow snowshoes of various sorts depending on the species. Their nostrils are hidden by feathers. Some members of this family are known for spectacular displays. Feed on seeds, insects, buds, and berries.

ROCK PTARMIGAN [PTARMIGAN] *Lagopus mutus* <Raichō> L 37cm. A grouse of high mountains. *White feathered legs* and *white wings* in all plumages. **Summer:** Male has richly mottled blackish-brown upperparts, breast, and flanks; white underparts; red wattle over eye. Female is much more tawny-yellow; red wattle smaller than that of male. **Winter:** Both sexes are *pure white* except for black on tail which is usually hidden at rest; male has black eye line. Not wary; often observed at close range. **Voice:** Harsh *gwa gwa gwa*. **Status:** Uncommon local resident on mountains over 2,400m.; Japanese Alps in central Honshu.

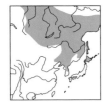

HAZEL GROUSE *Tetrastes bonasia* <Ezo-raichō> L 36cm. **Male:** *Short crest* on grayish-brown crown; upperparts grayish with dark brown and reddish-brown bars; conspicuous *broad white bands on sides of black throat* and *across scapulars;* underparts white with black and brown mottling. **Female:** Resembles male but is browner with whitish throat. Often observed in pairs or in family groups. Nests on the ground. **Voice:** Whistled *pew pew pew pew.* **Similar species:** Rock Ptarmigan is found in an entirely different area. **Status:** Locally uncommon resident only in Hokkaido; mixed woodlands with dense shrubs, often near streams.

Ptarmigans, Grouses

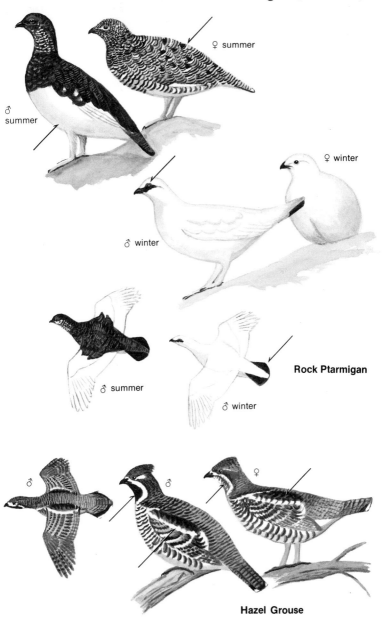

♂ summer

♀ summer

♀ winter

♂ winter

♂ summer

♂ winter

Rock Ptarmigan

♂

♂

♀

Hazel Grouse

Buttonquails

Family *Turnicidae* (World: 14 species; Japan: 1 species) Small quail-like birds that inhabit grasslands and cultivated fields. Ground-dwelling and polygamous. Females larger than males. Sex roles reversed.

BARRED BUTTONQUAIL *Turnix suscitator* <Mifu-uzura> L 14cm. Very small. **Female:** Crown black, spotted with white; face finely spotted with black and white; *throat and center of upper breast black; black bars on sides of breast.* **Male:** Slightly smaller and paler; chin, throat, and foreneck white. Difficult to observe; usually seen when flushed. In flight, distinct *contrast between primaries and wing coverts.* **Similar species:** Common Quail is larger and has no contrast between primaries and wing coverts. Shares same area only in winter. **Status:** Common resident in Amami Is. and Ryukyu Is.

Pheasants, Partridges, and Quails

Family *Phasianidae* (World: 180 species; Japan: 4 species.) Chicken-like, ground-dwelling birds with short stout bills and legs. Flight is fast and direct with rapid beats of short rounded wings. Feed on seeds, insects, buds, and berries. Pheasants have long sweeping tails. Partridges and quails are much smaller and plumper with short tails. Nest on the ground.

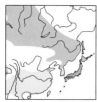

COMMON QUAIL *Coturnix coturnix* <Uzura> L 20cm. A small plump bird with striped head and short tail; blackish-brown upperparts strongly streaked with whitish buff; paler below with black streaks on breast and flanks; long creamy *white stripe* above eye. Flight is slow, usually brief. Usually seen only when flushed. **Voice:** Distinctive *gwa kuro.* **Similar species:** Barred Buttonquail is smaller, lacks strong streaking on back, has clearer contrast between primaries and wing coverts, and shares same area only in winter (Ryukyu Is.). **Status:** Common throughout Japan. Breeds from southern Hokkaido to central Honshu.

BAMBOO PARTRIDGE *Bambusicola thoracica* <Kojukei> L 27cm. Plump and brightly colored. *Brownish-orange of cheeks, chin, and throat;* long broad *gray stripe above eye; gray upper breast* are most conspicuous. Belly and flanks pale yellowish-brown with *black crescent markings.* Family flocks are often observed in parks and crossing country paths. Flight short, direct, and heavy. **Voice:** Loud *pi pi quee.* **Similar species:** Common Quail is smaller with paler plumage. Female Pheasant is larger with longer tail. **Status:** Common, Honshu south to Kyushu. Introduced in 1919 in Tokyo and Kanagawa; has spread widely. Subspecies *sonorivox* (gray face and upper breast, orange throat) introduced in Kobe area (Hyogo Pref.).

Quails, Partridges

♀

♂

♀

Barred Buttonquail

♀

♂ summer

♀

Common Quail

♀ (reduced)

♂

Bamboo Partridge

juv.

♂

subspecies *sonorivox*

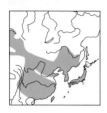

COMMON PHEASANT *Phasianus colchicus* <Kiji>
L Male 80cm. Female 60cm. Large with a long
sweeping pointed tail. **Male:** *Glossy dark green
head, back, and underparts; scarlet wattles on face;*
two feathered dark green ear tufts; long grayish-
green tail has blackish bars. **Female:** *Mottled brown;*
long pointed tail is diagnostic. Runs swiftly to cover
rather than taking flight. When flushed, rises with
loud whir of wings. Flight is strong but seldom sus-
tained or high. Feeds mostly on waste grains, seeds,
and berries. Often seen in the open. **Similar species:**
Male Copper Pheasant is much larger with reddish
underparts and lacks green or red of Common
Pheasant. Female Copper is similar to female
Common Pheasant but its tail is shorter and less
pointed, its back and tail are more reddish, and its
flight feathers are darker. **Status:** Common resident
throughout Japan except in Hokkaido. Subspecies
karpowi, Ring-necked Pheasant, is easily identified
by male's *white neck ring* and *chestnut-yellow
underparts.* All other characteristics are similar to
Common Pheasant. Introduced; locally common,
Tsushima I. and Hokkaido.

COPPER PHEASANT *Phasianus soemmerringii* <Ya
madori> L Male 125cm. Female 55cm. **Male:** Has
slightly larger body and much longer tail than
Common Pheasant. *Head and neck dark copper
brown, upperparts copper brown.* Underparts paler
with each feather edged with white, creating a white
net-like pattern on belly and flanks. *Long tail is
barred with chestnut.* When flushed, bursts straight
upward, then glides down into a low-lying area.
Mainly feeds on the ground but occasionally in
trees. **Female:** About half the size of the male and is
grayish brown mottled with reddish brown, black,
and white. **Similar species:** Compare females of
Common Pheasant and Bamboo Partridge. **Status:**
Common resident in Honshu, Shikoku, and Kyushu,
but no records from Hokkaido. Forests on hillsides
and mountains.

Pheasants

♂

♀

Common Pheasant

♂

♀

♂

subspecies *karpowi*

♂

Copper Pheasant

♀

♀

Sandgrouse
Family *Pteroclididae* (World: 15 species; Japan: 1 species) Plump, terrestrial birds with short feathered legs and pigeon-like gait; long pointed wings and tails; short bills. Flight is rapid with occasional glides. Noisy and gregarious.

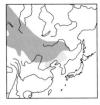

PALLAS'S SANDGROUSE *Syrrhaptes paradoxus* <Sakei> L 37.5cm. Sandy upperparts with black bars. *Long needle-like center tail feathers* and prominent *black patch on belly*. In flight the swept-back primaries make the wings appear crescent shaped. **Male:** Orange head with gray cheeks. **Female:** Yellow head with black spots on crown and cheeks. **Status:** Accidental to open grassland and cultivated fields.

Pigeons
Family *Columbidae* (World: About 300 species; Japan: 9 species) Pigeons and doves are names often used interchangeably. There is no technical distinction. Pigeons and doves have plump bodies, small heads, long pointed wings, short legs, and crooning voices. They walk frequently, bobbing their heads. Flight is rapid. Sexes are similar.

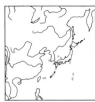

JAPANESE WOOD PIGEON *Columba janthina* <Karasu-bato> L 40cm. *Black plumage* overall, glossed with purple on head and shoulders, *green* on neck, back, and breast. Dark blue bill; reddish legs. **Status:** Uncommon resident Honshu southward in subtropical and warm temperate zones on islands and along coasts. Prefers broad-leaved evergreen woodlands.

BONIN WOOD PIGEON *Columba versicolor* <Ogasa wara-karasu-bato> L 45cm. Slate-gray plumage glossed with green and purple; pale crescent-shaped patch on breast. Yellow bill; reddish legs. **Status:** Extinct. Subtropical forests. (Four records from 1827, 1828, and 1889; Ogasawara Is.)

RYUKYU WOOD PIGEON *Columba jouyi* <Ryukyu-karasu-bato> L 45cm. Black plumage with purple gloss on head and breast and green gloss on neck and underparts. Pale crescent-shaped patch on upper back. Dark blue bill; red legs. **Status:** Apparently extinct. Last seen in Daito Is. in 1936 and on Okinawa in 1904. Subtropical forests.

RED TURTLE DOVE *Streptopelia tranquebarica* <Beni-bato> L 22.5cm. *Much smaller and redder* than Collared Turtle Dove, but similarly marked with a *black half-collar*. **Male:** Vinaceous-red upperparts, *gray head and throat*, paler vinaceous-red breast and belly, white under tail coverts. Gray tail with black outer feathers tipped with white. Dark bill and legs. **Female:** Plumage more brownish red. **Status:** Straggler; central Honshu southward. Open fields, forest edges, bamboo groves.

Sandgrouses, Pigeons, Doves

Pallas's Sandgrouse

Japanese Wood Pigeon

Ryukyu Wood Pigeon

Bonin Wood Pigeon

Red Turtle Dove

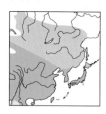

RUFOUS TURTLE DOVE *Streptopelia orientalis*
<Kiji-bato> L 33cm. Head, neck, and underparts
brownish to pinkish gray with black and gray
striped patch on sides of neck. Back and scapulars
blackish brown with *rufous edges.* Rump and upper
tail coverts gray; tail dark with a light gray tip. Bill
gray; legs dark red. **Voice:** *Deh deh, po po.* **Status:**
Common resident; parks, gardens, and forest edges.
Domestic Pigeon Introduced. Descended from the
Rock Dove, *Columba livia. Various colors and patterns.* Abundant in cities and on farms.

COLLARED TURTLE DOVE *Streptopelia decaocto*
<Shirako-bato> L 32.5cm. Pale dusty brownish-
gray plumage with *black half-collar* on nape; *dark
primaries;* white tips on outer tail feathers. Under
tail is black at base and white at tip. Black bill; red
legs. **Voice:** Deep *coo-cooo, coo,* with the accent on
the second beat. **Status:** Locally common resident,
Saitama Pref.; possibly introduced. Villages and cultivated fields with scattered trees.

EMERALD DOVE *Chalcophaps indica* <Kin-bato>
L 25cm. Striking colors. **Male:** *Glossy green back
and wings;* rich brown cheeks, neck, and underparts; bluish-gray crown and nape; *white forehead
and eyebrow;* white carpal joint; black rump and tail;
two whitish bars on rump; dark flight feathers; *red
bill;* purple legs. **Female:** Duller with gray forehead
and eyebrows. **Voice:** Deep *oo oo.* **Status:** Locally
uncommon resident, southern Ryukyu Is.; subtropical forests.

JAPANESE GREEN PIGEON *Sphenurus sieboldii*
<Ao-bato> L 33cm. Yellowish-green plumage darker
on crown and upperparts; slaty flight feathers; *white
belly; broad black streaks* on greenish-white flanks
and under tail coverts. Blue bill; red legs. **Male:**
Chestnut on wing coverts. **Female:** No chestnut on
wings. **Similar species:** See Red-capped Green
Pigeon. **Voice:** Slow *ah oh ah oh.* **Status:** Uncommon resident from Honshu southward; common
summer visitor to Hokkaido. Lowland forest; broad-
leaved mountain forests in Hokkaido; seacoasts.

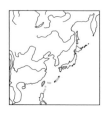

RED-CAPPED GREEN PIGEON *Sphenurus formo-
sae* <Zuaka-ao-bato> L 35cm. *Lesser and median
wing coverts are dark green with a brownish-purple
tint;* head and breast have *less yellow* tint; *green
belly;* whitish lower belly and under tail coverts with
blackish streaks; no red cap. Bright blue bill; red
legs. **Voice:** *Po po peh* with last at higher pitch. **Status:** Common resident in Ryukyu Is.; fields and subtropical forests.

Pigeons, Doves

Rufous Turtle Dove

Collared Turtle Dove

Emerald Dove

♂   ♀

♂

♂   ♀

Japanese Green Pigeon

Red-capped Green Pigeon

three phases of Domestic Pigeon

Cuckoos

Family *Cuculidae* (World: About 130 species; Japan: 6 species) Solitary, arboreal birds with long tails, slightly decurved bills, and usually long pointed wings. About 40% lay their eggs in other birds' nests. Calls are easily recognizable and the best means of identification.

COMMON CUCKOO *Cuculus canorus* <Kakkō> L 35cm. Head, throat, and upperparts slate gray; chin, throat, and upper breast gray; underparts white, *barred* with dark gray. In the rare red phase female's upperparts are chestnut with black bars, underparts pale rufous buff with black bars. **Voice:** Penetrating *cuc-coo*. **Similar species:** See Oriental Cuckoo. **Status:** Common summer visitor, Kyushu northward. Edges of woodlands, open lands with scattered trees; during migration, in city parks.

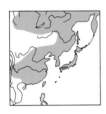

ORIENTAL CUCKOO [HIMALAYAN CUCKOO] *Cuculus saturatus* <Tsutsudori> L 32.5cm. Similar to Common Cuckoo but upperparts darker, *blackish bars* on underparts usually broader. Female red phase is more common than in Common Cuckoo. **Voice:** Monotone *po-po-po-po*. **Status:** Common summer visitor, Shikoku northward. Prefers deciduous forests; in city parks during migration.

INDIAN CUCKOO *Cuculus micropterus* <Segurokakkō> L 32.5cm. Resembles Common Cuckoo but *upperparts are browner,* tail has *black subterminal band.* **Voice:** *Ka ka ka ko,* with the fourth note lower. **Status:** Straggler; Tottori Pref. and Tsushima I. Forests and second-growth woods.

LITTLE CUCKOO *Cuculus poliocephalus* <Hototogisu> L 27.5cm. Similar to Oriental Cuckoo but *smaller;* bars on underparts more widely spaced. Red phase occurs. **Voice:** Loud five-note whistle, the first three at the same pitch, the fourth higher, the fifth lower. **Status:** Common summer visitor Kyushu northward; uncommon in Hokkaido. Forests on low mountains.

RED-WINGED CRESTED CUCKOO *Clamator coromandus* <Kanmuri-kakkō> L 45cm. Unusually large cuckoo, black above and white below with *long tail,* dark crest, and *chestnut wings.* **Status:** Accidental. One record, Tokara Is. Forests.

HORSFIELD'S HAWK-CUCKOO *Cuculus fugax* <Jū ichi> L 32cm. Slate-colored upperparts; *white band on nape; rufous* on breast and belly; dark bars on grayish tail; black bill with yellow tip and base. **Juvenile:** Brown upperparts; brown streaks on light underparts. Voice: Repeated *ju ichi, ju ichi, ju ichi, ju ichi.* **Status:** Uncommon summer visitor, Kyushu northward; mountain forests.

Cuckoos

♀ red phase

juv.

Common Cuckoo

juv.

Oriental Cuckoo

Little Cuckoo

♀ red phase

red phase ♀

♂

Indian Cuckoo

Horsfield's Hawk-Cuckoo

juv.

Red-winged Crested Cuckoo

205

Nightjars

Family *Caprimulgidae* (World: About 70 species; Japan: 1 species) Nightjars are nocturnal birds with mottled plumage in soft shades of brown, buff, black, gray, and white. Well camouflaged during the day when they sit motionless on the ground or lengthwise on a branch. They have large eyes, long wings and tails, flat heads, tiny bills, and huge gapes. Insect eaters, they feed at night on the wing.

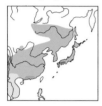

JUNGLE NIGHTJAR *Caprimulgus indicus* <Yotaka> L 29cm. Upperparts heavily speckled and barred in dead-leaf camouflage. Generally grayish brown; gray on scapulars; blackish-brown throat with buffy patch. *White patch* near wing tip and *white tips on outer tail feathers* are clear on male in flight. Black bill; brown legs. **Status:** Common summer visitor throughout Japan. Clearings and open woodlands on hillsides and mountains.

Swifts

Family *Apodidae* (World: About 70 species; Japan: 3 species) Small aerial birds somewhat like swallows but with longer, more slender, scythe-like wings and a different wingbeat. Flight is extremely rapid and continuous throughout the day as they catch insects in their wide mouths and even collect nesting material on the wing. Gregarious. Breed colonially. Sexes are similar.

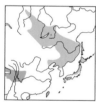

WHITE-THROATED NEEDLE-TAILED SWIFT *Chaetura caudacuta* <Hario-amatsubame> L 21cm. Largest of the Japanese swifts, has a short *square tail with sharp spines at the end.* Black or blackish-brown plumage with pale back and rump; *white throat,* chin, and forehead; *white under tail coverts;* white patches on tertiaries. **Status:** Summer visitor; breeds from central Honshu northward, mostly in mountains in Honshu and on wooded plains in Hokkaido.

HOUSE SWIFT *Apus affinis* <Hime-amatsubame> L 13cm. Small bluish-black swift with a *shallowly forked short tail; white rump and upper tail coverts;* white chin and throat; black bill and legs. **Similar species:** House Martin has white underparts. **Status:** Uncommon resident, central Honshu southward. Cities, rivers, low mountains.

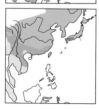

WHITE-RUMPED SWIFT *Apus pacificus* <Amatsubame> L 19.5cm. Markings are similar to those of House Swifts, but White-rumped Swifts are larger and have more deeply *forked tails.* Mostly blackish brown with a greenish-blue gloss on the upperwings. *Fine white bars* on the dark underparts are visible only at close range. **Status:** Common summer visitor to shoreline cliffs and mountains throughout most of Japan; also to open lowlands during migration.

Jungle Nightjar

White-throated
Needle-tailed Swift

perched on cliff

House Swift

White-rumped
Swift

Kingfishers

Family *Alcedinidae* (World: About 90 species; Japan: 6 species) Compact with large heads, short necks, and long massive straight bills which are sharply pointed. Most species have bright plumage with striking markings, and some have distinctive crests. They are solitary birds, often noisy. Some species live near water, feeding mainly on fish and often hovering before plunging into the water. Other species live in woodlands or grasslands, feeding on reptiles or amphibians.

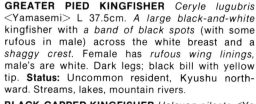

GREATER PIED KINGFISHER *Ceryle lugubris* <Yamasemi> L 37.5cm. *A large black-and-white* kingfisher with *a band of black spots* (with some rufous in male) across the white breast and a *shaggy crest.* Female has *rufous wing linings,* male's are white. Dark legs; black bill with yellow tip. **Status:** Uncommon resident, Kyushu northward. Streams, lakes, mountain rivers.

BLACK-CAPPED KINGFISHER *Halcyon pileata* <Yama-shōbin> L 28cm. *Black cap, white collar,* purplish-blue upperparts, white throat and upper breast, rufous underparts. Large *white wing patches;* black upper wing coverts and primaries. *Bright red bill* and legs. **Status:** Straggler in most of Japan; uncommon spring transient on Tsushima I. Usually seen near water; wooded rivers, mangroves, rice fields.

RUDDY KINGFISHER *Halcyon coromanda* <Aka-shōbin> L 27.5cm. *Striking rufous plumage* and *large red bill.* The red plumage has a *purple gloss* on the back and scapulars; *glossy blue feathers* on the rump; yellowish-rufous underparts with paler chin and throat; short red legs. **Status:** Summer visitor, common in warmer regions. Deciduous woods and near mountain streams.

MIYAKO KINGFISHER *Halcyon miyakoensis* <Miyako-shōbin> Somewhat smaller than Ruddy Kingfisher and browner in color with blue-green stripe extending from underneath the eye to the blue-green back, scapulars, and tail. Rump and upper tail coverts cobalt blue. Dark red legs. **Status:** Extinct. One specimen found on Miyako I. in southern Ryukyu Is., 1887.

COLLARED KINGFISHER *Halcyon chloris* <Nanyo-shōbin> L 23.5cm. *Bright blue-and-white coloring* is distinctive. Blue cap with *white eyebrow; black eyeline extends to the nape* and there separates the blue cap from the *white collar.* Upperparts are green to blue; upper side of wings *blue;* underparts *white.* Dark bill with pale base to lower mandible. Black legs. **Status:** Accidental, southern Ryukyu Is.; mangrove swamps and coastal forests.

Kingfishers

♀
hovering

♂

♂

Greater Pied Kingfisher

Black-capped
Kingfisher

Ruddy
Kingfisher

Miyako Kingfisher

Collared
Kingfisher

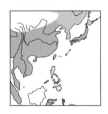

COMMON KINGFISHER *Alcedo atthis* <Kawasemi> L 17cm. *Smallest* Japanese kingfisher. Brilliant coloring with iridescent blue-green cap and upper-parts spotted with *bluish white* on cap and wings; bright blue stripe down middle of back; *bright rufous cheeks and underparts;* white chin, throat, and neck patch. Long pointed black bill is red on the base of the lower mandible in female; red legs. **Status:** Common resident throughout Japan; near ponds, marshes, quiet streams.

Bee-eaters
Family *Meropidae* (World: 25 species; Japan: 1 species) Bee-eaters are slender birds with long, decurved bills and brightly colored plumage, predominantly green. They feed on insects.

AUSTRALIAN BEE-EATER *Merops ornatus* <Ha chikui> L 26cm. *Green and blue with long decurved black bill,* black face stripe with blue edges, pale orange on throat with black stripe in center. Wire-like shafts of two central tail feathers extend beyond the end of tail, farther in male. In flight, distinct coppery flight feathers. **Status:** Accidental, Miyako I., southern Ryukyu Is.

Rollers
Family *Coraciidae* (World: 16 species; Japan: 1 species) Rollers are stout birds with large flat heads, strong bills with hooked tips, and broad wings. Name comes from spectacular courtship flights with much swooping, turning, and rolling. Often wait on exposed perches to catch insects in the air.

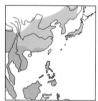

BROAD-BILLED ROLLER *Eurystomus orientalis* <Buppōsō> L 29.5cm. Stocky green and blue bird with a dark head and *prominent red bill; large white patches* on base of primaries are distinct in flight and show as a small mark on wings at rest. Emerald-green underparts; darker green above; dark tail feathers are edged with violet blue. Red legs. **Status:** Uncommon summer visitor and breeder; Kyushu, Shikoku, and Honshu. Forests with tall conifers.

Hoopoes
Family *Upupidae* (World: 1 species; Japan: 1 species) Medium-sized ground-feeding birds with long erectile crests, striking coloration, broad wings, and long decurved bills. Sexes similar.

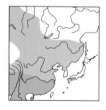

HOOPOE *Upupa epops* <Yatsugashira> L 28cm. Unmistakable. Pinkish-brown plumage with *boldly barred* black-and-white wings and tail. *Black-tipped erectile crest* looks like a large fan but is often held flat. The long black *decurved bill* has a flesh-colored base. **Status:** Uncommon transient in Ryukyu Is. and Tsushima; straggler elsewhere in Japan. Open woodlands, orchards, cultivated fields, and lawns.

Kingfishers, Rollers, Hoopoes

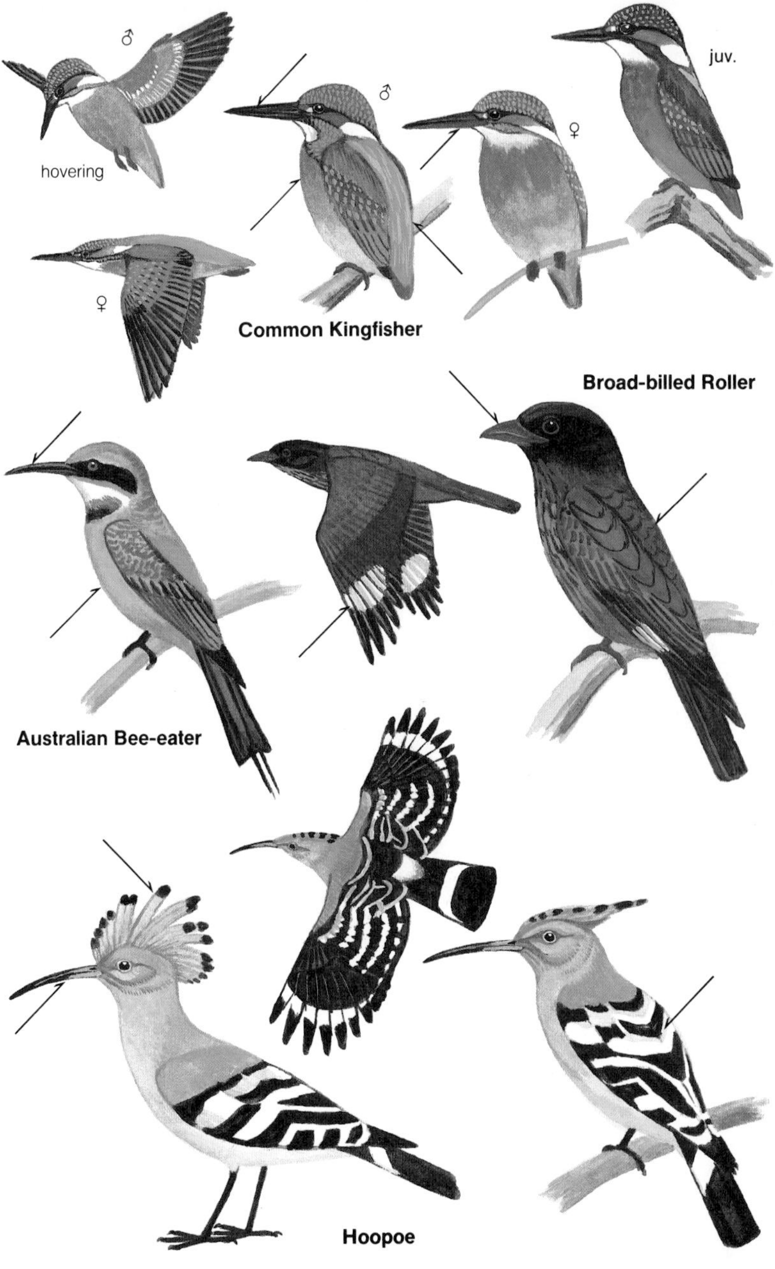

hovering

♂

♀

Common Kingfisher

♂

♀

juv.

Broad-billed Roller

Australian Bee-eater

Hoopoe

Woodpeckers

Family *Picidae* (World: About 180 species; Japan: 11 species) Most have strong bills, short stiff tails, and powerful feet with sharp claws. These features enable them to climb and cling to tree trunks and to bore for insects in the bark. Undulating flight.

JAPANESE GREEN WOODPECKER *Picus awokera* <Ao-gera> L 29cm. **Male:** *Bright red crown and nape; red and black moustachial stripe;* yellowish-green upperparts with white-speckled dark primaries and a yellow rump; pale underparts with *dense black bars on belly*. **Female:** Similar except *crown is gray*. **Voice:** Whistled *peoo peoo*. **Status:** Common resident, Honshu south to Kyushu; endemic to Japan. Mixed forests on hills and mountains.

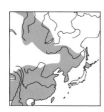

GRAY-HEADED WOODPECKER *Picus canus* <Yamagera> L 29.5cm. **Male:** Crimson on *forehead only;* greenish-gray crown and nape with dark streaks; narrow black moustachial stripe; pale greenish-gray *underparts with no markings; olive-green* upperparts with white spots on dark primaries. **Female:** No red on forehead; paler moustachial stripe. **Voice:** Accelerating and descending *pyo pyo pyo pyo*. **Similar species:** Japanese Green Woodpecker has black bars on belly; male is red on crown and nape. **Status:** Common resident, Hokkaido; straggler to Honshu. Deciduous forests on hills and low mountains; lowlands in winter.

BLACK WOODPECKER *Dryocopus martius* <Kumagera> L 45.5cm. *Large* with *black plumage*. **Male:** Red crown with slight crest. **Female:** Red patch on back of crown. Pale yellow eyes and bill. **Voice:** Loud and grating *kleea* or a high *krri-krri-krri-krri;* occasional loud drumming. **Status:** Uncommon resident, Hokkaido; coniferous forests. Has bred in northern Honshu (Akita Pref.)

WHITE-BELLIED BLACK WOODPECKER *Dryocopus javensis* <Kitataki> L 46cm. Similar to Black Woodpecker but with *white rump and belly*. **Male:** Red crest, crown, and moustachial stripe. **Female:** No red. **Status:** Formerly on Tsushima I., now extinct in Japan. Last specimens, from Tsushima I. in 1920.

WRYNECK *Jynx torquilla* <Arisui> L 17.5cm. Plumage mottled and barred in soft shades of brown and gray much like that of a nightjar. *Black* stripe runs from forehead across crown and down the back. Long gray tail is barred with brown. More like a passerine in the way it perches. Feeds on ground. **Status:** Uncommon breeder in northern Japan; uncommon winter visitor from central Honshu southward. Orchards, sparse woods, forest edges.

Woodpeckers

Japanese Green Woodpecker ♀

Gray-headed Woodpecker

Black Woodpecker

White-bellied Black Woodpecker

Wryneck

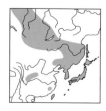

WHITE-BACKED WOODPECKER *Dendrocopos leucotos* <Ō-aka-gera> L 28cm. Resembles Great Spotted Woodpecker but is *larger,* with *longer bill, white rump, black streaks on flanks,* and no white patches on back. Pinkish on underparts; black wings barred with white. Male has red crown, but so does *juvenile* Great Spotted. Female's crown is black. **Voice:** Short, harsh *kyo kyo kyo.* **Status:** Common resident (but in smaller numbers than Great Spotted), Kyushu northward and Amami Is.; forests;

GREAT SPOTTED WOODPECKER *Dendrocopos major* <Aka-gera> L 23.5cm. Resembles White-backed with predominantly black-and-white plumage and white barring on black wings, but has *two large white patches on scapulars* visible in flight and at rest; *black rump;* pale buff underparts with red lower belly and under tail coverts. Male has black crown with red nape; female has all-black crown; juveniles of both sexes have red crowns. **Voice:** Similar to White-backed's *kyo kyo kyo.* **Status:** Common resident, Honshu northward. Mountain forests; in Hokkaido also at low elevations.

PRYER'S WOODPECKER *Sapheopipo noguchii* <Noguchi-gera> L 31cm. Mostly brown. **Male:** Dark red crown and nape streaked with blackish brown. **Female:** Blackish-brown crown. Dark brown upperwings with some white spots on primaries; pale face and neck. Back, rump, and underparts are dark gray with red tips to feathers. **Status:** Endemic to Japan. Uncommon local resident of the northern part of Okinawa I. in subtropical forests.

Woodpeckers

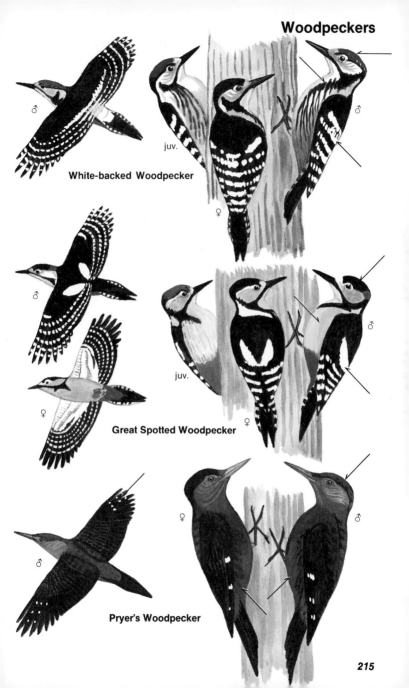

White-backed Woodpecker

juv.

♂

♀

♂

Great Spotted Woodpecker

♂

♀

juv.

♂

♀

Pryer's Woodpecker

♂

♀

♂

JAPANESE PYGMY WOODPECKER *Dendrocopos kizuki*<Ko-gera> L 15cm. *Smallest* Japanese woodpecker. Grayish-brown crown and nape; white eyebrow and moustachial stripe; *brown lores and cheeks;* whitish underparts with *brown streaks on flanks* and sides of breast; dark brown upperparts with white barring. **Male:** Small orange-red spot behind eye, not always visible. **Voice:** *Gi gi gi.* **Status:** Common resident Shikoku northward; woodlands, both in lowlands and low mountains.

LESSER SPOTTED WOODPECKER *Dendrocopos minor* <Ko-aka-gera> L 16cm. Much smaller than Great Spotted or White-backed Woodpeckers, but somewhat similar in coloring and markings. No white patches on scapulars; *no red on underparts; closely barred back;* buff-colored underparts without strong streaking. **Male:** Red crown. **Female:** Black crown. **Voice:** Similar to Great Spotted's; loud, high-pitched sharp *kyo kyo kyo.* **Status:** Uncommon resident in Hokkaido; woodlands.

(NORTHERN) THREE-TOED WOODPECKER *Picoides tridactylus* <Miyubi-gera> L 22cm. **Male:** *Yellow crown bordered with black.* **Female:** Black crown. *Broad white stripe down center of back;* black upperwings with white spots on flight feathers; black cheeks with white eyebrows and moustachial stripe; whitish underparts with *black bars on flanks. No red markings.* Feet have only three toes. Seldom vocal; may drum occasionally. **Status:** Rare resident of coniferous forests, Taisetsu Mts. in Hokkaido.

Pittas Family *Pittidae* (World: About 25 species; Japan: 1 species)

Pittas are small colorful birds with large heads, short necks and tails, and strong legs. They are mostly terrestrial. Their thick curved bills are well adapted to digging worms and insects out of the ground.

FAIRY PITTA *Pitta brachyura* <Yairochō> L 18cm. Unmistakable. *Emerald-green* back, shoulders, and secondaries; cobalt-blue rump, upper tail coverts, tip of tail, and lesser wing coverts; *red patch* on creamy yellow underparts; *broad black eyestripe;* brown crown; yellow eyebrow. **Status:** Uncommon summer visitor to low mountains in southern Japan. Records of breeding in Kochi, Nagasaki, and Miyazaki Prefs. and Tsushima I.

Woodpeckers, Pittas

Japanese Pygmy Woodpecker

Lesser Spotted Woodpecker

Fairy Pitta

Three-toed Woodpecker

217

Larks

Family *Alaudidae* (World: About 76 species; Japan: 5 species) Brown streaked songbirds. Feed on the ground, walking, not hopping. Hind claw usually elongated. Varied musical song.

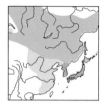

SKYLARK *Alauda arvensis* <Hibari> L 17cm. Slight *crest*, often raised. In flight shows distinct white outer tail feathers and *white rear edge on broad wings.* Slightly undulating, erratic flight. Soars and hovers, singing. Squats when alarmed. Is always flushed from the ground. **Voice:** A short *byur-rup.* Only bird which sings continuously from high in the sky; occasionally sings from song post. **Similar species:** Water Pipit is darker; heavily streaked on belly. Richard's Pipit is more slender with slightly erect stance and longer legs and tail; stripes on face; no crest. **Status:** Common breeder, Kyushu northward. Birds from snowy regions winter in warmer areas.

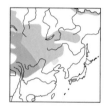

HORNED LARK [SHORE LARK] *Eremophila alpestris* <Hama-hibari> L 16cm. **Male:** Distinctive head pattern with *yellow on face and throat,* small *black horns,* black whisker marks, and black breast patch. Black tail with white outer feathers conspicuous in flight; unmarked whitish underparts. **Female and immature:** Duller; pattern evident but not conspicuous. **Status:** Rare winter visitor to Japan; seashores, sparsely grassed reclaimed lands.

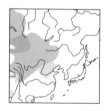

SHORT-TOED LARK *Calandrella cinerea* <Hime-kō tenshi> L 14cm. Smaller and paler than Skylark; sandy-brown upperparts with bold dark streaks; *tertiaries almost reach tip of primaries;* buffy tinge on pale underparts; variable darker patches on neck and breast are difficult to see, but are good field marks if there. Some may have *irregular* streaks. **Similar species:** See Lesser Short-toed Lark. **Status:** Rare transient; open wasteland, sandy seashores, riverbanks.

BIMACULATED LARK *Melanocorypha bimaculata* <Kubiwa-kōtenshi> L 16.5cm. About the size of Skylark with stout yellowish-brown bill and shorter tail with *white tip,* whitish eyebrow, small white patch below eye, no crest, conspicuous *black crescent* on each side of neck, buffy breast and flanks with blackish-brown streaks, white belly, pale brown legs. **Status:** Accidental. One record, Hachijo I.

LESSER SHORT-TOED LARK *Calandrella rufescens* <Ko-hibari> L 14cm. Difficult to separate from Short-toed Lark. *Finely and regularly streaked breast band* is visible at close range; streaks usually extend to flanks. *Tertiaries are shorter* and do not entirely cover the primaries. **Status:** Accidental to western Japan.

Larks

Skylark

Horned Lark

Short-toed Lark

Lesser Short-toed Lark

Bimaculated Lark

219

Swallows

Family *Hirundinidae* (World: About 80 species; Japan: 5 species) Graceful flyers which spend almost as much time in flight as swifts, but wingbeat is different and wings are broader and shorter. Gregarious. Sexes alike. Look for sure field marks; color often deceiving.

HOUSE MARTIN *Delichon urbica* <Iwa-tsubame> L 14.5cm. Glossy bluish-black upperparts with *white rump;* pure white underparts. **Similar species:** See Bank Swallow and House Swift. **Status:** Common summer visitor, Kyushu northward. Nests colonially under eaves and bridges from seacoast to mountains. Winters locally; southern Honshu, Shikoku, and Kyushu.

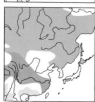

BANK SWALLOW [SAND MARTIN] *Riparia riparia* <Shōdo-tsubame> L 12.5cm. Only small brownish swallow. White underparts with *narrow breast band,* T-shaped when seen from front. Breeds colonially; nest holes bored in sand cliff. **Status:** Locally common breeder in Hokkaido. Migrant, Honshu southward. In flocks around river mouths and marshy lakes. Seldom seen at higher elevations.

RED-RUMPED SWALLOW *Hirundo daurica* <Koshi aka-tsubame> L 18.5cm. Deeply forked tail, *brick-colored rump, buffy underparts with fine black streaks,* narrow chestnut eyebrow. Gourd-shaped mud nest. **Similar species:** Barn Swallow is slightly smaller with dark rump, reddish-brown throat, and white band on tail. Pacific Swallow has shorter tail, no red on rump, and is found only in Ryukyu Is. **Status:** Common summer visitor to cities and villages in southwestern Japan; local in northern Honshu.

PACIFIC SWALLOW *Hirundo tahitica* <Ryukyu-tsubame> L 13cm. Looks like a small, *dirty Barn Swallow* with shallow forked tail, dark wing linings, reddish-brown forehead and throat, dull brown underparts with pale belly, black scaly markings on white tail coverts. **Similar species:** Immature Barn Swallow shows white wing linings and underparts, no scaly pattern on under tail coverts; only transient in Ryukyu Is. **Status:** Uncommon resident; cities, villages, seacoast in Ryukyu Is.

BARN SWALLOW [HOUSE SWALLOW] *Hirundo rustica* <Tsubame> L 17cm. Deeply forked tail with white band; *reddish-brown throat* bordered with black; *white wing linings.* Immature lacks long outer tail feathers; throat is duller with less sharp black border. **Similar species:** See Pacific Swallow. **Status:** Common summer visitor as far north as southern Hokkaido. During migration roosts in large flocks in marshes and along coasts. Some winter in warmer regions of central and southern Japan.

Swallows

House Martin

Bank Swallow

Pacific Swallow

Red-rumped Swallow

juv.

Barn Swallow

juv.

Red-rumped

Barn

House Martin

Pacific

Bank

221

Wagtails and Pipits

Family *Motacillidae* (World: 56 species; Japan: 13 species) Wagtails and pipits are slender, mostly terrestrial birds with long legs. They usually wag their tails up and down. Some have strongly undulating flight. Many commonly call during flight, which is a definite aid in identification. Wagtails have longer tails and unstreaked plumage. Pipits are brownish with streaked plumage.

YELLOW WAGTAIL *Motacilla flava* <Tsumenaga-sekirei> L 16.5cm. Four subspecies occur in Japan. All have *black legs, olive-green backs, greenish-yellow rumps, and clear white lines on the wings.* **Winter:** The subspecies are almost indistinguishable with brownish-gray upperparts, pale eyebrows, and buffish underparts. Subspecies *taivana* has olive-green cheek, yellow eyebrow. Juvenile resembles winter adult but has black malar stripe joining black line across upper breast. Subspecies *simillima* has dark bluish-gray face, white eyebrow. Subspecies *macronyx* has dark bluish-gray face with no white. Subspecies *plexa* has dark bluish-gray face, narrow white line behind eye. This subspecies is not officially recorded. **Voice:** *Jijit, jijit.* **Similar species:** Citrine Wagtail male has completely yellow head; female has paler cheek and two clear white wing bars. Gray Wagtail has longer tail; throat white in female, black in male; pale legs. **Status:** Rare migrant; uncommon in Ryukyu Is. and Tsushima I.; some winter in Ryukyu Is. Subspecies *taivana* breeds in northern Hokkaido. Prefers wet grasslands and riverbanks.

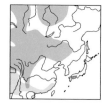

CITRINE WAGTAIL *Motacilla citreola* <Kigashira-sekirei> L 16.5cm. Black wings with two broad white wing bars. Dark gray back and rump, dark legs. **Male:** *Yellow head and underparts,* black hind neck. **Female:** Dark crown and nape, olive gray tinge on flanks. **Similar species:** Female resembles Yellow Wagtail subspecies *taivana* but has gray back, broad white wing bars, paler cheeks. **Status:** Accidental, mainly spring; wet cultivated land.

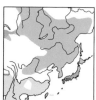

GRAY WAGTAIL *Motacilla cinerea* <Ki-sekirei> L 20cm. *Gray upperparts; yellow underparts; white eyebrow;* white chin and throat. Male in summer has black throat and white moustachial stripe. *Pale legs.* **Voice:** *Chichin, chichin,* often in flight. **Similar species:** From Yellow Wagtail by narrow white bar at base of secondaries, conspicuous in flight; yellowish rump; whitish throat (black in summer male); pale legs. Citrine Wagtail male has yellow head, female has yellow eyebrow and two white wing bars. **Status:** Common breeder in warmer regions from Kyushu northward. Found mostly near water.

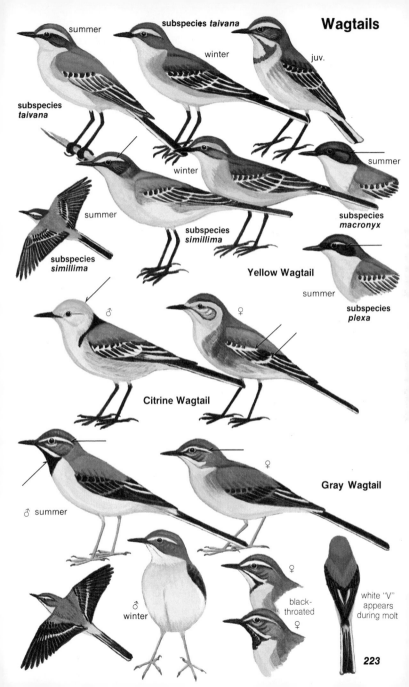

Wagtails

summer

subspecies *taivana*

winter

juv.

subspecies *taivana*

winter

summer

subspecies *simillima*

summer

subspecies *macronyx*

subspecies *simillima*

Yellow Wagtail

summer

subspecies *plexa*

♂

♀

Citrine Wagtail

♀

Gray Wagtail

♂ summer

♂ winter

♀

black-throated

♀

white "V" appears during molt

223

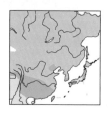

WHITE WAGTAIL *Motacilla alba* <Haku-sekirei> L 21cm. Black, gray, and white plumage. *White face with black eyestripe.* **Summer:** Black crown, nape, and back; white chin; black throat and upper breast. **Winter:** Gray back; white throat; black neck ring. Subspecies *ocularis* in summer has *light gray back and black chin;* in winter, light gray crown and nape. Subspecies *leucopsis* has white chin, black back, no black eyestripe. Subspecies *baicalensis* resembles *leucopsis* but has gray back and secondaries. **Voice:** *Chuchun, Chuchun.* **Similar species:** Japanese Wagtail has black face with white eyestripe and a different call. **Status:** Common; breeds central Honshu northward. Winters in warmer regions. Subspecies *ocularis* and *baicalensis* are rare transients in western Japan. Subspecies *leucopsis* is uncommon, western Japan; some breed in Kyushu. In winter roost in large flocks, often under bridges and in industrial parks. Prefer coastal plain, riverbanks, rice stubble fields, and cultivated land. Breeding sites are often near human habitation.

JAPANESE WAGTAIL *Motacilla grandis* <Seguro-sekirei> L 21cm. *White eyebrow; black upperparts, throat, and upper breast;* white belly. **Juvenile:** Gray hood and gray back. **Voice:** *Jujun Jujun.* **Similar species:** White Wagtail has white face with black eyestripe, black patch on throat. **Status:** Common, Kyushu northward, but uncommon in northern Hokkaido. Prefers water's edge on gravelly rivers, ponds, and inland lakes. Seldom on coast or at mouths of rivers. Breeds near human habitation in hilly countryside. Endemic to Japan.

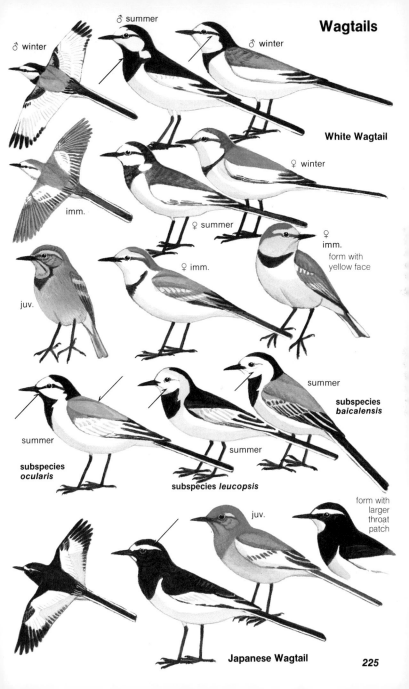

Wagtails

♂ winter

♂ summer

♂ winter

imm.

White Wagtail

♀ winter

juv.

♀ summer

♀ imm.

♀ imm.
form with
yellow face

summer

subspecies
baicalensis

summer

subspecies
oculis

summer

subspecies *leucopsis*

form with
larger
throat
patch

juv.

Japanese Wagtail

225

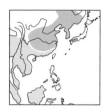

FOREST WAGTAIL *Dendronanthus indicus* <Iwami-sekirei> L 15.5cm. Brown upperparts; off-white underparts with *diagnostic black pattern on breast.* White eyebrow. Two white wing bars on black wing are distinctive. Sways body and tail from side to side. **Similar species:** Immature White Wagtail and Yellow Wagtail have brownish upperparts with dark whisker mark and breast line but lack diagnostic black pattern on breast. Different body movement. **Status:** Uncommon migrant and winter visitor mainly in western regions. Some breeding records from western regions. Feeds on ground in forest; often perches in tree.

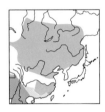

RICHARD'S PIPIT *Anthus novaeseelandiae* <Mami jiro-tahibari> L 18cm. Largest pipit. Walks swiftly on long legs; upright posture; wags tail up and down; long hind claw. **Voice:** *Byuun,* in flight. **Similar species:** Godlewski's Pipit is slightly smaller and has shorter claw, but is almost indistinguishable in the field. Some field guides point out the difference in call. Skylark is rather chunky with shorter tail. **Status:** Uncommon transient, probably regular to Tsushima I., Ryukyu Is., and Kyushu. Grassland, cultivated fields, rice stubble fields.

GODLEWSKI'S PIPIT *Anthus godlewskii* <Ko-mami jiro-tahibari> L 16.5cm. Resembles Richard's Pipit in color and posture but has grayish tinge and proportionally shorter tail and legs. **Similar species:** See Richard's Pipit. **Status:** Accidental. One specimen from southern Ryukyu Is.; one record from Hegura I.

PECHORA PIPIT *Anthus gustavi* <Sejiro-tahibari> L 14.5cm. Resembles Indian Tree Pipit but has yellowish tinge, especially on face and breast. *Two off-white streaks* on back are not always distinct. **Voice:** *Pit, pipit,* or *pwit,* usually repeated three times. **Similar species:** Not always safely distinguished from Indian Tree, Tree, and Water Pipits. **Status:** Straggler, some specimen records from southern Ryukyu Is. and central Honshu.

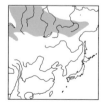

TREE PIPIT *Anthus trivialis* <Yōroppa-binzui> L 15cm. Resembles Indian Tree Pipit but has black streaks on back and finer streaks on breast. Probably indistinguishable in field. **Status:** Accidental. One specimen record from Niigata Pref.

Forest Wagtail

Richard's Pipit

Godlewski's Pipit

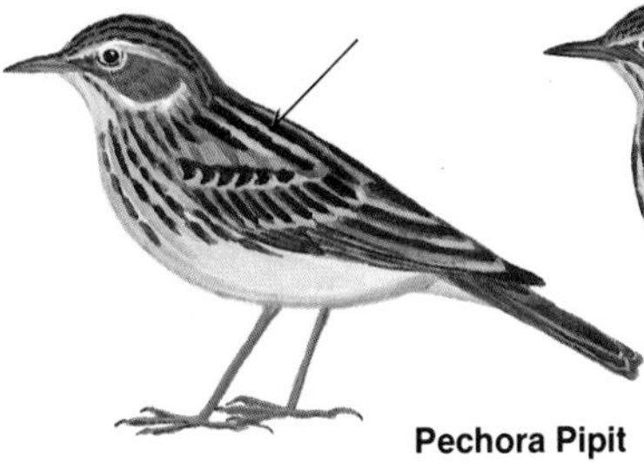

Pechora Pipit

Tree Pipit

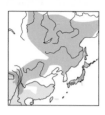

INDIAN TREE PIPIT [OLIVE-BACKED PIPIT] *Anthus hodgsoni* <Binzui> L 15.5cm. *Olive-yellow back* with indistinct black streaks; white underparts with distinct streaks; white eyebrow; may have *white spot behind ear*. **Voice:** Call, *tsui* or *zui*. Song, loud and melodious *chichiro tsuitsuitsui, chotpechibii*. **Similar species:** Water Pipit has brownish back; no white spot behind ear. Red-throated Pipit has distinct black streaks on back, different habitat, and different call. **Status:** Common breeder from Shikoku and central Honshu northward; mainly mountain forests, shrubs, and forest edges. Winter: Pine woods or forest edges on lowland. Perches in trees.

RED-THROATED PIPIT *Anthus cervinus* <Muneaka-tahibari> L 15cm. Resembles Water Pipit but has *paler back with distinct black streaks*. **Summer:** Reddish-cinnamon throat, upper breast, face, and eyebrows. Extent of reddish area and the intensity of color are highly variable depending on season and individual. **Winter:** Pinkish cheek. **Voice:** *Chii,* somewhat like White-eye's. **Similar species:** Indian Tree Pipit has greenish back with indistinct streaks; sometimes has white spot behind ear. In winter Water Pipit is darker with less distinct streaks on back, no pink cheek, different call. **Status:** Uncommon winter visitor or transient; relatively common in Ryukyu Is., western Kyushu, and Tsushima I. Seacoast, rice fields, wet lands.

WATER PIPIT *Anthus spinoletta* <Tahibari> L 16cm. *Dark brown back* with indistinct black streaks. Two narrow white lines on wing. **Summer:** Buffy underparts with faint spots and streaks on breast. **Winter:** Yellowish underparts with black whisker mark and heavy spotting and streaking on lower throat, breast, and sides. **Voice:** *Chichichit* or *pipipit*. **Similar species:** See Indian Tree Pipit and Red-throated Pipit. **Status:** Common winter visitor except in snow-covered regions. Rice stubble fields, riverbanks, wet land, and coast.

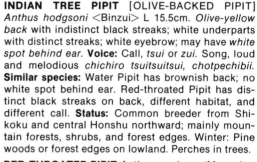

Pipits

Indian Tree Pipit

Red-throated Pipit

two color phases

summer

summer

winter

Water Pipit

winter

summer

Minivets

Family *Campephagidae* (World: About 70 species; Japan: 2 species) Arboreal birds of various sizes and colors. Sexes mostly differ. Thick bills and long wedge-shaped tails. Most species form loose flocks after breeding season.

ASHY MINIVET *Pericrocotus divaricatus* <Sanshō kui> L 20cm. Slender, with *gray upperparts and white underparts. White wing stripes* distinct in undulating flight. **Male:** White forecrown, black hindcrown and nape. **Female:** Gray crown and nape. Subspecies *tegimae* has more black on face, darker breast and belly. Upperparts black in male, dark gray in female. **Voice:** *Hee ree reen,* usually in flight. **Similar species:** Gray Wagtail has more distinctly undulating flight, yellow underparts, different voice. **Status:** Common summer visitor, Honshu northward. Subspecies *tegimae* is common resident in Ryukyu Is. Stays in treetops, seldom coming to lower branches or ground.

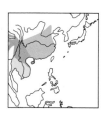

LESSER CUCKOO-SHRIKE *Coracina melaschistos* <Asakura-sanshōkui> L 23.5cm. **Male:** *Dark bluish gray* with black flight feathers, paler underparts, grayish-white under tail coverts. Small white spots on tip of outer tail feathers accentuate wedge-shaped black tail. **Female:** Brownish with heavily barred underparts. White spots on tail as male. **Status:** Accidental. Only 2 records, Miyazaki Pref. (1971) and southern Ryukyu Is. (1975).

Bulbuls

Family *Pycnonotidae* (World: about 120 species; Japan: 2 species) Medium-sized arboreal birds with short round wings and long tails. Gregarious and noisy. Sexes alike.

CHINESE BULBUL *Pycnonotus sinensis* <Shiroga shira> L 18.5cm. Smaller than Brown-eared Bulbul. Olive-brown upperparts; light underparts; white throat. *Large white patch on nape and sides of black head* and small one on cheek are diagnostic. **Status:** Common local resident found only in southern Ryukyu Is. (abundant in Yonakuni I.) and southern tip of Okinawa I. Prefers open fields and gardens with shrubs.

BROWN-EARED BULBUL *Hypsipetes amaurotis* <Hiyodori> L 27.5cm. Dark brown, medium-sized bird with long tail. Silvery streaks make the head look frosty; *chestnut ear patch;* gray streaking on underparts. Undulating flight. Visits feeders. Gregarious. **Voice:** Sometimes very noisy, *peet peet, pii yieyo.* **Status:** Abundant in low mountain forests, city parks, and gardens throughout Japan. Northern breeders move south in winter in flocks.

Minivets, Bulbuls

♂

♀

♂

subspecies
tegimae

Ashy Minivet

Lesser
Cuckoo-Shrike

♂

♀

Chinese Bulbul

Brown-eared
Bulbul

Shrikes

Family *Laniidae* (World: 73 species; Japan: 5 species) Distinctive shape with large head, hooked bill, and long tail. Often perch on poles or wires in open country. Undulating flight, gliding upward before perching. Sometimes impale prey on thorns or barbed wire. Solitary.

BULL-HEADED SHRIKE *Lanius bucephalus* <Mozu> L 20cm. **Male:** Brown crown and nape, black eyestripe, gray back, and a tiny *conspicuous white spot on primaries.* Most birds in summer have paler heads and whitish underparts. **Female:** Browner than male with fine wavy bars on underparts, *no* white spot on wing. **Voice:** A high-pitched shriek. Mimics songs of other passerines. **Similar species:** Brown Shrike has reddish-brown back and white underparts; occurs in Japan only in summer. Brown Shrike subspecies *lucionensis,* found Kyushu southward, resembles summer Bull-headed, but has creamy-buff underparts, no spot on wing, and no brown on head. Thick-billed Shrike has gray head, rufous back, and white underparts; no eyebrow; no white spot on wing; is summer visitor. Rare Northern Shrike is larger; only gray, black, and white; has white outer tail feathers. **Status:** Common breeder throughout Japan. Those which breed in the north or at higher elevations move to warmer regions in winter. Open country, roadsides with shrubs and trees, low mountain plateaus.

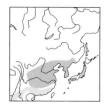

THICK-BILLED SHRIKE *Lanius tigrinus* <Chigomozu> L 18.5cm. Brightly colored with thicker bill than other shrikes. **Male:** Finely barred *rufous back,* white underparts, *bluish-gray crown,* no white eyebrow. **Female:** Duller with black bars on sides. **Similar species:** Brown Shrike has brown crown and conspicuous white eyebrow. Northern Shrike is larger; has white patch on wing and white outer tail feathers; no brown coloration. **Status:** Uncommon summer visitor. Breeds locally, central Honshu northward; light deciduous and mixed forests from lowlands to low mountains.

BROWN SHRIKE *Lanius cristatus* <Aka-mozu> L 20cm. *Reddish-brown upperparts* and whitish underparts; conspicuous white eyebrow, black eyestripe. **Immature:** Barred sides. Subspecies *lucionensis* has grayish crown, brownish-gray back, narrower eyebrow, and creamy-buff underparts. Female and immature have fine wavy grayish-brown bars on flanks. **Similar species:** Thick-billed has bluish-gray crown, no white eyebrow. Female Thick-billed has barred sides. See Bull-headed Shrike. **Status:** Common summer breeder, Kyushu northward. Open fields with thickets, ranging from lowlands to low mountain plateaus.

Shrikes

♂ summer

Bull-headed Shrike

♂

♀

Thick-billed Shrike

♀

♂

Brown Shrike

subspecies *lucionensis*

♀

♂

233

NORTHERN SHRIKE [GREAT GRAY SHRIKE] *Lanius excubitor* <Ō-mozu> L 24.5cm. Gray above, white below, narrow white eyebrow, broad black eyeline, *white spots on black wing,* white outer tail feathers, *whitish upper tail coverts.* Some have faint brown wavy bars on breast, much more noticeable in female and immatures. Sometimes hovers. **Immature:** Gray-brown. **Similar species:** See Chinese Great Gray Shrike. White outer tail feathers will distinguish it from all other shrikes except Chinese Great Gray. **Status:** Winter visitor; uncommon in Hokkaido, rare Honshu southward. Immature was reported in Hokkaido, 1974. Open fields with scattered trees and shrubs; forest edges.

CHINESE GREAT GRAY SHRIKE *Lanius sphenocercus* <Ō-kara-mozu> L 31cm. Like large, long-tailed Northern, with *larger white wing patches* which form a white stripe in flight; *gray upper tail coverts.* This largest of the shrikes hovers. **Status:** Accidental. The latest records, 1974-80, from Kumamoto, Ishikawa, and Hyogo Prefs. Found in cultivated fields and reclaimed land with grass and shrubs.

Waxwings

Family *Bombycillidae* (World: 3 species; Japan: 2 species) Sleek birds with prominent crests. Silky plumage predominantly fawn to gray. The number fluctuates greatly each year. Highly gregarious fruit eaters. Sexes alike.

JAPANESE WAXWING *Bombycilla japonica* <Hirenjaku> L 17.5cm. Like Bohemian Waxwing, but *with red band on tail;* noticeable yellow tinge on the center of belly; no white spots on wing. Black eyeline extends to end of crest. The crest is more often erect than that of Bohemian Waxwing. **Voice:** Like Bohemian Waxwing's and a delicate high trilling *hee hee hee.* **Status:** Common winter visitor to parks and low mountains; often perches on wires and TV antennas. More numerous in southwestern Japan than Bohemian Waxwing.

BOHEMIAN WAXWING *Bombycilla garrulus* <Kirenjaku> L 19.5cm. Crested gray bird with diagnostic *yellow band* on tip of tail which is gray at base, black near the end. Black eyeline extends only to nape. White spots on wings. **Voice:** Weak repeated trill, *zhrie.* **Similar species:** See Japanese Waxwing. **Status:** Common winter visitor to Japan.

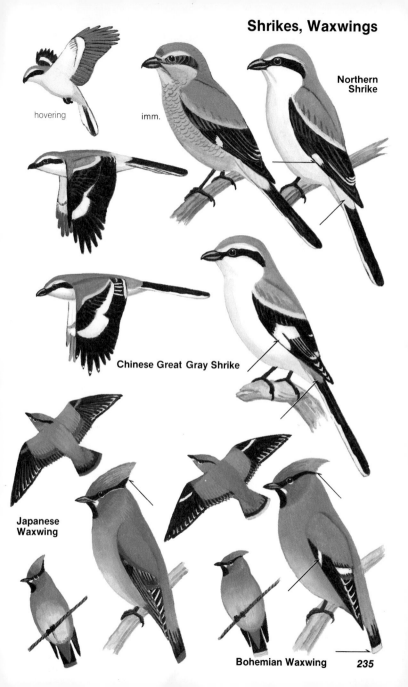

Shrikes, Waxwings

hovering

imm.

Northern Shrike

Chinese Great Gray Shrike

Japanese Waxwing

Bohemian Waxwing

235

Dippers
Family *Cinclidae* (World: 4 species; Japan: 1 species)
Medium-sized birds of swift-flowing mountain streams. Perch on rocks and swim or walk on stream beds, searching for aquatic insects and fish. Flight low and fast along the stream. Solitary. Sexes alike.

BROWN DIPPER *Cinclus pallasii* <Kawagarasu> L 22cm. *Chubby chocolate-brown* bird with pointed bill and short tail. Immature has whitish spots. **Voice:** Short, strong beeping call. **Similar species:** Wren has similar shape, but Brown Dipper is much larger with uniformly dark body. **Status:** Common resident, Kyushu northward.

Wrens
Family *Troglodytidae* (World: 59 species; Japan: 1 species)
One of the smallest birds in Japan. Elaborate song is loud. Sexes alike.

WINTER WREN [WREN] *Troglodytes troglodytes* <Misosazai> L 10.5cm. Small, dark, finely-barred brown bird with *short cocked tail.* Forages on or near forest floor. **Similar species:** Short-tailed Bush Warbler is light brown and unbarred with more conspicuous eyebrow. **Status:** Common resident, Kyushu northward. Prefers rocky, moist ground in forests.

Accentors
Family *Prunellidae* (World: 12 species; Japan: 3 species) Small brownish birds with thin pointed bills. Feed on ground. Usually solitary. Sexes alike.

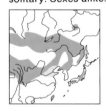

ALPINE ACCENTOR *Prunella collaris* <Iwa-hibari> L 18cm. Dark gray and brown; irregular double white bar on wings; *chestnut streaks on flanks;* whitish tips to outer tail feathers. *Walks.* Takes no notice of human presence. **Status:** Common in alpine zone of central and northern Honshu. Winters lower.

JAPANESE ACCENTOR *Prunella rubida* <Kaya kuguri> L 14cm. Inconspicuous and nondescript with chocolate-brown and dark gray streaked plumage. Seldom away from cover. *Hops.* **Similar species:** Gray Bunting's habitat is similar in winter but winter male is darker gray, has thick pale bill, and different call. **Status:** Common breeder, high mountains up to timber line; Shikoku and central Honshu northward. Winters on hillsides and along streams in low mountains.

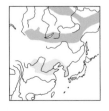

SIBERIAN ACCENTOR *Prunella montanella* <Yama-hibari> L 14cm. Brown with black cheeks, *brownish-yellow eyebrow and underparts,* streaked chestnut flanks, bluish-gray sides of neck, and brownish-gray rump. **Status:** Rare winter visitor, Honshu and Hokkaido; bushes and forest edges in mountains.

Dippers, Wrens, Accentors

juv.

Brown Dipper

Winter Wren

Alpine Accentor

Japanese Accentor

Siberian Accentor

Thrushes, Warblers, and Flycatchers

Family *Muscicapidae* (World: 1,375 species; Japan: 57 species) A diverse group of small to medium-sized insectivorous songbirds; represented in Japan by thrushes and their allies, Bearded Tit, Old World warblers, and Old World flycatchers.

Small Thrushes

Subfamily *Turdinae* in part. A group of small, mainly terrestrial birds including robins, redstarts, and wheatears. Compact with long legs and slender bills; many have habit of cocking or twitching tail when perched. Sexes differ; juveniles like female but spotted or speckled.

JAPANESE ROBIN *Erithacus akahige* <Komadori> L 14cm. **Male:** Upperparts dark reddish-brown; *face, throat, and upper breast dark orange.* Underparts white with dark breast band and slate-gray flanks. Tail chestnut. **Female:** Duller; lacks dark breast band. **Voice:** Characteristic trill. **Similar species:** Song of Siberian Blue Robin is preceded by a series of *chit-chit-chit* notes. **Status:** Common summer visitor, Kyushu northward. Mixed or deciduous forests at higher elevations. Secretive; keeps to dense undergrowth.

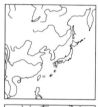

RYUKYU ROBIN *Erithacus komadori* <Akahige> L 14cm. **Male:** Entire upperparts dull orange; *throat and upper breast black;* rest of underparts white. **Female:** Lacks the black throat; underparts mottled with gray. **Voice:** Song similar to Japanese Robin's but more varied. **Status:** Locally common resident, Ryukyu Is. north to Osumi Is.; also on Danjo Is. Skulking bird in deep forests.

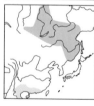

SWINHOE'S RED-TAILED ROBIN *Erithacus sibilans* <Shima-goma> L 13cm. Brown with *chestnut on tail;* off-white underparts with scaly grayish-brown mottlings often forming an *irregular breast band.* Sexes similar. **Similar species:** Female Rubythroat has distinct eyebrows and is slightly bigger. **Status:** Rare transient, along coast of the Sea of Japan mainly on spring migration. Skulks on passage.

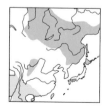

SIBERIAN RUBYTHROAT *Erithacus calliope* <Nogoma> L 15.5cm. **Male:** Upperparts olive brown; eyebrow and moustachial stripe white; *striking red throat;* breast and flanks grayish-brown; belly dirty white. **Female:** Like male but has white throat; some females may show some pink on the throat. **Status:** Common summer visitor to Hokkaido, from coastal lowlands to high mountains. Uncommon summer visitor to Mt. Hayachine, northern Honshu. Uncommon transient elsewhere. Open grassland with scattered thickets. Skulks on passage.

Small Thrushes

Japanese Robin ♂ ♀

Ryukyu Robin ♂ ♀

Swinhoe's Red-tailed Robin

form with pale red throat ♀

Siberian Rubythroat ♂ ♀

239

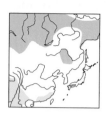

BLUETHROAT *Erithacus svecicus* <Ogawa-koma dori> L 15cm. Upperparts brown, streaked with black. *Base of outer tail feathers chestnut.* Conspicuous *white eyebrows.* **Male:** In summer, *blue throat and upper breast* with chestnut spot in center; black and chestnut breast bands. In winter the throat becomes white but retains the summer pattern. **Female:** Upperparts like male; *black moustachial stripe, black breast band,* and streaked underparts. **Status:** Rare winter visitor, western Japan; scrub and reedbeds near water. Feeds on insects on open ground.

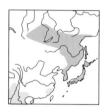

SIBERIAN BLUE ROBIN *Erithacus cyane* <Ko-ruri> L 14cm. Posture more horizontal than in other robins. **Male:** *Upperparts dull blue, underparts pure white;* black from lores to side of neck. **Female:** Upperparts and flanks olive brown; underparts white mottled olive brown; tail bluish. **Immature:** Like female with some blue on back. **Voice:** Song resembles Japanese Robin's, but lacks its ringing quality. **Status:** Common summer visitor, central Honshu northward. Hills, usually at lower elevations than Japanese Robin. Lives on dense forest floor. Transient, Shikoku southward.

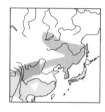

DAURIAN REDSTART *Phoenicurus auroreus* <Jō-bitaki> L 14cm. Conspicuous; often perches on fence posts or bare branches, quivering its tail and giving characteristic call. **Male:** *Black face, chestnut underparts, silver-gray head* with lighter brown markings; chestnut rump and sides of tail; *white wing spot.* **Female:** Brown overall except for chestnut rump, lower underparts, and sides of tail; white wing spot. **Voice:** Series of soft whistles followed by soft *tac-tac* notes. **Status:** Common winter visitor throughout Japan; hillsides, open cultivated fields, parks, and gardens.

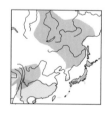

SIBERIAN BLUECHAT [RED-FLANKED BLUETAIL] *Tarsiger cyanurus* <Ruri-bitaki> L 14cm. **Male:** *Bright blue upperparts and tail;* whitish underparts with white throat and *bright orange flanks.* Immature males are like females but show varying amounts of blue. **Female:** Olive brown above with *blue only on tail;* white throat and eye-ring. **Voice:** Short and monotonous warble, often given from exposed perch. **Similar species:** Female Daurian Redstart has chestnut tail and white wing spot. **Status:** Common summer breeder in subalpine mixed forests with dense undergrowth, Shikoku northward. Uncommon wintering bird, Honshu southward. Prefers coniferous forests on hillsides near streams.

Small Thrushes

Bluethroat

♂

♀

♂ winter

♂ imm.
winter

Siberian Blue Robin

♂

♂ imm.

♀

Daurian Redstart

♂

♀

♂

Siberian Bluechat

♂

♂ imm.

♀

241

WHEATEAR *Oenanthe oenanthe* <Hashiguro-hitaki> L 14.5cm. **Summer male:** Unmistakable with *pale gray head and mantle, black eyestripe, and white eyebrow.* **Female and winter male:** Sandy brown above, paler below with buffy wash on breast; wings blackish brown with broad pale brown feather edges; rump and base of tail white; tail shows characteristic *black T* in flight. **Similar species:** Isabelline. Wheatear is slightly longer with thicker bill; broader black band on tail. Pied Wheatear is brownish below, not buffy; black tail band is narrower. **Status:** Accidental; only three records. Grasslands and newly reclaimed land.

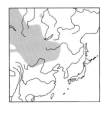

ISABELLINE WHEATEAR *Oenanthe isabellina* <Inaba-hitaki> L 16cm. Largest and thickest-billed wheatear recorded in Japan. Sexes alike. Pale sandy brown above. Brown wings with buffy feather edges; *white eyebrows and dark lores* are more pronounced than in other wheatears; white rump; black-and-white tail showing the wheatear tail pattern. Buffy underparts with yellowish-orange wash on breast. **Similar species:** See Wheatear. **Status:** Accidental; only one old record from Tottori Pref. Open woodlands and grasslands.

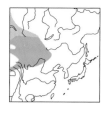

DESERT WHEATEAR *Oenanthe deserti* <Sabaku-hitaki> L 14.5cm. Pale sandy brown *above and below;* pale eyebrows; black wings with narrow pale feather edges; *rump and basal half of tail off-white, rest of tail black.* Male in summer has black face and throat which are lacking in winter and in females. **Similar species:** All winter and female wheatears are similar, but this species can be recognized by its predominately *black tail which does not show the usual T.* **Status:** Accidental; only three records. Open grasslands, riverbanks.

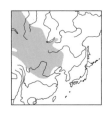

PIED WHEATEAR *Oenanthe pleschanka* <Seguro-sabaku-hitaki> L 14.5cm. **Male:** In summer distinct with *white head and back of neck;* black on face and throat *joined* to black of mantle and wings. These features are not present in females or in winter males. **Female:** Pale brown, resembles Desert Wheatear though darker in color. Rump and tail white with thin black T in all seasons; *the black tail band is narrow but usually wider on outer tail feathers.* **Similar species:** Winter Wheatear is buffy underneath; winter Desert Wheatear has different tail pattern. **Status:** Accidental; five records from Honshu and outlying islands in Sea of Japan, all males in summer plumage. Open sandy fields, cultivated land, seacoasts.

Wheatears

♂summer

♀

imm.

♂

Wheatear

Isabelline Wheatear

Desert Wheatear

♀

♂
summer

♀

Pied Wheatear

♂summer

♂ summer

♀

243

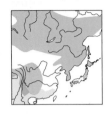

STONECHAT *Saxicola torquata* <No-bitaki> L 13cm. **Male:** In summer, *black and orange with white on neck, shoulders, rump, and belly;* varying amount of orange on underparts, darkest on breast. In winter, black turns to brown; some males may retain black around eye in fall. **Female:** Brown head and upperparts streaked with black; pale eyebrows; some white on shoulders; light yellowish-brown rump; pale yellowish-brown underparts with white on throat. **Voice:** Call, loud grating *tsch-tsch,* sometimes with whistling note. Song, short squeaking warble. **Status:** Common summer visitor, central Honshu northward. Grassy highlands in Honshu down to coastal plains in Hokkaido. Migrant elsewhere; paddy fields, riverbanks, and reedbeds.

GRAY BUSHCHAT *Saxicola ferrea* <Yamazaki-hitaki> L 15cm. **Male:** Upperparts blue gray with black streaks; wings black with white patch; tail black with white outer tail feathers; *white eyebrow* contrasts with *black mask;* underparts pale gray. **Female:** Upperparts brown with rump and outer tail feathers reddish brown; no white wing patch; eyebrows buffy; throat and belly white; rest of underparts uniformly brown. **Similar species:** Female Stonechat has white on wing. **Status:** Accidental; one record from Yakushima I., south of Kyushu.

Rockthrushes

Birds of the genus *Monticola* are medium-sized thrushes with characteristic blue plumage. Some species live in forests while others inhabit rocky country in mountains or on seacoasts. Sexes differ.

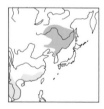

WHITE-BREASTED ROCKTHRUSH *Monticola gularis* <Hime-isohiyo> L 18.5cm. **Male:** Top of head, nape, and lesser wing coverts *powder blue;* back, wings, and tail bluish black; throat and wing patch white; rest of underparts, cheeks, and rump orange chestnut. **Female:** Upperparts brown barred with black; *underparts white barred with black;* throat white. *White throat* in both sexes is distinctive. **Status:** Accidental; one record, Akita Pref. Forests.

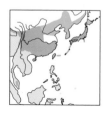

BLUE ROCKTHRUSH *Monticola solitarius* <Iso-hiyodori> L 25.5cm. Upright posture; labored wingbeats. **Male:** Head, breast, back, and rump *slate blue;* underparts *chestnut;* wings and tail dark blackish brown. **Female:** Dark brown, spotted dark yellow below. **Immature male:** Plumage scaled with white and black. **Status:** Common resident; rocky seashore. Birds in northern Japan move to warmer climate in winter. May appear on riverbanks, cliffs, or even on concrete buildings in cities.

Small Thrushes, Rockthrushes

Stonechat
♂ summer
♀
winter
winter
♂ summer

White-breasted Rockthrush
♂
♀

Gray Bushchat
♂
♀

Blue Rockthrush
♂
♂ imm.
♀

Large Thrushes

Birds of the genus *Turdus* are medium to large thrushes of well balanced proportions. Most species live in forests and feed on insects, earthworms and other invertebrates, and berries. Nest usually in bushes or trees. Sexes differ to some extent.

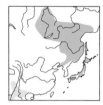

SIBERIAN THRUSH *Turdus sibiricus* <Mamijiro> L 23.5cm. In flight both sexes show conspicuous *white bar on underwing*. **Male:** Black with prominent *white eyebrows;* some white barring on lower belly and under tail coverts. **Female:** Upperparts dark brown with *whitish eyebrow; throat white;* underparts spotted pale yellow. **Voice:** Song a disyllabic *krrn-tzeep* repeated; call similar to Brown Thrush's. **Similar species:** White's Ground Thrush also shows white on underwing but body is bigger and generally paler. **Status:** Uncommon summer visitor to wooded hillsides from central Honshu northward.

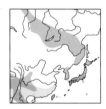

WHITE'S GROUND THRUSH *Turdus dauma* <Toratsugumi> L 29.5cm. Largest thrush in Japan. Sexes alike. Body *pale yellowish-brown, finely barred with crescent-shaped black marks* above and below. Conspicuous *white underwings* with black bar; tip of tail white; bill black; legs yellowish. **Voice:** Song is a high thin whistle and an even higher whistle given alternately at very slow pace. Usually sings at night. **Status:** Common in wooded hills throughout Japan; northern birds move to warmer parts in winter. Feeds chiefly on forest floor.

BLACKBIRD *Turdus merula* <Kuro-utadori> L 28cm. **Male:** *Body black; bill, legs, and eye-ring yellow* or horn colored. **Female:** Brown with some mottling on underparts; bill and legs dark; no eye-ring. **Similar species:** Male Gray Thrush is smaller with white belly. **Status:** Accidental; one record from the Ryukyu Is. Habits resemble those of Brown and Pale Thrushes.

FIELDFARE *Turdus pilaris* <Nohara-tsugumi> L 25.5 cm. *Head, neck, ear coverts, and rump gray,* contrasting with *reddish-brown back;* tail black; underparts white with black markings; breast buffy orange; wing linings white; bill yellow; legs dark. Sexes alike. Call is said to resemble Dusky Thrush's. **Status:** Accidental; one record from Nagano Pref. Open country in winter.

BONIN ISLANDS THRUSH *Turdus terrestris* <Ogasawara-gabichō> Olive brown with black streaks on back and breast. Throat white; tail reddish brown. **Status:** Extinct; Ogasawara Islands. Only four specimens were collected, 1828.

Thrushes

Siberian Thrush

White's Ground Thrush

Blackbird

Fieldfare

Bonin Islands Thrush

247

BROWN THRUSH *Turdus chrysolaus* <Akahara> L 23.5cm. **Male:** Upperparts, chin, and throat dark olive brown; darker on head and tail; thin yellowish eye-ring. *Underparts rufous;* center of belly and under tail coverts white; wing linings white to pale gray. **Female:** Duller with whitish chin and throat streaked with brown; indistinct eyebrow stripe. **Immature:** Like female but spotted on underparts. **Voice:** Song, a three-syllable *krrn-krrn-zee;* call, a series of harsh *chuck-chuck.* **Status:** Common summer visitor to wooded hills from central Honshu northward, lowland forests in Hokkaido. Common in winter, central Honshu southward; lowland woods. May feed in open but stays near cover.

IZU ISLANDS THRUSH *Turdus celaenops* <Akako kko> L 23cm. Resembles Brown Thrush but is darker. **Male:** Upperparts dark brown with head, throat, and upper breast *black,* rest of underparts rich *brick red;* white area on belly narrow; tail black. **Female:** Like female Brown Thrush but richer color on upperparts and underparts; chin and throat white with black streaks. Some are similar to male. **Voice:** Like Brown Thrush's but grating. **Status:** Abundant resident on Izu Is. except on Oshima I. and Torishima I.; winter visitor on Oshima I. Lives in woods ranging from dense forests to light open second growth.

GRAY-HEADED THRUSH [EYE-BROWED THRUSH] *Turdus obscurus* <Mamichajinai> L 21.5cm. **Male:** Resembles Brown Thrush with *white eyebrow* and chin; grayish brown head; rest of upperparts brown to olive brown; throat and breast dark brown merging into russet brown of upper belly and flanks; belly white. **Female:** Like female Brown Thrush but with *distinct white eyebrow;* white on throat more prominent with black streaks. **Voice:** Thin *zee,* often given in flight; difficult to distinguish from flight note of Pale and Brown Thrushes. **Status:** Common fall migrant, appears as early as September; rare in spring. Some winter in southern Japan.

GRAY-BACKED THRUSH *Turdus hortulorum* <Kara-akahara> L 23cm. **Male:** Head, breast, and upperparts gray, darker on wings and tail (throat whitish in some birds); *flanks orange;* rest of underparts white; wing linings orange. **Female:** Upperparts browner; black spots on breast and flanks; grayish wash on white throat and breast. **Similar species:** Gray-headed Thrush has white eyebrows; female Gray Thrush is blackish brown above with *dark* bill. **Status:** Rare migrant; recorded mainly from the coast and islands of Sea of Japan.

Thrushes

juv.

Brown Thrush

Izu Islands Thrush

Gray-headed Thrush

Gray-backed Thrush

249

GRAY THRUSH *Turdus cardis* <Kuro-tsugumi> L 21.5cm. **Male:** *Black upperparts,* neck, and breast; rest of *underparts white* spotted black on upper belly and flanks; *bill bright yellow;* thin yellow eye-ring. **Female:** Blackish brown above with grayish tinge on rump and tail; underparts white spotted black; *sides of breast and flanks orange; bill dark.* **Voice:** Song rich in quality, long and warbling; given from tops of high trees. **Similar species:** Female Gray-backed is browner with yellow bill. **Status:** Summer visitor to wooded hills from Kyushu northward; common north, rarer south. In lowland woods on migration. Some winter in southern Japan.

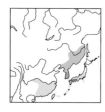

PALE THRUSH *Turdus pallidus* <Shirohara> L 24cm. **Male:** *Head and throat dark brownish gray;* rest of upperparts olive brown, tinged with chestnut on mantle; underparts pale brown, darker *brown on flanks.* Tail shows *conspicuous white tips.* **Female:** Duller with pale throat. **Voice:** Call like Brown Thrush's *chuck-chuck;* also curious harsh bubbling alarm note. **Similar species:** Resembles Brown Thrush, but lacks rufous on flanks. **Status:** Common migrant in northern Japan. Common winter visitor to rest of Japan. Wooded hillsides, park woods, and gardens.

BLACK-THROATED THRUSH *Turdus ruficollis* <No doguro-tsugumi> L 23.5cm. **Male:** Distinctive with *slate-gray upperparts; black face, throat, and breast;* white belly. In winter, black is mottled with white. Legs blackish brown. **Female:** Ashy gray above, whitish below with black mottling on sides of throat and breast; faint eyebrows. Subspecies *ruficollis* male has *gray upperparts; rufous face, throat, and breast;* rest of underparts white; *rufous in tail.* **Similar species:** Male Gray Thrush has black upperparts, black spots on underparts, and yellow legs. Pale Thrush has white in tail. Dusky Thrush subspecies *naumanni* has mottled red area extending down to belly; *brown* on upperparts. **Status:** Accidental; four records, from Hokkaido to s. Ryukyu Is.

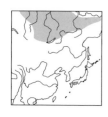

REDWING *Turdus iliacus* <Wakiaka-tsugumi> L 20cm. Small thrush; sexes alike. Upperparts *dark brown* with distinct *white eyebrows;* underparts white, heavily *streaked blackish brown;* flanks and wing lining *bright chestnut.* **Similar species:** Distinguished from female Gray and Gray-backed by white eyebrow, streaked rather than spotted underparts; from some forms of Dusky Thrush subspecies *naumanni* by chestnut restricted to flanks, not extending onto rest of underparts. **Status:** Accidental; two records from Honshu.

Thrushes

Gray Thrush

♂

♀

♀

Pale Thrush

♂

♀

♂

Black-throated Thrush

♂

subspecies *ruficollis*

Redwing

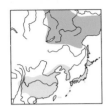

DUSKY THRUSH *Turdus naumanni* <Tsugumi> L 24cm. By far the most common thrush in winter. Plumage variable but always with *brown upperparts, rufous on wings, creamy white* eyebrows and malar area, white underparts *heavily blotched with black.* Bill yellowish with dark tip; legs pale. The amount of black on underparts varies from mere streaks to broad breastband. Subspecies *naumanni* has *heavy orange instead of black mottlings on underparts; uniformly brown wings; chestnut on tail.* Wide range of intermediates occurs between this and Dusky showing characteristics of both forms. **Voice:** Call, harsh *ket-ket-ket* or *kwa-kwa-kwa;* song can be heard in spring just before the birds migrate north. **Status:** Abundant winter visitor but absent in coldest parts of Hokkaido in middle of winter. Bird of open cultivated fields, open woods, riverbanks, city parks, gardens. Arrives in fall from Siberia to woody hills, gradually coming down to lower levels. Not gregarious, but may form large parties at favorable feeding places.

Bearded Tits
Subfamily *Paradoxornithinae*. A group close to babblers (*Timaliinae*) with main population in southeast Asia. Small to medium long-tailed birds with characteristic strong parrot-like bills. Gregarious, moving about dense vegetation in noisy flocks.

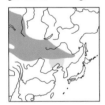

BEARDED TIT *Panurus biarmicus* <Hige-gara> L 16.5cm. Bill short and thin, yellow to orange. **Male:** Distinctive with gray head and *thick black moustache;* rufous-brown upperparts and flanks; black-and-white wing bar at rest; long reddish-brown tail; black under tail coverts. **Female:** Lacks gray head, black moustache, and black under tail coverts of male. **Voice:** Like clicking stones; noisy. **Status:** Accidental; two records. Birds of reedbeds, actively moving about with weak, undulating flight.

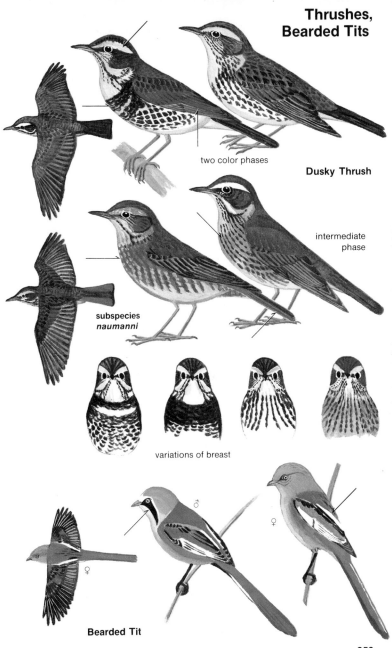

Thrushes, Bearded Tits

two color phases

Dusky Thrush

intermediate phase

subspecies *naumanni*

variations of breast

♀

♂

♀

Bearded Tit

Warblers

Subfamily *Sylviinae*. Small and active with thin bills adapted for catching insects. Can be confusing and difficult to identify. Most have distinctive songs. Many are migratory. Sexes alike.

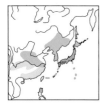

BUSH WARBLER *Cettia diphone* <Uguisu> L 15.5cm. *Olive brown above; dusky below.* Pale off-white eyebrows. Same posture as *Phylloscopus* but tail rather long and movements more deliberate. **Voice:** Song, distinctive up-ending low whistle followed by loud *hot-ket-kyot*, the last two syllables often repeated many times; call, repeated *chick-chuck*. **Status:** Common resident; throughout Japan. In summer, lowland hills to high mountains; prefers bamboo thickets. In winter, lowland with bushes.

SHORT-TAILED BUSH WARBLER *Cettia squameiceps* <Yabusame> L 10.5cm. *Appears tailless.* Dark brown above with pronounced white eyebrows. Pale brown below. **Voice:** High, insect-like, persistent *see-see-see-see* becoming louder toward end. **Similar species:** Winter Wren is darker; lacks eyebrows; different posture. **Status:** Uncommon summer visitor, Kyushu northward. Densely wooded lowland hills. Skulks in lower foliage.

JAPANESE MARSH WARBLER *Megalurus pryeri* <Ō-sekka> L 13cm. *Streaked brown above;* pale brown below; pale eyebrows; rounded tail. **Voice:** Series of chirruping notes given in circling song-flight. **Similar species:** Fan-tailed Warbler is yellowish with white-tipped tail. **Status:** Locally common; breeds only in three places in northern Honshu. Some winter records from warm areas along Pacific coast, central Japan southward. Reedbeds; coastal grasslands.

FAN-TAILED WARBLER *Cisticola juncidis* <Sekka> L 12.5cm. Yellowish brown with dark crown, wings, and tail; streaked back; graduated *tail with white tip* is opened like a fan in song flight; pale eyebrows. **Voice:** In song flight, a series of whistling *hit-hit-hit* as the bird ascends, *chat-chat-chat-chat* as it descends. **Status:** Common; Honshu southward. Coastal and riverside reedbeds and grasslands; also highland grasslands in summer. Winters central Honshu southward.

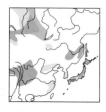

GOLDCREST *Regulus regulus* <Kikuitadaki> L 10cm. Dark olive green above, paler below. *Crown stripe* bright yellow with orange-red center in male. White eye-ring. Black wings with white feather edges. **Voice:** Thin *tzee*. **Status:** Common resident, Honshu northward. Coniferous forests, hills to subalpine zones in summer, low hills in winter. May be in parties with tits in non-breeding seasons.

Warblers

Bush Warbler

Short-tailed Bush Warbler

Japanese Marsh Warbler

Fan-tailed Warbler

summer

winter

Goldcrest

♂

♀

MIDDENDORFF'S GRASSHOPPER WARBLER
Locustella ochotensis <Shima-sennyū> L 15.5cm.
Resembles Bush Warbler, but has browner plumage, graduated white-tipped tail, thicker bill, upright posture, different habitat. **Voice:** Song, a series of unmelodious short warbles given from tops of low bushes or tall grass; also a short song flight. **Status:** Common summer visitor, grasslands of Hokkaido; also in Izu Islands and islands off northern Kyushu. Transient elsewhere. Skulks in the grass.

LANCEOLATED GRASSHOPPER WARBLER *Locustella lanceolata* <Makino-sennyū> L 12cm. *Heavily streaked* brown upperparts, paler underparts; off-white eyebrows and throat. **Voice:** Insect-like thin trill sometimes given from open perch. Sings both day and night. **Status:** Common summer visitor, northern Hokkaido; uncommon transient elsewhere. Grassy plains. Skulks on ground.

GRAY'S GRASSHOPPER WARBLER *Locustella fasciolata* <Ezo-sennyū> L 18cm. Dark grayish brown above, brownish gray below, paler on belly; distinct pale eyebrow. Tail decidedly rounded. **Voice:** Loud and distinctive *top-pin, kat-kat;* from hidden perch. Sings day and night. **Status:** Common summer visitor, Hokkaido; transient elsewhere. Forest edges on wooded plains and hills. Skulks in lower foilage.

GREAT REED WARBLER *Acrocephalus arundinaceus* <Ō-yoshikiri> L 18.5cm. Yellowish brown above; paler below with whitish throat and belly; *distinct eyebrows; blackish lores.* Feathers on nape often raised slightly. **Voice:** Loud, grating *ket-ket-shi, ka-ka-ka,* from open perch. **Status:** Common summer visitor, Kyushu northward; coastal and inland reedbeds and marshes.

THICK-BILLED REED WARBLER *Acrocephalus aedon* <Hashibuto-ō-yoshikiri> L 20cm. Resembles Great Reed Warbler, but *whitish lores* and absence (or near absence) of eyebrow stripe separate the species. Thickness of bill is no help in field. **Status:** Accidental; one record, from Nagano Pref.

BLACK-BROWED REED WARBLER *Acrocephalus bistrigiceps* <Ko-yoshikiri> L 13.5cm. Resembles Great Reed Warbler but is smaller, has browner upperparts and *black and white double eyebrows.* **Voice:** Complex warbling including harsh notes and trills, given from open perch. **Status:** Common summer visitor, Kyushu northward; grasslands with scattered bushes and thickets. From sea level in Hokkaido to higher elevations in Honshu and Kyushu.

Warblers

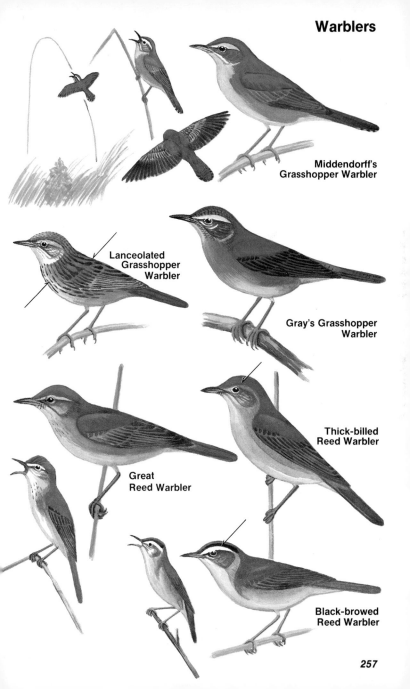

Middendorff's
Grasshopper Warbler

Lanceolated
Grasshopper
Warbler

Gray's Grasshopper
Warbler

Great
Reed Warbler

Thick-billed
Reed Warbler

Black-browed
Reed Warbler

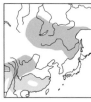

PALLAS'S WILLOW WARBLER *Phylloscopus proregulus* <Karafuto-mushikui> L 10cm. Greenest of the *Phylloscopus*. Green above; pale yellow below. *Yellow eyebrows, crown stripe, double wing bars, and rump.* Often hovers. **Voice:** Call note, soft *see-see.* **Similar species:** Yellow-browed Warbler lacks yellow rump. **Status:** Accidental; one record, Yamaguchi Pref. Forests, especially coniferous.

YELLOW-BROWED WARBLER *Phylloscopus inornatus* <Kimayu-mushikui> L 10.5cm. Similar to Pallas's but browner, *lacks yellow rump.* Eyebrows pale yellow; yellowish crown stripe often indistinct or absent. One and a half or two whitish wing bars. **Voice:** Call, *zit-zit* repeated. **Status:** Rare migrant; more frequent in Ryukyu Is.

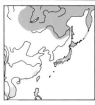

ARCTIC WARBLER *Phylloscopus borealis* <Meboso-mushikui> L 13cm. Dark olive green above with whitish eyebrows. Underparts grayish, tinged *yellow.* May show no wing bars. **Voice:** Song, monotonous buzzing trill; call, similar but shorter *tzyut.* **Status:** Common summer visitor, subalpine forests of Honshu and Shikoku. Migrant elsewhere. Migrants include northern subspecies *borealis* which is slightly smaller and less yellowish underneath; song higher in pitch.

PALE-LEGGED WILLOW WARBLER *Phylloscopus tenellipes* <Ezo-mushikui> L 11.5cm. Brown above, lacks greenish tinge; dirty white below, washed pale brown. White eyebrows. No noticeable wing bar. **Voice:** Song, clear drawn-out *hee-stooo-keee;* call, loud *peet.* **Status:** Common summer visitor, central Honshu northward. High hill forests in Honshu; any woods in Hokkaido. Migrant elsewhere.

CROWNED WILLOW WARBLER *Phylloscopus occipitalis* <Sendai-mushikui> L 12.5cm. *Olive green* above, dirty white below; white eyebrow topped by black stripe, so *crown looks pale;* some birds show paler crown stripe; indistinct white wing bar. **Voice:** Song, fast chitter ending with *beet* or *been;* call, soft *phit-phit.* **Similar species:** Ijima's Willow Warbler lives in restricted locality. **Status:** Common summer visitor, Kyushu northward; deciduous and mixed forests. Migrant, Kyushu southward.

IJIMA'S WILLOW WARBLER *Phylloscopus ijimae* <Ījima-mushikui> L 11.5cm. Closely resembles Crowned Willow Warbler with darker back and crown stripe. **Voice:** Song is more varied and richer in quality than Crowned's and lacks ending *beet.* **Status:** Common summer visitor to *Izu Islands only.*

Warblers

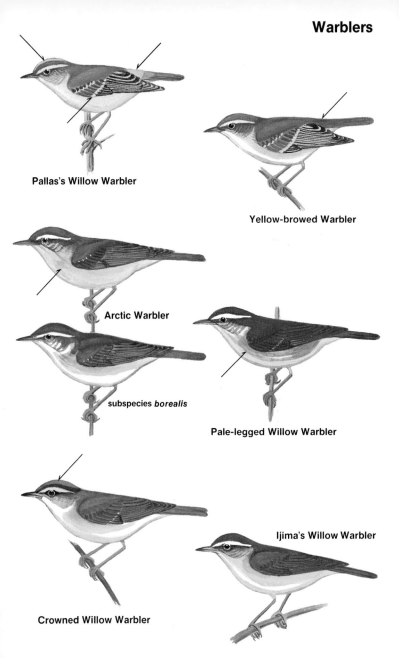

Pallas's Willow Warbler

Yellow-browed Warbler

Arctic Warbler

subspecies *borealis*

Pale-legged Willow Warbler

Ijima's Willow Warbler

Crowned Willow Warbler

Flycatchers

Subfamily *Muscicapinae*. Small migratory birds with thin bills broad at base, adapted for catching insects on wing. Often seen sitting upright on exposed perches, flying after passing prey, and returning to the same vantage point. Legs short, usually invisible at rest. Eyes are proportionally large. Sexes differ, except *Muscicapa*.

TRICOLOR FLYCATCHER *Ficedula zanthopygia* <Mamijiro-ki-bitaki> L 13cm. **Male:** Closely resembles Narcissus Flycatcher, but eyebrow is *white, throat more yellow than orange*. **Female:** Differs from Narcissus by *white patch on wings* and *yellow rump*. **Status:** Rare migrant, mainly western Japan. Open deciduous woods. Habits and voice resemble those of Narcissus.

NARCISSUS FLYCATCHER *Ficedula narcissina* <Ki-bitaki> L 13.5cm. **Male:** Black upperparts with *yellow-orange eyebrows* and yellow rump; conspicuous white patch on wing; bright yellow underparts; *orange on throat;* white under tail coverts. Immature birds are paler overall. **Female:** Olive brown above, browner on tail; wings have pale feather edges; underparts pale brownish gray, mottled brown on breast. **Voice:** Melodious warble with repeated three-syllable whistling notes. **Status:** Common summer visitor throughout; deciduous and mixed hill forests.

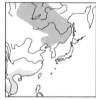

MUGIMAKI FLYCATCHER *Ficedula mugimaki* <Mu gimaki> L 13cm. **Male:** Black above with *white spot behind eye;* broad white patch on wings; tail has white on base of outer feathers; underparts chestnut orange; belly white. Immature birds are paler. **Female:** Grayish brown above, no white on tail; pale orange on throat, breast, and flanks; white belly. **Status:** Rare migrant throughout; woodlands.

FERRUGINOUS FLYCATCHER *Muscicapa ferruginea* <Miyama-bitaki> L 12.5cm. Head, nape, and face sooty. Wings and back dark brown; rump and tail rufous. Flanks and under tail coverts orange; rest of underparts white. White eye-ring and half-collar. **Status:** Accidental; one record, Danjo Is.

RED-BREASTED FLYCATCHER *Ficedula parva* <Ojiro-bitaki> L 11.5cm. **Male:** Upperparts grayish brown with face and side of breast slaty gray; *tail black with base of outer feathers white; throat orange; upper breast gray;* rest of underparts white. **Female:** Upperparts grayish brown; tail as in male; underparts white with creamy wash on throat and breast. Both sexes show distinct white eye-ring. **Status:** Rare migrant and winter visitor, mainly western Japan; woodlands.

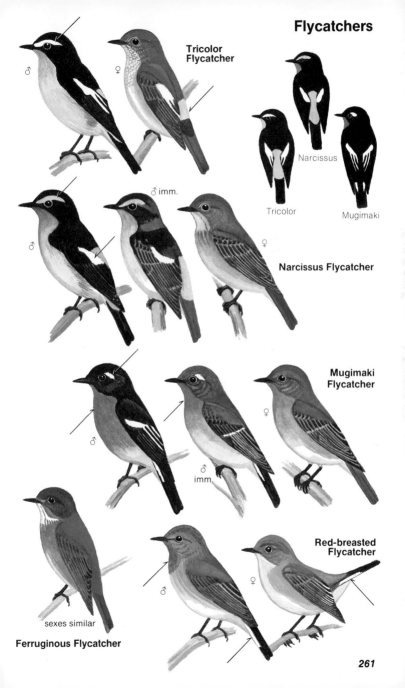

Flycatchers

Tricolor Flycatcher

♂ ♀

Narcissus

Tricolor Mugimaki

Narcissus Flycatcher

♂ ♂ imm. ♀

Mugimaki Flycatcher

♂ ♂ imm. ♀

Ferruginous Flycatcher

sexes similar

Red-breasted Flycatcher

♂ ♀

BLUE-AND-WHITE FLYCATCHER *Cyanoptila cyanomelana* <Ō-ruri> L 16.5cm. **Male:** *Glossy blue upperparts; black face and breast;* white underparts. Young males like females with variable amount of blue. **Female:** Brown with distinct white eye-ring; white throat and center of belly. **Voice:** Melodious warble with distinctive *jit-jit* ending notes. **Status:** Common summer visitor, Kyushu northward; absent from northern and eastern Hokkaido. Deciduous and mixed hill forests near streams.

BLACK PARADISE FLYCATCHER *Terpsiphone atrocaudata* <Sankōchō> A *long-tailed* flycatcher with overall length of 44.5cm. in male, 17.5cm. in female; young males have shorter tails. Black hood with bright *blue eye-ring* and base of bill; shaggy crest on head. Back and tail brownish-black in male, brown in female. Underparts white. **Voice:** Three-syllable chitter followed by fast, whistling *hoy-hoy-hoy.* **Status:** Uncommon summer visitor to forests and woods of lower hills, Shikoku northward. Common, Kyushu southward.

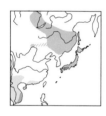

BROWN FLYCATCHER *Muscicapa latirostris* <Ko-same-bitaki> L 13cm. Grayish brown above with lores and eye-ring white or pale buff. *Underparts whitish or pale gray* with indistinct brownish streaks on breast and flanks. Immatures may show pale wing bar and pale feather edges on secondaries. Juveniles are spotted. **Similar species:** See Sooty Flycatcher and Gray-spotted Flycatcher. Female Narcissus has grayer upperparts and almost unmarked underparts. **Status:** Common summer visitor and migrant, Kyushu northward. Breeds in open wooded hills up to about 1,500m.

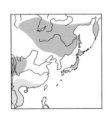

SOOTY FLYCATCHER *Muscicapa sibirica* <Same-bitaki> L 13.5cm. Resembles Brown Flycatcher, but upperparts dark brown; distinct pale wing bar; *dark on sides of breast* meets at center; pure white throat. **Similar species:** Female Narcissus has olive-brown upperparts; throat washed brownish and generally looks more untidy. Female Blue-and-White is larger and browner, tail tinged with reddish brown. **Status:** Common summer visitor and migrant, central Honshu northward. Breeds at higher elevation than Brown.

GRAY-SPOTTED FLYCATCHER *Muscicapa griseisticta* <Ezo-bitaki> L 14.5cm. Resembles Sooty Flycatcher, but breast and flanks heavily *streaked with dark grayish brown.* **Status:** Common transient, mostly in fall. Woodlands and edges of forests in plains and low hills.

Flycatchers

Blue-and-White Flycatcher

♂

♂ imm.

♀

Black Paradise Flycatcher

♀

♂

Brown   Sooty   Gray-spotted

Sooty Flycatcher

Gray-spotted Flycatcher

Brown Flycatcher

juv.

263

Tits

Family *Paridae* (World: 46 species; Japan: 5 species) Small active birds of woods and forests; feed on insects, seeds, nuts, and berries. Conical bills; strong legs and feet; can hang acrobatically from twigs. Often in mixed parties. Sexes alike.

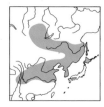

MARSH TIT *Parus palustris* <Hashibuto-gara> L 12.5cm. Crown, nape, and throat black; adult has *glossy black crown.* Cheeks white; underparts dirty white; back, wings, and tail grayish brown. **Voice:** Song resembles combined songs of Great and Coal Tits with some jarring notes; call, harsh and scolding. **Similar species:** Adults can be separated from Willow Tit at close range, but are best identified by voice. **Status:** Common resident in Hokkaido. Woodlands, gardens, reedy marshes near woods. In summer often at lower elevations than Willow Tit.

WILLOW TIT *Parus montanus* <Ko-gara> L 12.5cm. Like Marsh Tit but crown *sooty* black, sometimes brownish; often shows *pale patch on secondaries.* **Voice:** Song, fluty *chee-hoo-chee;* call, soft and nasal *eez-eez-eez.* **Status:** Common resident, Kyushu northward. Mixed and deciduous woods in central Honshu above 1,000m., slightly lower levels in winter; in Hokkaido can be seen in lowlands.

COAL TIT *Parus ater* <Hi-gara> L 11cm. Smallest tit, with short tail. *Crown black; nape white;* upperparts dark gray; tail almost black; *double white wing bar.* Cheeks white; throat black; underparts off-white. **Voice:** Resembles Great Tit's, but much faster and higher in pitch. **Status:** Common resident, Kyushu northward; coniferous and mixed hill forests.

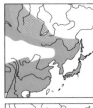

GREAT TIT *Parus major* <Shijū-kara> L 14.5cm. Black on crown and throat encircles white cheek. *Black line* down the center of white underparts is broad in male, narrow in female. Back bluish gray, tinged olive on mantle; wing dark gray with white wing bar; tail dark gray. **Voice:** Repeated *chuppi-chuppi* notes. **Status:** Common resident throughout. Forest, woodlands, and gardens.

VARIED TIT *Parus varius* <Yama-gara> L 14cm. Only tit in Japan with *russet plumage.* Top of head to neck black; face and large nape patch creamy. Back rusty; mantle, wings, and tail slate gray. Throat black; rest of underparts russet brown. Subspecies *owstoni* in southern Izu Islands is very dark overall. **Voice:** Song is slow, repeated *tsn-tsn-wheee,* with accent on the last nasal whistle; call is nasal *bee-bee.* **Status:** Common in evergreen and deciduous forests of southern Japan; uncommon in Hokkaido.

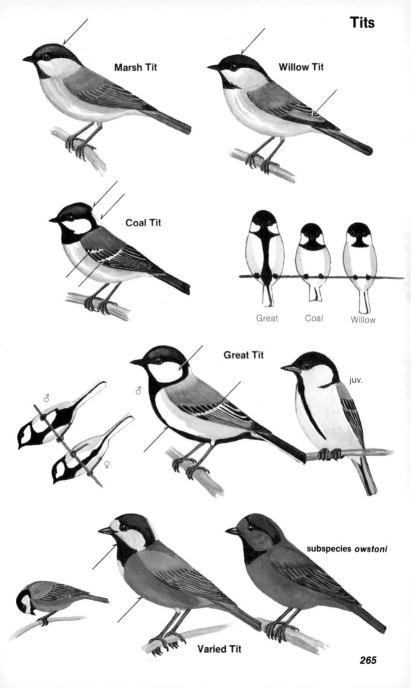

Tits

Marsh Tit

Willow Tit

Coal Tit

Great   Coal   Willow

Great Tit

♂   ♂   juv.

♀

subspecies *owstoni*

Varied Tit

Long-tailed Tits
Family *Aegithalidae* (World: 7 species; Japan: 1 species) Small birds with long tails. Resemble true tits, are active and restless, often moving around in mixed parties. Sexes alike.

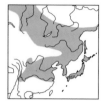

LONG-TAILED TIT *Aegithalos caudatus* <Enaga> L 13.5cm. Head and underparts white with broad black eyestripe. Back is black and pinkish chestnut, wings black with broad white feather edges. *Long tail* black with white outer tail feathers. Coloration of young birds less striking, face smudged with blackish. In subspecies *japonicus,* inhabiting Hokkaido, adult birds lack black eyestripe; whole head is white. **Voice:** Thin *tzee-tzee*. **Status:** Common resident, Kyushu northward; in wooded lowland hills.

Nuthatches
Family *Sittidae* (World: 17 species; Japan: 1 species) Small tree-climbing birds with dagger-like bills, strong legs, and short tails. Freely walk up or down vertical tree trunks without the aid of tail. Sexes alike.

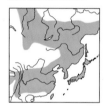

NUTHATCH *Sitta europaea* <Gojū-kara> L 13.5cm. *Upperparts bluish gray; narrow white eyebrow and thick black eyestripe;* rest of face and underparts white with flanks, lower belly, and under tail coverts rufous. The race inhabiting Hokkaido is less rufous on underparts, almost pure white in some birds. **Voice:** Typical call is *chwit-chwit* or *chit-chit;* in early spring and throughout breeding season, loud whistling *tweee*. **Status:** Common resident in wooded hills, Kyushu northward; also in lowland woods in Hokkaido. Usually found in pairs or alone; may accompany mixed flocks of tits in winter.

Tree Creepers
Family *Certhiidae* (World: 6 species; Japan: 1 species) Slender brownish birds with thin decurved bills and stiff pointed tails. Creep about on tree trunks using tail to help grip. Sexes alike.

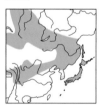

BROWN CREEPER [TREE CREEPER] *Certhia familiaris* <Kibashiri> L 13.5cm. *Upperparts dark sandy brown* streaked white and light brown. Distinct whitish eyebrow. Underparts white; tail brown. **Voice:** Call is a high-pitched thin *tseeee*. Has thin but somewhat melodious song. **Similar species:** Small woodpeckers climb trees rather jerkily, but Brown Creeper is quite smooth, almost running, like a mouse. **Status:** Common in rather deep mixed and coniferous forests in Honshu, Shikoku, and Hokkaido. Found at high elevations in Honshu and Shikoku, down to sea level in northern Hokkaido. Solitary outside breeding season, but may accompany parties of tits.

Tits, Nuthatches, Creepers

Long-tailed Tit

juv.

subspecies *japonicus*

Nuthatch

Brown
Creeper

267

Penduline Tits
Family *Remizidae* (World: 9 species; Japan: 1 species) Small birds with habits resembling true tits, but penduline tits inhabit open country rather than woods. The species which occurs in Japan inhabits marshes and reedbeds. Sexes alike.

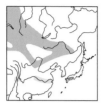

PENDULINE TIT *Remiz pendulinus* <Tsurisu-gara> L 11cm. **Male:** *Gray head* with broad *black eyestripe; chestnut back* contrasting with black wings and tail; white underparts with brown mottling on flanks. **Female:** Brownish on head; eyestripe browner and thinner. **Voice:** Thin *tsee-tsee.* **Status:** Uncommon winter visitor; western Japan, mainly Kyushu. Coastal reedbeds and marshes.

White-Eyes
Family *Zosteropidae* (World: 80 species; Japan: 2 species) Small, greenish arboreal birds with thin bills. Resemble willow warblers in shape but tails are short; have conspicuous white eye-rings from which the vernacular name is derived. Feed on insects, fruits, and nectar. Sexes alike.

JAPANESE WHITE-EYE *Zosterops japonica* <Mejiro> L 11.5cm. Bright olive-green above, wings may look darker; *white eye-ring;* yellow throat merges into white of underparts; sides of breast and flanks washed brown. **Voice:** Call is a bell-like *tzee* or *chwee,* often ending higher, sounding like a Siskin. **Status:** Common resident throughout Japan, rare north and numerous southwest. Wooded lowland hills; also parks and gardens in winter.

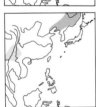

CHESTNUT-FLANKED WHITE-EYE *Zosterops erythropleura* <Chōsen-mejiro> L 10.5cm. Resembles Japanese White-eye, but is *grayer* on upperparts and sides, has distinct *chestnut patch on flanks.* **Status:** Accidental; a few records from coastal areas of Sea of Japan.

Honeyeaters
Family *Meliphagidae* (World: 169 species; Japan: 1 species) A tropical family primarily of Australia. Most are drab-colored birds dwelling in forests, feeding mainly on flower nectar and insects. Sexes alike.

BONIN ISLANDS HONEYEATER *Apalopteron familiare* <Meguro> L 13.5cm. An aberrant species endemic to Ogasawara Islands. Mainly olive-green above with yellowish tinge, pale yellow below with grayish wash on flanks. Head and throat yellow with distinctive *triangular black eye patch.* **Voice:** Various whistling calls; song is like that of Siberian Bluechat in quality.**Similar species:**Japanese White-eye is only similar bird in same area. **Status:** Known only from Haha-jima group of islands in the Ogasawara Is. where it is very common. Open forests.

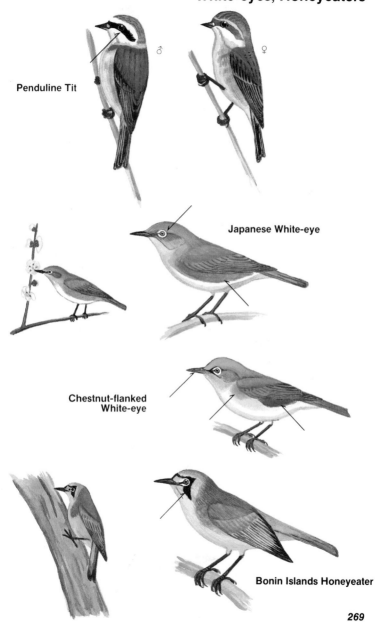

Penduline Tit

♂

♀

Japanese White-eye

**Chestnut-flanked
White-eye**

Bonin Islands Honeyeater

Buntings
Family *Emberizidae* (World: 553 species; Japan: 24 species) A large family of seed eaters of which only one subfamily, *Emberizinae,* occurs in Japan. Most species of this subfamily are small, brownish, ground-feeding birds with varying amounts of white on outer feathers of longish tails. Some sexual and seasonal differences.

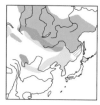

PINE BUNTING *Emberiza leucocephala* <Shiragahōjiro> L 17cm. **Summer male:** *White crown,* cheek, collar, and breast patch; *chestnut eyebrow* and *throat.* **Winter male:** Dark streaks on crown, less chestnut. **Female:** Grayish-brown head with pale eyebrows and brown cheeks. In both sexes brown back streaked black; chestnut rump; chestnut breast band (brown in female) streaked black; white underparts; long notched tail. **Status:** Rare migrant and winter visitor; mainly northern Japan. Forest edges and scrublands.

SIBERIAN MEADOW BUNTING *Emberiza cioides* <Hōjiro> L 16.5cm. Chestnut crown; black face (brown in female); white eyebrow, malar area, and throat; *unstreaked reddish-brown underparts;* reddish-brown back streaked blackish; chestnut rump. **Voice:** Call, clear and metallic *chi-chi.* Song given from exposed perch is a series of rusty chitters. **Status:** Common resident, Kyushu northward; open countryside. Absent only from high mountains and southern offshore islands.

RUSTIC BUNTING *Emberiza rustica* <Kashira daka> L 15cm. Distinctive *short crest and whitish appearance.* **Female and winter male:** Crown and nape brown; dark brown cheeks and moustachial stripe; brown above streaked with black; chestnut rump; white underparts with brown breast band and streaks. **Summer male:** Black head with white eyebrow and throat; chestnut back streaked black. **Voice:** Monosyllabic *chit* or *tzit* often repeated, lacking metallic quality of Siberian Meadow Bunting's. **Status:** Common winter visitor to open lowland woods, paddyfields, and riverbanks.

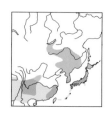

GRAY-HEADED BUNTING *Emberiza fucata* <Hō aka> L 16cm. Head and nape *brownish gray streaked black,* with *chestnut ear coverts* and shoulder patch; back grayish brown streaked black. Throat and breast white with two breast bands, one black and the other chestnut; rest of underparts brown and white with heavy black streaks in summer, faint streaks in winter. **Voice:** Resembles Rustic Bunting's. **Status:** Common breeder on mountain grasslands, central Honshu northward; lowland plains in Hokkaido. Common in winter in snowless lowlands, central Honshu southward.

Buntings

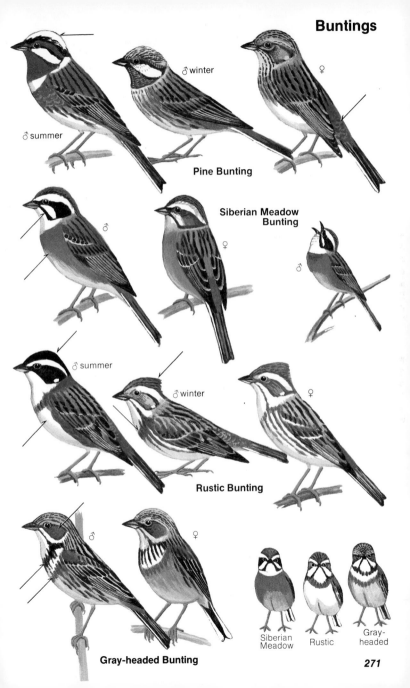

♂ summer
♂ winter
♀

Pine Bunting

♂
♀

Siberian Meadow Bunting

♂

♂ summer
♂ winter
♀

Rustic Bunting

♂
♀

Gray-headed Bunting

Siberian Meadow
Rustic
Gray-headed

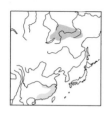

YELLOW-BROWED BUNTING *Emberiza chryso-phrys* <Kimayu-hōjiro> L 15.5cm. **Male:** Black head with white crown and malar stripe and *yellow eye-brow;* upperparts grayish brown, lighter on neck, streaked blackish; underparts white washed pale brown on sides of breast and flanks; throat, upper breast, and flanks streaked blackish brown. **Female:** Like male but eyebrow yellowish buff; black on face replaced by dark brown. **Voice:** *Tzit* or *chit.* **Similar species:** See Tristram's Bunting. **Status:** Rare transient, western Japan.

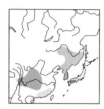

YELLOW-THROATED BUNTING *Emberiza elegans* <Miyama-hōjiro> L 15.5cm. Distinctive *black-and-yellow head with short crest.* **Male:** Head and throat yellow with black face mask and blackish-brown crest; triangular *black breast patch;* back brown streaked black; underparts white with chestnut streaks on sides of breast and flanks. **Female:** Brown crest and cheeks, paler eyebrow and throat, and no black on breast; underparts yellowish brown with light brown streaks on breast and flanks; belly white. **Status:** Common winter visitor, western Japan; uncommon in east and north. Open woods and forest edges; usually stays in cover.

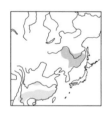

TRISTRAM'S BUNTING *Emberiza tristrami* <Shiro hara-hōjiro> L 15cm. **Male:** Head and throat black with crown, eyebrow, and malar stripe white; back brown and streaked; rump and tail reddish brown; sides of breast and flanks brown with black streaks; rest of underparts white. In winter black replaced by dark brown; resembles female but with darker throat. **Female:** Like male with black and white on head replaced by brown and buff; throat white with fine dark streaks. **Similar species:** Female Yellow-browed has whiter breast, yellowish eyebrow, and is generally less reddish. **Status:** Rare transient, mainly on Hegura I. and Tsushima I.

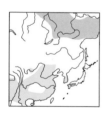

LITTLE BUNTING *Emberiza pusilla* <Ko-hōaka> L 12.5cm. Smallest bunting; sexes alike. **Winter:** Upperparts grayish brown to brownish gray streaked black, reddish on crown and rump; facial pattern distinctive with *thick buffy-white eyebrow* and malar stripe and *black-bordered chestnut ear coverts;* underparts white streaked blackish on breast and flanks. **Summer:** Head and upper throat heavily washed with chestnut; the rest like winter but generally redder; black stripes on sides of crown. **Voice:** Similar to Rustic's but thinner. **Status:** Rare transient and winter visitor; regular uncommon spring migrant to Tsushima I. Open lowlands.

Buntings

♂ summer

Yellow-browed Bunting

♀

♂

♀

Yellow-throated Bunting

♂ summer

♀

Tristram's Bunting

♂ summer

♀ winter

Little Bunting

273

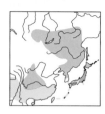

BLACK-FACED BUNTING *Emberiza spodocephala* <Aoji> L 16cm. **Male:** *Head dark gray washed yellow green;* creamy malar stripe; back dark brown streaked with cream and black; rump brown; tail dark brown; underparts greenish yellow streaked brown. **Female:** Head dark brown with creamy-yellow eyebrow and malar stripe; underparts creamy yellow heavily streaked dark brown; upperparts like male. **Voice:** Monosyllabic metallic *tzit* or *tzee.* **Status:** Common breeder in open hill forests from central Honshu northward. In winter common in lowland woods, also parks and gardens with dense cover. Keeps within vegetation. Continental subspecies *spodocephala,* with dark slate-gray head in male and no yellow in either sex, is a rare migrant in the Ryukyu Is., Kyushu, and islands of northwestern Japan.

JAPANESE YELLOW BUNTING *Emberiza sulphurata* <Nojiko> L 14cm. **Male:** Upperparts dark greenish gray streaked black; *white eye-ring* and *two pale wing bars* distinctive; underparts dull yellow, paler on throat; light streaking on flanks. **Female:** Like male but paler, especially on upperparts. **Status:** Uncommon summer visitor to deciduous and mixed forests in the lower mountains of central Japan. Uncommon migrant in west and south.

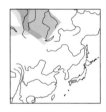

YELLOWHAMMER *Emberiza citrinella* <Ki-aoji> L 16cm. **Male:** *Head and underparts yellow;* stripe at sides of crown and border around ear coverts black; back brown streaked black; rump reddish brown; breast and flanks washed brown streaked darker. **Female:** Like male but duller and less yellow. **Similar species:** Female distinguished from female Black-faced by yellowish crown, russet rump, and yellower underparts streaked with brown, not black. **Status:** Accidental; one record from Nagano Pref.

BLACK-HEADED BUNTING *Emberiza melanocephala* <Zuguro-chakinchō> L 16cm. Both sexes lack white in tail. **Male:** *Black cap,* chestnut upperparts, and *unmarked yellow underparts* distinctive; wings black with broad white feather edges; tail black. **Female:** Upperparts brown streaked black; rump russet brown; buff eyebrow; unstreaked underparts pale yellow washed with olive. **Status:** Accidental; two records only, both from Hachijo Island in Izu Islands. Some possibility of escapees.

Buntings

♂

♀

Black-faced Bunting

♂

♀

subspecies *spodocephala*

Japanese Yellow Bunting

♂

♀

♂

Yellowhammer

♀

♂ summer

Black-headed Bunting

♀

275

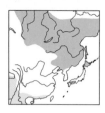

YELLOW-BREASTED BUNTING *Emberiza aureola* <Shima-aoji> L 14cm. **Male:** In summer, distinctive with *black face and throat;* chestnut crown, nape, back, and *breast band;* white shoulder patch; *yellow underparts.* In winter, white shoulders are lost and all other markings become obscure; face dark with pale feather edges; back brown with black streaks; two narrow whitish wing bars; broken breast band. **Female:** Upperparts brown, streaked dark brown; broad creamy-white eyebrow and pale crown stripe together with unmarked lemon-yellow underparts distinctive. Both sexes show some brown streaks on flanks and only a little white in tail. **Voice:** Song is fluty and melodious, given from open perch. **Status:** Common summer visitor, coastal plains of Hokkaido. Rare transient elsewhere. Open grasslands with scattered bushes.

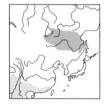

CHESTNUT BUNTING *Emberiza rutila* <Shima-nojiko> L 13.5cm. **Male:** In summer, *chestnut hood,* back, and wing coverts. In winter, chestnut feathers have buffy edges giving mottled appearance. Rest of underparts *yellow* with some dark streaks on flanks. **Female:** Upperparts olive brown streaked black, *rump dull chestnut;* eyebrow buff; ear coverts brown; throat buff; rest of underparts pale yellow with brownish streaks on flanks. No noticeable white in tail. **Similar species:** Female distinguished from female Yellow-breasted by chestnut (not brown) rump and lack of white in tail. **Status:** Rare transient, mainly Tsushima I. and Hegura I. Open cultivated land with cover nearby.

GRAY BUNTING *Emberiza variabilis* <Kuroji> L 17cm. or smaller. Variable in size. **Male:** In summer, *dark slate gray overall* except for white under tail coverts and horn-colored bill and legs. In winter, upperparts become dark brown, streaked black. **Female:** Upperparts dark brown, streaked black and buff; brown ear coverts with black border; pale eyebrow and malar stripes; pale underparts, heavily streaked; whitish on throat. Both sexes lack white in tail. **Voice:** Series of loud fluty notes. Call resembles Black-faced's. **Status:** Locally uncommon breeder in open hill forests of central Honshu and Hokkaido. In winter, central Japan southward in low hill forests with dense undergrowth.

Buntings

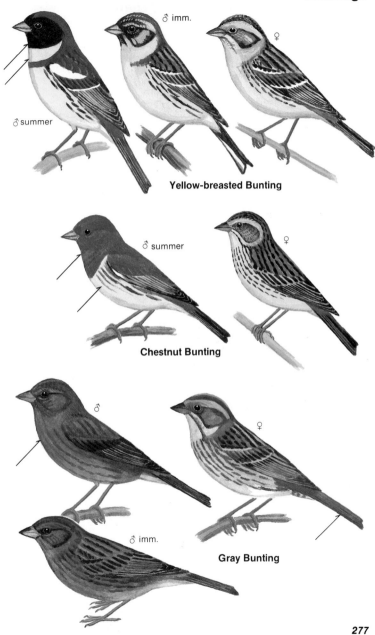

♂ imm.

♀

♂ summer

Yellow-breasted Bunting

♂ summer

♀

Chestnut Bunting

♂

♀

♂ imm.

Gray Bunting

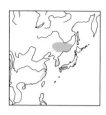

JAPANESE REED BUNTING *Emberiza yessoensis* <Ko-jurin> L 14.5cm. Upperparts dark brown streaked black, grayish on wing coverts; rump chestnut; *unstreaked* underparts are off-white with brown wash on breast and flanks. **Summer male:** Distinctive with *black hood;* some birds may show whitish patch behind eye. **Female and winter male:** Head dark brown with buffy eyebrow, buffy and black malar stripes. **Voice:** Call *chit-chit,* quite distinct from Reed Bunting's. Song similar to Meadow Bunting's. **Similar species:** Reed Bunting is larger, female has streaked underparts. See Pallas's Reed Bunting. **Status:** Locally uncommon breeder on highland meadows of Mt. Aso in Kyushu, Kirigamine area of Nagano Pref., and Mt. Fuji; also in Kasumigaura Marsh and coastal lakes in n. Honshu. Winters in grasslands and reedbeds of warmer parts of Japan.

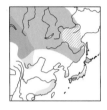

REED BUNTING *Emberiza schoeniclus* <Ō-jurin> L 16cm. **Male:** In summer, *black hood; white malar stripe,* collar, and underparts. Back *brown* streaked black; rump grayish; wing dark brown with *russet-brown* wing coverts. In winter resembles female; may show dark feathers on throat. **Female:** Head brown with pale eyestripe and whitish malar stripe; back brown streaked whitish and black; rump grayish; wing coverts russet; underparts dirty white with some brown streaks. **Similar species:** See Japanese Reed and Pallas's Reed Buntings. **Voice:** Call is a distinct up-ending *tzween.* Song rather short, mellow, and monotonous. **Status:** Common summer visitor to wet grasslands of Hokkaido; also in small numbers to n. Honshu. Common winter visitor for rest of Japan; in lowland grasslands near water, especially reedbeds.

PALLAS'S REED BUNTING *Emberiza pallasi* <Shiberia-jurin> L 14cm. Closely resembles Reed Bunting in all plumages but is smaller with *upperparts brownish gray* instead of brown, pale *slate blue on wing coverts,* and pale streaking on underparts is restricted to flanks. **Similar species:** Japanese Reed is brown on upperparts instead of grayish, has russet-brown rump, unstreaked flanks. **Status:** Rare winter visitor to western Japan. Habits and habitat same as for Reed Bunting.

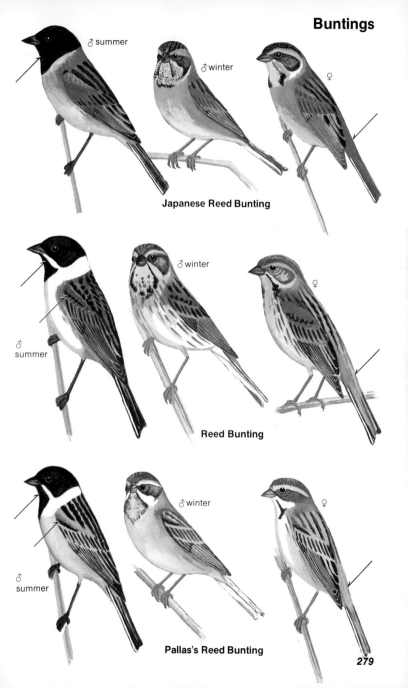

Buntings

♂ summer ♂ winter ♀

Japanese Reed Bunting

♂ summer ♂ winter ♀

Reed Bunting

♂ summer ♂ winter ♀

Pallas's Reed Bunting

LAPLAND LONGSPUR [LAPLAND BUNTING] *Calcarius lapponicus* <Tsumenaga-hōjiro> L 15.5cm. Appears fatter and shorter-tailed than *Emberiza* buntings. The long hind toe is visible only at very close range. Terrestrial, walks and runs on ground. **Summer male:** Black on crown, face, throat, and upper breast; white line starting from behind eye joins the white on neck; *nape chestnut;* back brown, streaked with light brown and black; belly white, flanks streaked black. **Winter male:** Resembles female but *some black* is retained on sides of throat and breast, *some chestnut on nape.* **Female:** Upperparts light brown, streaked with blackish brown, *chestnut tinge on nape* and greater wing coverts; pale eyebrow and malar area; underparts white, streaked black on sides of breast and flanks. Bill yellowish or horn-colored; *legs dark.* **Similar species:** Rustic Bunting has crest. **Voice:** A short trill. **Status:** Rare winter visitor to coastal barren lands of Hokkaido and northern Honshu.

SNOW BUNTING *Plectrophenax nivalis* <Yuki-hōjiro> L 16cm. *Whitish,* with long wings. **Summer male:** Distinctly black and white, with black on back, tail, wing tips, and carpal joints. **Winter male:** Black on back becomes mottled with white and brown; white on face, crown, and breast suffused with rusty brown. **Female:** Like winter male but more brownish overall; wing coverts brown; less white in wing than male. **Voice:** Flight note *krrirr-krrirr;* other calls include *phit* and *twee.* **Status:** Uncommon winter visitor to coastal barren land of northern Japan, regular in Hokkaido. Numbers vary greatly from year to year. Gregarious.

Buntings

♂ summer
♀
♂ winter

Lapland Longspur

♂ summer
♀
♂ winter

Snow Bunting

♂ winter
♀

WHITE-CROWNED SPARROW *Zonotrichia leucophrys* <Miyama-shitodo> L 15cm. *Broad white crown and white eyebrow;* black stripes on sides of crown; black eyestripe; face, neck, and underparts unstreaked gray; back streaked brown and pale brown. Bill pinkish or yellowish. Two white wing bars. **Immature:** Black and white on the head is replaced by dark brown and light buff; brown ear coverts; generally buffier. **Status:** Accidental; a few records from various parts of Japan in non-breeding season. Edges of woods, open fields, and grasslands with dense cover.

GOLDEN-CROWNED SPARROW *Zonotrichia atricapilla* <Kigashira-shitodo> L 16cm. Adults distinctive with *yellow crown and thick black eyebrow stripes* meeting on forehead and nape; back brown streaked black and pale brown; two white wing bars; face and underparts gray; brownish flanks. **Immature:** May be difficult to separate in field from larger female buntings; head brown with pale crown; buffy eyebrow; back streaked brown; two white wing bars; throat white, rest of underparts unstreaked pale brown. Bill pale brown. **Status:** Accidental; one record from Tokyo. Grasslands with dense cover.

FOX SPARROW *Zonotrichia iliaca* <Gomafu-suzume> L 17cm. A large North American sparrow with many races, varying in size and color. Dark slaty gray or dark brown upperparts; *heavy blackish-brown streaks* on white underparts cluster on upper breast forming an irregular dark breast spot. Tail is rusty, though in the darkest races there is not a strong contrast between the colors on the back and tail. A brighter rufous form occurs more commonly in eastern North America. **Status:** Accidental; one record from Nikko, Tochigi Pref. Dense scrub and undergrowth.

SAVANNAH SPARROW *Ammodramus sandwichensis* <Sabanna-shitodo> L 14cm. Rather small with short *notched tail.* Upperparts sandy brown to dark brown, streaked black; striped crown; blackish-brown eyestripe and moustachial streak; eyebrow or lores sometimes yellowish; malar stripe white. Streaked underparts may have a small spot in center of breast. **Status:** Accidental; a few records. Dried paddy fields and grasslands.

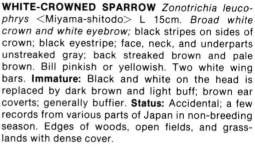

Sparrows

imm.

White-crowned Sparrow

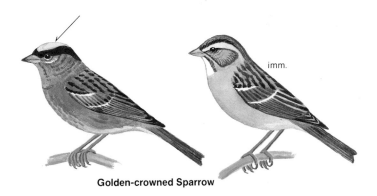

imm.

Golden-crowned Sparrow

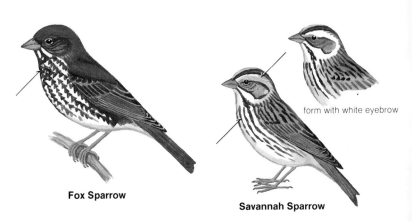

form with white eyebrow

Fox Sparrow

Savannah Sparrow

Finches

Family *Fringillidae* (World: About 125 species; Japan: 17 species) Typical seed eaters with thick bills. In Japan they range in size from the Siskin to the Japanese Grosbeak. Most species inhabit forests and make cup-shaped nests on branches. They are found mainly in cultivated areas and at forest edges. Males are excellent singers.

ORIENTAL GREENFINCH *Carduelis sinica* <Kawarahiwa> L 14.5cm. **Male:** Greenish brown with greenish head. Base of outer tail feathers and *base of flight feathers are bright yellow* and conspicuous both in flight and at rest. **Female:** Resembles male but is more brown than green. **Juvenile:** Like female with fine black streaks above and below, paler yellow on wing and tail. **Similar species:** Siskin is smaller and much yellower with black streaks above and below. **Status:** Breeds from Hokkaido to Kyushu; those in Hokkaido migrate southward in winter. Abundant in open forests, along riverbanks, and in urban areas. Often comes to feeders.

SISKIN *Carduelis spinus* <Ma-hiwa> L 12.5cm. **Male:** Black crown and dark yellow-green back with black streaks; two yellow wing bars; *yellow face and breast.* Black streaks on flanks. **Female:** *Much more streaked* than male; pale yellow underparts; crown is not black. **Similar species:** Common Redpoll has no yellow, and forehead is red. **Status:** Common winter visitor; small population breeds in Hokkaido. In small flocks in forests; often calls in flight.

COMMON REDPOLL *Acanthis flammea* <Beni-hiwa> L 13.5cm. **Male:** *Forehead bright red;* back pale gray brown with black streaks; underparts whitish with conspicuous dark streaks on flanks and rump; *breast pink;* flanks and rump a little pinkish. Two white wing bars. **Female:** No pink on breast and flanks. **Similar species:** Hoary Redpoll is whiter with *unstreaked white rump.* **Status:** Uncommon winter visitor mainly to Hokkaido and northern Honshu. The number varies greatly from year to year. Often seen in forests and fields.

HOARY REDPOLL [ARCTIC REDPOLL] *Acanthis hornemanni* <Ko-beni-hiwa> L 13cm. Resembles Common Redpoll but generally whiter. **Male:** Bright red patch on forehead is smaller than in Common Redpoll. Rump is white with *no streaks,* may be tinged with pink in male. White underparts with fewer dark streaks on flanks than in Common Redpoll. **Female:** Browner than male, more like Common Redpoll. **Status:** Rare winter visitor to Hokkaido and northern Honshu. Usually occurs in flocks of Common Redpolls.

Finches

Oriental Greenfinch

♀

♂

juv.

Siskin

♂

♂

♀

Common Redpoll

♂

♀

♀

Hoary Redpoll

sexes similar

285

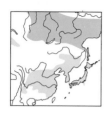

BRAMBLING *Fringilla montifringilla* <Atori> L 16cm. **Male:** In summer, black upperparts with white rump, black tail. *Rufous breast and shoulders* are diagnostic. In winter, head is gray with two black stripes from crown to nape; back grayish brown. **Female:** Resembles winter male but is browner and duller. **Similar species:** In flight resembles Bullfinch, but Bullfinch has gray upper wing coverts and breast. **Status:** Common winter visitor, western Japan. Open woodlands and cultivated fields; sometimes in large flocks.

ROSY FINCH *Leucosticte arctoa* <Hagi-mashiko> L 16cm. **Male:** Forehead, face, and throat black; nape pale brown; back dark reddish brown with black streaks; underparts *spotted with rosy pink* and dark gray. **Female:** Generally duller with brown nape; paler rosy pink on underparts. Blackish-brown legs. **Similar species:** Alpine Accentor has reddish-brown underparts and light brown legs. **Status:** Locally common winter visitor to northern Japan. Rare in western Japan. Cliffs in mountains and along coast; snow-covered grassland. Forms small flocks and feeds on the ground.

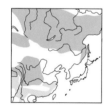

SCARLET FINCH *Carpodacus erythrinus* <Aka-mashiko> L 14cm. **Male:** *Upperparts, throat, and breast are red* with brown on back and cheeks; wings and tail are blackish brown; no wing bars; belly and flanks are white. Red varies individually. It is impossible to distinguish the first-winter male from female in the field. **Female:** Upperparts dark brown with black streaks; underparts white with black streaks. **Similar species:** Red Crossbill's head looks bigger; tail shorter; large crossed bill. **Status:** Rare transient and winter visitor.

Finches

♂ winter

♀

♂ summer

♂ winter

Brambling

♂

♀

Rosy Finch

♂ imm.

♂

♀

Scarlet Finch

PINE GROSBEAK *Pinicola enucleator* <Ginzan-mashiko> L 20cm. Large finch with *heavy dark conical bill* and long tail. **Male:** Rosy red above and below; darker on back and wings; two white wing bars. **Female:** Red of male is replaced by yellow brown. **Immature:** Resembles female but with irregular red patches on upperparts. **Voice:** Call, *pee pee pyui.* **Similar species:** Red Crossbill is smaller with crossed bill, no white wing bars. **Status:** Locally uncommon breeder and winter visitor in Hokkaido; coniferous mountain forests. In small flocks in winter.

WHITE-WINGED CROSSBILL [TWO-BARRED CROSSBILL] *Loxia leucoptera* <Naki-isuka> L 15cm. **Male:** Red with black wings and tail, two conspicuous *white wing bars,* white edges on the tertiaries, and *crossed black bill.* **Female:** Olive yellow with brownish streaks, two white wing bars, and yellow rump. **Voice:** Call, short *giyo giyo giyo.* **Similar species:** Red Crossbill has no white wing bars and female has no dark brown streaks on breast and flanks. **Status:** Rare winter visitor found in flocks of Red Crossbills.

RED CROSSBILL [CROSSBILL] *Loxia curvirostra* <Isuka> L 16.5cm. **Male:** Red with blackish-brown wings and tail, dark brown on back. *Crossed black bill.* Male of the *rubrifasciata* type has red edges on the greater and median coverts making two pale red wing bars. This type resembles White-winged Crossbill but the edges of the tertiaries are not white. **Female:** Plumage yellow brown. **Juvenile:** Resembles the female but has conspicuous dark brown streaks on the underparts. **Voice:** Call *pee* and *cho cho.* **Similar species:** See White-winged Crossbill. **Status:** Uncommon winter visitor to Japan; number varies considerably from year to year. Some breeding records from mountains of Honshu. Pine forests.

BONIN ISLANDS GROSBEAK *Chaunoproctus ferreorostris* <Ogasawara-mashiko> L 18.5cm. Large finch with *very large bill.* **Male:** Red face and reddish-brown back. **Female:** Upperparts olive brown; underparts olive. **Status:** Distributed in Bonin Is. None have been found since 1828. Considered extinct.

Finches

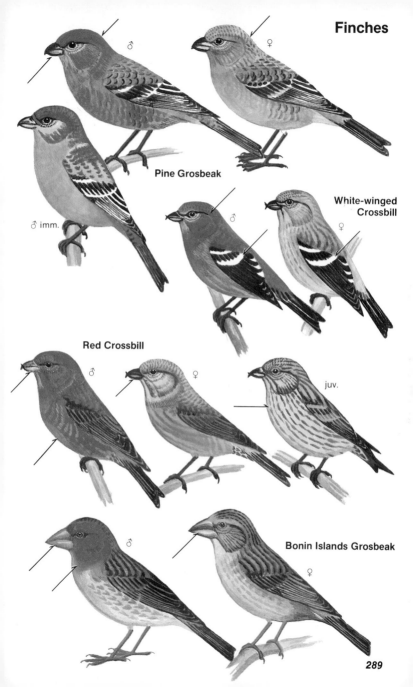

Pine Grosbeak

♂

♀

♂ imm.

White-winged
Crossbill

♂

♀

Red Crossbill

♂

♀

juv.

Bonin Islands Grosbeak

♂

♀

289

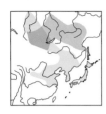

PALLAS'S ROSY FINCH *Carpodacus roseus* <Ō-mashiko> L 17.5cm. **Male:** Rosy red above and below, white lower belly. *Forehead and throat are silver white;* black streaks on back; pale rosy edges on the greater and median coverts. **Female:** Pale brown with black streaks on back and underparts. Head, throat, and back tinged with red; unstreaked red rump. **Immature:** Resembles female but more red on face and breast. **Similar species:** Scarlet Finch has no markings on wings, no silver white on forehead. Female has no red. Long-tailed Rose Finch is smaller with a longer tail, two white wing bars, and white face. Female is not reddish. **Status:** Uncommon winter visitor to Japan; forests.

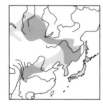

LONG-TAILED ROSE FINCH *Uragus sibiricus* <Beni-mashiko> L 15cm. **Male:** In summer, *whitish head* with red lores and forehead, scarlet back with brown streaks, and scarlet belly. Wing black with two conspicuous *wing bars;* tail black with white outer feathers. In winter, scarlet on the belly becomes dull. **Female:** Pale brown above and below. Wing and tail are same as male's. **Similar species:** See Pallas's Rosy Finch. **Status:** Common; breeds in Hokkaido and migrates to southern Japan in winter. Reedbeds or bushes on hills.

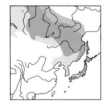

BULLFINCH *Pyrrhula pyrrhula* <Uso> L 15.5cm. **Male:** *Black cap* and *red cheek* are diagnostic. Gray above and below with black wings and tail. *White wing bar* and *white rump* are conspicuous in flight. **Female:** Dark brown above and below with gray nape. **Juvenile:** Gray brown; no black cap. Subspecies *rosacea* has some reddish on breast; subspecies *cassinii* has red breast and belly. **Similar species:** Hawfinch has no black cap. **Status:** Common breeder in coniferous forests of high mountains in northern Japan, migrates southward or to lower elevations in winter. Subspecies *rosacea* is a rare winter visitor, often seen in flocks of Bullfinches. Subspecies *cassinii* is a rare winter visitor.

Finches

Pallas's Rosy Finch

♂   ♂ imm.   ♀

Long-tailed Rose Finch

♂ summer   ♂ winter   ♀

♂   ♀   juv.

Bullfinch

♂

subspecies *cassinii*

♂   ♂ subspecies *rosacea*

291

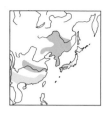

CHINESE GROSBEAK *Eophona migratoria* <Koikaru> L 18.5cm. **Male:** *Glossy blue-black head with large yellow bill*. Nape and back are gray brown, rump is pale gray, and tail is black. Underparts gray brown; flanks rufous. *Tips of primaries, secondaries, and tertiaries are white*. White tips to primary coverts make small white wing patch. White trailing edge of wing and pale rump are conspicuous in flight. **Female:** Head gray brown; tips of primaries black with white edges. **Similar species:** Japanese Grosbeak is larger and grayer; black area on head is smaller; pattern of white on wing is different. **Status:** Uncommon but regular winter visitor to western Japan.

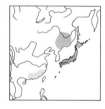

JAPANESE GROSBEAK *Eophona personata* <Ikaru> L 23cm. Largest finch in Japan. Glossy blue-black head and wings. *Large yellow bill* is conspicuous in the field. Back and rump are brownish gray; underparts gray; *white patch on wings*. Sexes alike. **Juvenile:** Grayish-brown head; black wings and tail. Bill is not as bright yellow as adult's. **Similar species:** Hawfinch has no black on head, underparts brown, tip of the tail white, color of bill is different. **Status:** Common resident in the forests of low mountains in Japan. Those in snowy regions migrate southward in winter.

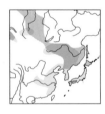

HAWFINCH *Coccothraustes coccothraustes* <Shime> L 18cm. **Male:** Brown head with gray nape; back and rump are dark brown; underparts pale brown; tip of the tail is white. *White wing bar* is conspicuous. Bill is dark gray in summer, pale brown in winter. **Female:** Generally duller. **Similar species:** See Japanese Grosbeak. **Status:** Common winter visitor to Japan; forests, gardens, and parks. Usually seen alone. Small population breeds in broad-leaved deciduous forests in Hokkaido.

Finches

♂

♀

♂

Chinese Grosbeak

juv.

Japanese Grosbeak

♂ summer

♀ winter

♂ winter

Hawfinch

Weaver Finches
Family *Ploceidae* (World: 263 species; Japan: 2 species) The genus *Passer* consists of 19 species and are small-sized members of this family. Often roost in big flocks.

RUSSET SPARROW *Passer rutilans* <Nyūnai-suzume> L 14cm. **Male:** In summer, reddish-brown head and back; black streaks on back; underparts slightly grayish. *White face.* In winter, *white line* appears on the crown. **Female:** Upperparts olive brown; conspicuous black eyestripe and *white eyebrow.* **Similar species:** See Tree Sparrow. **Status:** Locally common breeder in northern Honshu and Hokkaido; migrates to southern Japan in winter. Nests in holes in trees; in Hokkaido some birds nest under the eaves of houses.

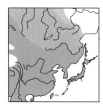

TREE SPARROW *Passer montanus* <Suzume> L 14.5cm. Most familiar bird in Japan. Sexes alike. Head and back are dark brown; white line on nape; two white wing bars; *white cheek with black spot* is diagnostic. **Juvenile:** Dull-colored; spot on cheek is much paler. **Similar species:** Male Russet Sparrow has more reddish on upperparts. Female has conspicuous white eyebrow. Both sexes lack black spot on cheeks. **Status:** Abundant throughout Japan in areas of human habitation. In large flocks except when breeding.

Starlings
Family *Sturnidae* (World: 106 species; Japan: 7 species) Medium-sized birds with short tails. Often in large flocks.

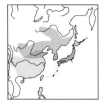

GRAY STARLING *Sturnus cineraceus* <Mukudori> L 24cm. Glossy black head with white markings. White portion of the face varies individually. *Orange bill and legs* are conspicuous. *White rump* is conspicuous in flight. Sexes alike. **Juvenile:** Generally browner. **Similar species:** Red-cheeked Myna is smaller with black legs and bill. **Status:** Abundant resident in northern Japan; uncommon resident in western Japan; summer visitor in Hokkaido.

RED-CHEEKED MYNA *Sturnus philippensis* <Ko-mukudori> L 19cm. **Male:** White forehead and chin, *reddish-brown cheeks, and white wing bar* are diagnostic. Back is black with violet gloss. Wings, tail, bill, and legs are black. **Female:** Head and underparts pale brown, back brown, tail black. **Similar species:** Gray-backed Myna has gray cheeks and back; conspicuous white shoulders. Daurian Myna is gray headed with black spot on nape; cheek is gray. **Status:** Common summer visitor to northern Japan.

Weaver Finches, Starlings

♂ summer

♂ winter

♀

Russet Sparrow

Tree Sparrow

juv.

juv.

Gray Starling

♂

♀

Red-cheeked Myna

♂

GRAY-BACKED MYNA *Sturnus sinensis* <Kara-mukudori> L 19cm. **Male:** Upperparts and breast gray, belly white. Conspicuous *white patch on the shoulders.* Bill and legs are blue gray. **Female:** Upperparts darker gray than in male, white patch on shoulder is smaller. **Similar species:** Female Silky Starling does not have white shoulders; color of bill and legs is different. **Status:** Rare winter visitor to Japan. Small number regularly winters in Ryukyu Islands.

SILKY STARLING *Sturnus sericeus* <Gin-mukudori> L 24cm. Whitish head with *reddish-yellow bill. Legs are dull orange.* **Male:** Back and belly are dark gray. **Female:** Head is a little darker and back and belly are duller than in male. **Similar species:** Female Gray Starling has dark brown head. Female Red-cheeked Myna has black bill and legs. **Status:** Rare winter visitor to southern Ryukyu Is.

(EUROPEAN) STARLING *Sturnus vulgaris* <Hoshi-mukudori> L 21cm. A little smaller than Gray Star-ling. *Black with violet gloss.* Bill is yellow in summer, brown in winter. *Many white or brown spots appear on body in winter.* Legs are dark orange. **Similar species:** Gray Starling has white head and rump. **Status:** First seen at Arasaki in southern Kyushu in 1969. Since then small numbers found regularly in Kyushu and Ryukyu Is. Often seen in flocks of Gray Starlings.

DAURIAN MYNA *Sturnus sturninus* <Shiberia-mukudori> L 16.5cm. Head and underparts gray, *black spot on nape,* black back, buffy upper tail coverts, black bill, and gray-brown legs. Conspicu-ous *wing bars.* Female is dark brown on back and nape. **Similar species:** Gray-backed Myna has white shoulders and different colored bill. **Status:** Acci-dental to western Japan.

CRESTED MYNA *Acridotheres cristatellus* <Ha kkachō> L 26cm. *Black bird with crest* on forehead. Bill is white to orange and legs are orange. *White patch on wings;* white marks on under tail coverts; tip of tail is narrowly white. **Status:** Rare visitor to western Japan. This species is distributed in Taiwan and China. Many are imported to Japan and some of them have been released.

Starlings

Gray-backed Myna

♂

♀

♂

Silky Starling

♀

summer

winter

Starling

Crested Myna

♂

Daurian Myna

♀

297

Drongos
Family *Dicruridae* (World: 20 species; Japan: 1 species)
Arboreal birds usually with glossy black plumage, varied tails. Swoop out from exposed perches to catch flying insects. Sexes alike.

BLACK DRONGO *Dicrurus macrocercus* <Ōchū> L 28cm. Long-tailed black bird, glossy on nape, back, and breast. *Tail is deeply forked.* Undulating flight. **Status:** Straggler to Kyushu and Ryukyu Islands. This species is abundant in Taiwan.

Orioles
Family *Oriolidae* (World: 28 species; Japan: 1 species)
Medium-sized birds with colorful plumage. Generally, female is duller than male or a different color.

BLACK-NAPED ORIOLE *Oriolus chinensis* <Kōrai-uguisu> L 26cm. A striking bird, unmistakable in the field. **Male:** *Golden yellow with black eyestripes meeting on nape,* black tail with yellow tip. *Bill is pale reddish violet.* **Female:** Black eyestripe is narrow and back is greenish yellow. **Status:** Rare transient to Japan; broad-leaved forests.

Wood-Swallows
Family *Artamidae* (World: 10 species; Japan: 1 species) Distributed from southern China to Australia. Catch insects in flight; make cup-shaped nests on branches or in holes in trees. Gregarious.

WHITE-BREASTED WOOD-SWALLOW *Artamus leucorhynchus* <Mori-tsubame> L 17.5cm. Smaller than Red-cheeked Myna. Black upperparts, throat, and tail; white underparts and rump. Long wings and short tail are diagnostic. Bill is grayish blue and legs are black. **Status:** Only one record, southern Ryukyu Is. in 1973.

Black Drongo

♂

♀

Black-naped Oriole

White-breasted Wood-Swallow

Crows

Family *Corvidae* (World: About 100 species; Japan: 10 species) Crows, nutcrackers, magpies, and jays are included. Most of them do not migrate. Sexes alike.

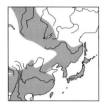

JAY *Garrulus glandarius* <Kakesu> L 33cm. *White cap with black streaks,* white throat, white eye. Back, shoulder, and belly are dark brown. Tail is black. *Blue on wing coverts* is diagnostic. White spot on wing and *white rump* are conspicuous in flight. Subspecies *brandtii* in Hokkaido has brown head and dark brown eye. **Voice:** *Jah-jah;* often imitates the songs of other birds and sometimes cats. **Similar species:** Azure-winged Magpie has black head and long blue tail. **Status:** Common resident in the forests of low mountains from Hokkaido to Kyushu.

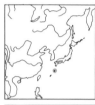

LIDTH'S JAY *Garrulus lidthi* <Ruri-kakesu> L 38cm. Head, wings, and tail are *dark blue;* back and underparts are *brown;* white tips on wings and tail. Easy to identify in the field. **Status:** Endemic species only on Amami Island and Tokunoshima Island off southern Kyushu. Common on Amami I. in evergreen forests; rare on Tokunoshima I. Nests in hollows of cliffs or sometimes gaps in roofs of houses.

AZURE-WINGED MAGPIE *Cyanopica cyana* <Onaga> L 37cm. *Black cap,* gray mantle and belly, *blue wings and tail.* Tip of tail is white. Bill and legs are black. **Voice:** Hoarse *gueei* or *gei.* **Similar species:** See Jay. **Status:** Common resident from central to northern Honshu. Mountain forests and urban areas with many trees. Common in parks and gardens in Tokyo. In small flocks when not breeding.

BLACK-BILLED MAGPIE [MAGPIE] *Pica pica* <Kasasagi> L 45cm. *Black upperparts, throat, breast,* and under tail coverts. Wings and tail are glossed with green. *Shoulders and belly are white.* White primaries are edged with black and conspicuous in flight. Bill and legs are black. Easy to identify in the field. **Status:** Locally common, northern Kyushu; cultivated areas. Makes nests on the branches of high trees or poles. Often feeds on the ground.

Jays, Magpies

Jay

subspecies *brandtii*

Lidth's Jay

Azure-winged Magpie

Black-billed Magpie

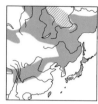

NUTCRACKER *Nucifraga caryocatactes* <Hoshi-garasu> L 34.5cm. Crow-shaped. *Black with many white streaks or spots.* Under tail coverts and tip of tail are white. Bill is black and pointed. **Status:** Uncommon resident in high mountains of Hokkaido, Honshu, and Shikoku; coniferous forests. In winter, some birds move to low mountains. A few reports from Kyushu.

JACKDAW *Corvus monedula* <Kokumaru-garasu> L 33cm. *Small crows* the size of doves, with small bills. Dark phase is entirely black except for slightly gray nape. Light phase has black face, back, wings, and tail; *white nape, breast, and belly.* Intermediate phase has gray nape and belly. **Voice:** *Kyaa kyaa.* **Status:** Rare winter visitor, mainly to Kyushu. Often seen in flocks of Rooks. The number varies greatly from year to year.

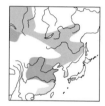

ROOK *Corvus frugilegus* <Miyama-garasu> L 47cm. A little smaller than a Carrion Crow. Black plumage. *Bill is pointed and somewhat whitish at the base.* Legs black. **Immature:** Bill is entirely black. **Voice:** *Kararara* or *guwaa* like Carrion Crow but weaker. **Similar species:** Carrion Crow is a little bigger and thicker billed. Base of the bill is not whitish. **Status:** Locally common winter visitor mainly to Kyushu. Sometimes forms flocks of several hundred. Cultivated areas.

Nutcrackers, Crows

Nutcracker

(reduced)

intermediate phase

dark phase

light phase

Jackdaw

imm.

Rook

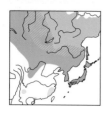

CARRION CROW *Corvus corone* <Hashiboso-gara su> L 50cm. Black plumage with greenish gloss. *Bill is thinner* than that of Jungle Crow. Forehead does not protrude. **Similar species:** Bill of Jungle Crow is thicker and its forehead protrudes obviously. This is an important field mark. Posture when calling is also different. **Status:** Abundant resident, Kyushu northward; roosts in large flocks in winter. Usually this species is abundant in cultivated areas, along riverbanks, and on reclaimed lands.

JUNGLE CROW *Corvus macrorhynchos* <Hashibuto-garasu> L 56.5cm. Same color as Carrion Crow and Raven but *bill is thicker and forehead protrudes*. Often seen with Carrion Crow. **Similar species:** See Carrion Crow. Raven is bigger with wedge-shaped tail; long bill is not as thick as Jungle Crow's. **Status:** Abundant resident throughout Japan especially in urban areas, along coast, and in mountains.

(NORTHERN) RAVEN *Corvus corax* <Watari-garasu> L 61cm. Largest crow. Bill is big but not as thick and not as curved as Jungle Crow's. Tail is *wedge-shaped*. **Similar species:** See Jungle Crow. **Status:** It is said Raven breeds in the northern islands of Hokkaido, but there are no recent records. A few birds winter regularly on Shiretoko Peninsula of eastern Hokkaido. Inhabit cliffs at seaside; feed on dead seals and fish.

Crows

Carrion Crow

Jungle Crow

Raven

Java Sparrow \<Bunchō\>
Padda oryzivora

Scaly-breasted Munia \<Amihara\>
Lonchura punctulata

White-headed Munia \<Hekichō\>
Lonchura maja

brown-bellied form
\<Kinpara\>

white-bellied form
\<Ginpara\>

Black-headed Munia *Lonchura malacca*

Black-rumped Waxbill \<Kaedechō\>
Estrilda melpoda

Orange-cheeked Waxbill \<Hōkōchō\>
Estrilda troglodytes

♂   ♀

Red Avadavat \<Beni-suzume\>
Amandava amandava

306

Escapees

♂

♀

Budgerigar
<Sekisei-inko>
*Melopsittacus
undulatus*

Rose-ringed Parakeet
<Wakake-honsei-inko>
Psittacula krameri

Pin-tailed Whydah
<Tenninchō>
Vidua macroura

♂

Masked Weaver
<Men-hataoridori>
Ploceus intermedius

Red-crested Cardinal
<Kōkanchō>
Paroaria cucullata

♀

♂

Red Bishop <Kinranchō>
Euplectes orix

Bibliography

Ali, S. *The Book of Indian Birds*. Bombay Natural History Society. Bombay, 1968.

Brown, L. and Amadon, D. *Eagles, Hawks and Falcons of the World*. 2 vols. Country Life. Felthem, 1968.

Bruun, B. *The Hamlyn Guide to Birds of Britain and Europe*. Hamlyn. London, 1978.

Burton, J.A. *Owls of the World*. E.P. Dutton. New York, 1973.

Chang, J. Wan-Fu. *A Field Guide to the Birds of Taiwan*. Taichung, 1980.

Cheng, Tso-Hsin. *A Distribution List of Chinese Birds*. Science Publishing House. Peking, 1976.

Gore, M.E.J. and Won, Pyong-Oh. *The Birds of Korea*. Royal Asiatic Society. Seoul, 1971.

Cramp, S. and Simmons, K.E.L. *Handbook of the Birds of Europe, the Middle East, and North Africa*. Vols.1—2. Oxford University Press. Oxford, 1977, 1980.

Delacour, J. and Scott, P. *The Waterfowl of the World*. 4 vols. Country Life. London, 1975.

Dement'ev, G.P. and Gladkov, N.A. et al. *Birds of the Soviet Union*. 6 vols. Moscow, 1951—1954. (Israel Program for Scientific Translation, Jerusalem, 1966—1970).

du Pont, J.E. *Philippine Birds*. Delaware Museum of Natural History. 1971.

Etchecopar, R.D. and Hüe, F. *Les Oiseaux de Chine, Non Passereaux*. les éditious du pacifique. 1978.

Fleming, R.L., Sr., Fleming, R.L., Jr., and Bangdel, L.S. *Birds of Nepal with Reference to Kashmir and Sikkim*. Fleming. Bombay, 1976.

Gabrielson, I.N. and Lincoln, F.C. *Birds of Alaska*. Stackpole Company. Harrisburg, 1959.

Glenister, A.G. *The Birds of the Malay Peninsula*. Oxford University Press. Oxford, 1974.

Goodwin, D. *Pigeons and Doves of the World*. Cornell University Press. New York, 1977.

Gruson, E.S. *A Checklist of the Birds of the World*. Collins. London, 1976.

Heinzel, H., Fitter, R., and Parslow, J. *The Birds of Britain and Europe with North Africa and the Middle East*. Collins. London, 1972.

Keith, S. and Gooders, J. *Collins Bird Guide, A photographic guide to the birds of Britain and Europe*. Collins. London, 1980.

King, B., Woodcock, M., and Dickinson, E.C. *A Field Guide to the Birds of South-East Asia*. Collins. London, 1975.

Kiyosu, Y. *The Birds of Japan*. 3 vols. Kodansha. Tokyo, 1965.

Lakagul, B. and Cronin, E.W., Jr. *Bird Guide of Thailand*. Kuruspha

Ladprao Press. Bangkok, 1974.

Medland, L. *Birds of New Guinea*. 2 vols. Georgian House. Melbourne, 1956.

Merne, O.J. *Ducks, Geese and Swans*. Hamlyn. London, 1974.

Morony, J.J., Jr., Bock, W.J., and Farrand, J., Jr. *Reference List of the Birds of the World*. Department of Ornithology, American Museum of Natural History. New York, 1975.

Nelson, J.B. *The Sulidae—Gannets and Boobies*. Oxford University Press. Oxford, 1978.

Ornithological Society of Japan. *Check-list of Japanese Birds*. Gakken. Tokyo, 1974.

Peters, J.L. *Check-list of Birds of the World*. Vols. 1—10, 12—15. Museum of Comparative Zoology. Cambridge, 1962—1979.

Peterson, R.T. *A Field Guide to the Birds, East of the Rockies*. Houghton Mifflin. Boston, 1980.

Prater, A.J., Marchant, J.H., and Vuorinen, J. *Guide to the Identification and Ageing of Holarctic Waders*. British Trust for Ornithology. Tring, 1977.

Ripley, S.D. *Rails of the World*. David R. Godine. Boston, 1977.

Robbins, S., Bruun, B., and Zim, H.S. *A Guide to Field Identification, Birds of North America*. Golden Press. New York, 1966.

Sharrock, J.T.R. *Frontiers of Bird Identification, A British Birds Guide to some difficult species*. Macmillan Journals Ltd. London, 1980.

Slater, P. *A Field Guide to Australian Birds*. 2 vols. Rigby. Sydney, 1970, 1974.

Smythies, B.E. *The Birds of Burma*. Oliver & Boyd. Edinburgh and London, 1953.

Smythies, B.E. *The Birds of Borneo*. Oliver & Boyd. Edinburgh and London, 1968.

Takano, S. *Handbook of the Field Identification of Japanese Birds*. Wild Bird Society of Japan. Tokyo, 1980.

Takano, S. *Birds of Japan in Photographs*. Tokai University Press. Tokyo, 1981.

Tuck, G. and Heinzel, H. *A field Guide to the Seabirds of Britain and the World*. Collins. London, 1978.

Udvardy, M.D.F. *The Audubon Society, Field Guide to North American Birds, Western Region*. Knopf. New York, 1977.

Vaurie, C. *The Birds of the Palearctic Fauna, Non-Passeriformes*. H.J. & G. Witherby. London, 1965.

Viney, C. and Phillipps, K. *A Colour Guide to Hong Kong Birds*. J.R. Lee. Hong Kong.

Webster, M. and Phillipps, K. *A New Guide to the Birds of Hong Kong*. Sino-American. Hong Kong, 1977.

Wildash, P. *Birds of South Vietnam*. Tuttle. Tokyo, 1968.

Wild Bird Society of Japan. *The Breeding Bird Survey in Japan*. Wild Bird Society of Japan. Tokyo, 1978.

Wild Bird Society of Japan. *Where to Go Birdwatching in Japan*. Wild Bird Society of Japan. Tokyo, 1977.

Yamashina, Y. *A Natural History of Japanese Birds*. Tokyo, 1980 (Reprint).

Birdwatching Guide for Japan

There are many birdwatching spots in Japan. The ones given here are well known among Japanese birdwatchers.

Most of the locations suitable for birdwatching are far from the towns and cities and often difficult for foreigners to find. Foreigners are advised to attend the weekend birdwatching tours held by the local chapters of the Wild Bird Society of Japan. A detailed birdwatching guide (in Japanese) is available at the headquarters of the society.

In general, the best seasons for each species are as follows: ducks, geese, and swans: November—February or March; other winter visitors: November—March; summer visitors (songbirds): May—June (July in Hokkaido); migration of birds of prey: early October; waders: late April—mid-May and mid-August—late September.

HOKKAIDO

Nopporo
Forest Park

Sapporo
Akan-cho Kushiro
Shunkunitai Area
around Lake Furen

Tomakomai Lake Utonai
Cape Ochiishi

Shimokita Peninsula

Lake Izunuma

Mt. Zao
Sendai

HONSHU

Ferryboat Trips

aruizawa

Mt. Takao
Tokyo Kasumigaura, Ukishima Marsh
Yatsu-higata Mudflat

Oi Bird Park
Meiji Shrine
Tama River

Miyake Island

ountain Side of Mt. Fuji

Amami Island

Naha Manko in Okinawa Island

R y u k y u Is.

Iriomote and Ishigaki Islands

311

•**Lake Utonai** (Hokkaido)

<Birds and Seasons> Late March—early April: White-fronted Goose, Bean Goose, Whooper Swan, Pintail and other ducks (about 10,000), White-tailed Eagle, Steller's Sea-Eagle, Marsh Tit, and Great Tit. June—July: Yellow-breasted Bunting, Siberian Rubythroat, Latham's Snipe, Brown Thrush, Marsh Harrier, Hobby, Gray Heron. <Habitat> Swamp, marsh, deciduous forest. <Transportation> 20 minutes by car from Sapporo (Chitose) Airport. <Memo> This is the first bird sanctuary in Japan established by the Wild Bird Society of Japan. Information is available from rangers at the Nature Center. (The center is closed on Tuesdays and Wednesdays.)

•**Akan-cho** (Hokkaido)

<Birds and Seasons> November—March: flocks of Japanese Cranes. <Habitat> Farmland. <Transportation> 20 minutes by car from Kushiro Airport. <Memo> Artificial feeding during the winter. Visitors may use the observatory.

•Cape Ochiishi (Hokkaido)

<Birds and Seasons> Late June—July: Tufted Puffin, Red-faced Cormorant, Temminck's Cormorant, Slaty-backed Gull, Spectacled Guillemot, Yellow-breasted Bunting, Siberian Rubythroat, Latham's Snipe. December-March: Red-faced Cormorant, Slaty-backed Gull, Glaucous-winged Gull, Peregrine Falcon, Pigeon Guillemot, and sea ducks. <Habitat> Cape with cliffs facing the ocean, grasslands, and forest on the headlands. <Transportation> 2½ hours by train from Kushiro Stn. to Ochiishi Stn. Then walk for 30 minutes to the cape.

•Shunkunitai Area around Lake Furen (Hokkaido)

<Birds and Seasons> Late June—July: Japanese Crane, Black Wood-pecker, Redshank, Yellow-breasted Bunting, Siberian Rubythroat Japanese Reed Bunting. August—September: waders such as Sharp-tailed Sandpiper, Wood Sandpiper, Rufous-necked Stint. Bean Goose migrates from the north at the end of August. October—November: big flock of Whooper Swans. December—March: Steller's Sea-Eagle, White-tailed Eagle, Snow Bunting. <Habitat> Wetland and forest. <Transporta-

tion> 2½ hours by express train from Kushiro Stn. to Attoko Stn. and 30 minutes by bus for Nemuro from Attoko Stn. Get off at Tobai bus stop.

●**Nopporo Forest Park** (Hokkaido)

<Birds and Seasons> June—July: Gray Heron, Black Woodpecker, tits, Common Cuckoo, Mandarin Duck, Red-cheeked Myna, Ruddy Kingfisher, Hazel Grouse, Ural Owl. <Habitat> Extensive forest. <Transportation> 30 minutes by car from Sapporo (Chitose) Airport.

●**Ferryboat Trips (Tokyo ↔ Kushiro and Tokyo ↔ Tomakomai)** (Pacific Ocean)

<Birds and Seasons> March—September: Laysan Albatross, Black-footed Albatross, Fulmar, skuas and jaegers, Streaked Shearwater, Short-tailed Shearwater, Sooty Storm Petrel, Slaty-backed Gull, Black-tailed Gull, Black-legged Kittiwake. Sometimes Stejneger's Petrel, Fork-tailed Storm Petrel. <Habitat> Open sea. <Transportation> Boat service to Kushiro is twice every 3 days. Boat service to Tomakomai is daily. <Memo> The ferries on both routes are very big, and restaurant and bath facilities are available.

●**Shimokita Peninsula** (Aomori)

<Birds and Seasons> December—March: Brant, Whooper Swan, Oldsquaw, Falcated Teal, Yellow-billed Loon, Pelagic Cormorant, Temminck's Cormorant, White-tailed Eagle. June—August: Japanese Reed Bunting, Japanese Marsh Warbler, Great Crested Grebe, Chinese Little Bittern. <Habitat> Bay and rocky coastline with many lakes along the coast. <Transportation> 8 hours by limited express train from Tokyo to Noheji Stn. Change there to the Ominato Line and get off at Ominato Stn. <Memo> A rental car is useful for birdwatching in such a huge area.

●**Mt. Zao** (Miyagi)

<Birds and Seasons> June—July: Japanese Robin, Narcissus Flycatcher, Indian Tree Pipit, Arctic Warbler, House Martin, White-rumped Swift, Gray Bunting. <Habitat> Conifererous deciduous forest at the foot of the mountain, sub-alpine zone at the summit. <Transportation> 2 hours from Tokyo to Sendai by limited express train (Shinkansen) and 1 hour by bus for Kattadake from Sendai Stn.

•Lake Izunuma (Miyagi)

<Birds and Seasons> November—mid-February: thousands of White-fronted and Bean Geese, some Canada Geese and Snow Geese, swans, various ducks such as Smew and Gadwall, Peregrine Falcon, Marsh Harrier, Japanese Wagtail. <Habitat> Two lakes with rice fields around the lakes. <Transportation> 2 hours from Tokyo to Sendai by limited express train (Shinkansen). Change to a local train at Sendai Stn., then 2 more hours to Nitta Stn.

•Kasumigaura, Ukishima Marsh (Ibaraki)

<Birds and Seasons> June—August: Japanese Reed Bunting, Black-browed Reed Warbler, Great Reed Warbler, Fan-tailed Warbler, Chinese Little Bittern, Schrenck's Little Bittern, Common Cuckoo, Coot. Japanese Reed Bunting and Schrenck's Little Bittern are difficult to see in other places in the Kanto Area. <Habitat> Wetland along the lake. <Transportation> 1½ hours from Tokyo by limited express train to Sawara Stn., then 30 more minutes by bus for Edosaki. Get off at Oppori bus stop.

•Miyake Island (Izu Islands)

<Birds and Seasons> Late April—June: Izu Islands Thrush, Ijima's Willow Warbler, Middendorff's Grasshopper Warbler, Japanese Wood Pigeon, Varied Tit, Japanese Robin, Collared Scops Owl, Bush Warbler, Siberian Meadow Bunting. Sea birds also appear on the way to and from the island: Streaked Shearwater, Japanese Murrelet, jaegers, phalaropes, and gulls. <Habitat> 60% of the island is evergreen forest. <Transportation> 6 hours from Tokyo by ship or 50 minutes by plane. There are many small pensions. <Memo> Tairoike Pond and Izumisaki Cape are especially good for birdwatching.

•Mt. Takao (Tokyo)

<Birds and Seasons> Resident: Azure-winged Magpie, Siberian Meadow Bunting, Brown-eared Bulbul, Japanese Green Woodpecker, Varied Tit, Japanese Wagtail. May—June: Short-tailed Bush Warbler, Bush Warbler, Broad-billed Roller, Narcissus Flycatcher, Gray-faced Buzzard-Eagle. January—February: Black-faced Bunting, Gray Bunting, Japanese Accentor, Daurian Redstart. <Habitat> Mountains reaching 600m. The walking path is well developed. <Transportation> 1 hour from the center

of Tokyo (Shinjuku Stn.) by Keio Line to Takaosanguchi Stn. <Memo>
This is a very famous birdwatching spot in the suburbs of Tokyo. Early
morning is best. It is a suitable day trip from Tokyo.

●**Meiji Shrine** (Tokyo)

<Birds and Seasons> Resident: Rufous Turtle Dove, Brown-eared Bulbul,
Varied Tit, Japanese White-eye, Gray Starling, Common Pheasant,
Bamboo Partridge. November—March: Mandarin Duck, Pale Thrush, Jay,
Siberian Bluechat. <Habitat> Forest in the central area of Tokyo.
<Transportation> 5 minutes by train from Shinjuku to Harajuku Stn. 5
minutes' walk from Harajuku Stn. <Memo> This is a dense forest and the
best spot for birdwatching in Tokyo. Mandarin Ducks can be seen at close
range in winter.

●**Oi Bird Park** (Tokyo)

<Birds and Seasons> June—July: Great Reed Warbler, Common
Gallinule, Coot, Chinese Little Bittern, Little Tern, Siberian Meadow
Bunting. August—October: Ruff, Marsh Sandpiper, Wood Sandpiper,

Black-tailed Godwit, Great Egret, Little Egret, Garganey. November—March: Black-tailed Gull, Herring Gull, Gadwall, Shoveler, Spot-billed Duck, Japanese Reed Bunting, Long-eared Owl. Sometimes Japanese Marsh Warbler is seen. <Habitat> Wetland in the reclaimed land of Tokyo Bay. <Transportation> 15 minutes by train from Tokyo to Hamamatsu-cho Stn. Transfer to monorail and get off at Ryutsu Center Stn. The park is within 15 minutes' walk. <Memo> This park is owned by the Tokyo Metropolitan Government. The Wild Bird Society of Japan is in charge of the management. Rangers of the society are there on the weekends. The marsh outside the park is also a good birdwatching spot.

•**Tama River** [near the Seisekisakuragaoka Stn. of Keio Line] (Tokyo)

<Birds and Seasons> November—February: Mallard, Spot-billed Duck, Wigeon, Pintail, Smew, Long-billed Ringed Plover, Black-headed Gull, Japanese Wagtail, Common Kingfisher, Daurian Redstart, Siberian Meadow Bunting, Rustic Bunting, Oriental Greenfinch. <Habitat> Riverbed. <Transportation> 30 minutes by train from the center of Tokyo (Shinjuku Stn.) to Seisekisakuragaoka Stn. (Keio Line) and 10 minutes' walk from the station to the river bank. <Memo> Good birdwatching spot in the suburbs of Tokyo, especially for waterfowl.

•**Yatsu-higata Mudflat** (Chiba)

<Birds and Seasons> April—May and August—October: waders such as Bar-tailed Godwit, Curlew, Black-bellied Plover. November—March: Snowy Plover, Black-bellied Plover, Curlew, and several kinds of ducks and egrets. <Habitat> Tidal flat surrounded by reclaimed land. <Transportation> 1 hour by train from Tokyo to Funabashi Stn. (Sobu Line). Take the bus to the terminal stop, Wakamatsu-Danchi. About 10 minutes' walk to the mudflat.

•**Karuizawa** (Nagano)

<Birds and Seasons> Mid-May—mid-June: Blue-and-White Flycatcher, Narcissus Flycatcher, Siberian Blue Robin, Siberian Thrush, Gray Thrush, Arctic Warbler, Siberian Meadow Bunting, Little Cuckoo, Horsfield's Hawk-Cuckoo, Oriental Cuckoo, Common Cuckoo, Brown Flycatcher. Excellent place to enjoy bird songs. December—March: Pallas's Rosy Finch, Long-tailed Rose Finch, Red Crossbill, Japanese Accentor.

Sometimes Solitary Snipe is seen. <Habitat> A popular summer resort; mixed forest. <Transportation> 2 hours from Tokyo (Ueno Stn.) by limited express train to Naka-karuizawa Stn. There are many hotels and pensions. Hoshino Spa area is excellent for birdwatching. <Memo> Chorus of the many songbirds is splendid in early summer, late May to early June.

●**Mountain Side of Mt. Fuji** [Gogo-me] (Yamanashi)
<Birds and Seasons> June—July: Siberian Bluechat, Bullfinch, Indian Tree Pipit, Arctic Warbler, Nutcracker, Goldcrest, Alpine Accentor. Birds of subalpine zone are seen. <Habitat> Virgin forest of the highest mountain in Japan. <Transportation> 3½ hours from Tokyo by bus from Shinjuku Stn. (center of Tokyo).

●**Cape of Irago** (Aichi)
<Birds and Seasons> Late September—early October: Best season to enjoy the hawk migration: Gray-faced Buzzard-Eagle, Honey Buzzard, Peregrine Falcon, Hobby, Goshawk, Sparrow Hawk, Japanese Lesser Sparrow Hawk. Other small birds, such as Brown-eared Bulbul, Barn Swallow, White Wagtail, are also migrating through the cape at this same time. <Habitat> Tip of the Atsumi Peninsula. <Transportation> 4½ hours from Tokyo by a combination of limited express train (Shinkansen), local train, and bus. <Memo> Shiokawa tidal flat on the same peninsula is good for waders in the same season as the hawk migration.

●**Yatomi Bird Park in Nabeta** (Aichi)
<Birds and Seasons> April—May: Little Egret, Wigeon, Tufted Duck, Common Pheasant, Common Gallinule, Spotted Redshank, Gray-headed Lapwing. August—September: Great Cormorant, Chinese Little Bittern, Pintail, Little Ringed Plover, Marsh Sandpiper, Black-tailed Godwit, Bank Swallow, Bull-headed Shrike. November—March: ducks, Northern Harrier, Marsh Harrier, Snowy Plover, Gray-headed Lapwing, Brown-eared Bulbul, Dusky Thrush, Long-eared Owl. <Habitat> Man-made habitat for waterfowl. <Transportation> 1½ hours from Nagoya Stn. by train or bus.

●**Bird Forest of the Japan World Exposition Commemorative Park** (Osaka)

<Birds and Seasons> Resident: Common Pheasant, Brown-eared Bulbul, Rufous Turtle Dove, Bull-headed Shrike, Japanese Wagtail, Little Grebe,

Common Kingfisher. November—March: Dusky Thrush, Rustic Bunting, Black-faced Bunting, Daurian Redstart. <Habitat> Bird Park. <Transportation> 30 minutes from Osaka Stn. to Senri-chuo Stn. by train and 10 minutes by taxi to the park. <Memo> Parks and museum were built in commemoration of the World EXPO '70.

●**Mino** (Osaka)
<Birds and Seasons> May—July: Blue-and-White Flycatcher, Short-tailed Bush Warbler, Crowned Willow Warbler, Black Paradise Flycatcher, Ashy Minivet. November—February: Bullfinch, Red Crossbill, Siberian Bluechat, Japanese Green Pigeon, Siskin, Long-tailed Rosy Finch. <Habitat> Virgin evergreen forest. <Transportation> 30 minutes from Osaka Stn. to Mino Stn. by train.

●**Chidori-hama** (Yamaguchi)
<Birds and Seasons> April—May and August—October: waders such as Dunlin, Whimbrel, Gray-tailed Tattler, Wood Sandpiper. November—March: Wigeon, Mallard, Mew Gull, Black-tailed Gull, Black-headed Gull, Brambling, Japanese Reed Bunting. <Habitat> Tidal flat. <Transportation> 1 hour by train from Hakata Stn. (Fukuoka) to Chofu Stn.

●**Mt. Ishizuchi** (Ehime)
<Birds and Seasons> May—June: Japanese Robin, Nutcracker, Hodgson's Hawk-Eagle, White's Ground Thrush, Siberian Bluechat. <Habitat> Virgin forest. <Transportation> Matsuyama Airport to Matsuyama Stn. by bus. Transfer to bus for Omogokei bus terminal. 2 hours.

●**Arasaki** (Kagoshima)

<Birds and Seasons> Mid-November—mid-February: thousands of Hooded and White-naped Cranes, several Common Cranes. Sometimes other cranes such as Demoiselle and Siberian White Cranes are seen.

White-tailed Eagle, Marsh Harrier, Penduline Tit, Chinese Grosbeak, Starling, Gray-headed Bunting, Japanese Reed Bunting, Rook, Jackdaw, Water Rail, Ruddy Crake. <Habitat> Farmland on reclaimed land. <Transportation> 1 hour by bus from Kumamoto Airport to Kumamoto Stn., 2 hours by express train from Kumamoto Stn. to Izumi Stn., 10 minutes by taxi from the station to the cranes' feeding area.

●**Amami Island** (Kagoshima)

<Birds and Seasons> Resident: Lidth's Jay, Amami Woodcock (these two species are endemic to this island), Ryukyu Robin, Japanese White-eye. March—May is the best for these birds' songs. <Habitat> Virgin forest. <Transportation> 1 hour flight from Kagoshima Airport. <Memo> Do not step into the forest because of a poisonous snake called Habu. Birdwatching only along the main road is strongly recommended.

●**Manko in Okinawa Island** (Okinawa)

<Birds and Seasons> September—April: Lesser Golden Plover, Dunlin, Rufous-necked Stint, Spot-billed Duck, Great Egret, Little Egret, Gray Heron, Black-winged Stilt. In winter, Black-faced Spoonbill, Saunders's Gull, Common Shelduck are also seen. <Habitat> Tidal flat. <Transportation> Manko is located in Naha City, 10 minutes by taxi from the Naha Airport. <Memo> Okinawa Rail, Pryer's Woodpecker (these two species are endemic to this island), and Ryukyu Robin are seen in the mountains of northern Okinawa.

●**Ishigaki and Iriomote Islands** (Okinawa)

<Birds and Seasons> Resident: Crested Serpent Eagle, Cinnamon Bittern, Purple Heron, Malay Night Heron, Chinese Bulbul, Emerald Dove, Banded Crake, Barred Buttonquail, Red-capped Green Pigeon. October—March: Yellow Wagtail, Gray-faced Buzzard-Eagle, Kestrel, White Stork, waders. June—August: Greater Crested Tern, Black-naped Tern, Roseate Tern, Ruddy Kingfisher, Black Paradise Flycatcher, Watercock. <Habitat> Wetland and ricefields. <Transportation> 1 hour flight from Naha Airport to Ishigaki Airport. It takes 1 or 2 hours by ship from Ishigaki I. to Iriomote I. <Memo> Hoopoe and Black-capped Kingfishers are recorded often during the migration season (March and October).

Index Scientific and English Names

The page numbers in the index refer to the text. The illustration appears on the opposite page. For escapees only, the page number refers to the illustration.

Index Japanese Names

MAP OF JAPAN

0   100   500 km.

YELLOW SEA

SEA OF JAP

Oki

Shimane — Tottori   Hy
Mishima   Okayama
Tsunoshima   Hiroshima   Ay
Tsushima   Yamaguchi   Kagawa
Iki   Ehime   Tokush
Goto Is.   Fukuoka   SHIKOKU
Saga   Oita
Nagasaki   Kochi
Danjo Is.   Kumamoto
KYUSHU
Koshiki
Miyazaki
EAST CHINA SEA   Kagoshima
Kusagaki
Mageshima
Osumi Is.   Tanegashima
Tokara Is.
Yakushima

Amami Is.   Amami
Tokunoshima
Okinoerabu
Senkaku Is.   Kume   Yoron

Okinawa   Okinawa
Yonaguni   Kita-daito
Nakano   Irabu   Miyako
oganjima-   Iriomote   R y u k y u   Is.   Minami-daito
Hateruma   Ishigaki   Daito Is.
Taketomi
Oki-daito

Tropic of Cancer

124°   128°   132°